ROLLING

COMEDY & CULTURE

Nick Marx and Matt Sienkiewicz, *series editors*

ROLLING

BLACKNESS

AND

MEDIATED

COMEDY

Edited by
Alfred L. Martin, Jr.

INDIANA UNIVERSITY PRESS

This book is a publication of

Indiana University Press
Office of Scholarly Publishing
Herman B Wells Library 350
1320 East 10th Street
Bloomington, Indiana 47405 USA

iupress.org

Manufactured in the United States of America

First printing 2024

Library of Congress Cataloging-in-Publication Data

Names: Martin, Alfred L., Jr. editor.
Title: Rolling : Blackness and mediated comedy / edited by Alfred L. Martin Jr..
Description: Bloomington, Indiana : Indiana University Press, 2024. | Series: Comedy & culture | Includes bibliographical references and index.
Identifiers: LCCN 2023045183 (print) | LCCN 2023045184 (ebook) | ISBN 9780253068873 (hardback) | ISBN 9780253068880 (paperback) | ISBN 9780253068897 (ebook)
Subjects: LCSH: African Americans on television. | African American wit and humor—History and criticism. | Black people—Race identity. | Television comedies—History and criticism. | African Americans in mass media. | African American comedians. | BISAC: SOCIAL SCIENCE / Media Studies | PERFORMING ARTS / Comedy | LCGFT: Television criticism and reviews.
Classification: LCC PN1992.8.A34 R65 2024 (print) | LCC PN1992.8.A34 (ebook) | DDC 791.45/61708996073—dc23/eng/20231213
LC record available at https://lccn.loc.gov/2023045183
LC ebook record available at https://lccn.loc.gov/2023045184

To my Potluck Crew for always keeping me rolling.

CONTENTS

ACKNOWLEDGMENTS

I begin these acknowledgments with a thanks to Black culture writ large. The ingenuity of Black humor, particularly in the face of the return of overt racism in an alleged postracial world, keeps me going. In particular, I thank my Black friends who keep me laughing, laughter that was partly the inspiration for this collection: Omari Gardner, Demetrius Bady, T. Tara Turk-Hayes, Stephanie Holloway, Tiffany Langford, Dee Blackmon, Krystal Villanosa, Khary Lawson, and Curtis Rowe.

Thank you to Matt Sienkiewicz and Nick Marx for soliciting the collection. Matt has been a cheerleader since I was a grad student trying to make my way in this field. And for that, I remain appreciative. Thanks to Allison Blair Chaplin and Sophia Hebert at Indiana University Press for their support for the project.

Thank you to this collection's contributors. Y'all were mostly on time and, more importantly, provided essays that helped me think about Blackness and comedy in new and exciting ways. You made editing these essays truly enjoyable. I am indebted to Pete Kunze and Adrien Sebro for reading the introduction to this collection. Thank you both for your generosity.

The study of Blackness and comedy would be nearly impossible without the work of Mel Watkins. And Bambi Haggins has provided a language to talk about the intersections of media studies, comedy, and Blackness. Your contributions to the field are immeasurable.

Last, but not least, I thank my husband, Tom, for always giving me the space to work *and* knowing when I need a break and masterfully getting me to take one.

ROLLING

INTRODUCTION

Finding the Funny: Recentering the *Comedy* in Black Comedy

Alfred L. Martin, Jr.

Iwant to begin this introduction with a joke I saw on Facebook from user Bella Devereaux because, after all, this collection is about the intersections of Blackness, media, and humor.

Bella Devereaux is with **Shameka Green** and **2 others**.   •••
Apr 13 at 9:42 PM • 🌐

Since y'all so SMART ‼️ 5 members were in a group called, The Temptations all of whom were named Paul, Eddie, Blue, Otis & David Ruffin. 2 went to see about David. 3 saw Eddie leave off stage. 1 went to Blue's funeral. 5+ saw Paul drunk.

How many came to see Otis?

😀 567   602 Comments • 6.6K Shares

Fig. 0.1 This Twitter joke uses "inside" knowledges about the mini-series *The Temptations* for its brand of Black humor.

This joke uses the logic of "word problems" that many of us grew up solving as part of math classes in elementary school. And through that logic, the answer is obvious: no one came to see Otis. Although The Temptations were (and are) a successful crossover music group, for some (most, or perhaps all) of their white fans, this "joke" may not be funny at all. And perhaps, it may be sad that no one came to see Otis. For many Black people, the joke might induce rolling because it draws on culturally specific knowledges to, as this introduction is titled, "find the funny." Rolling explains not simply Black laughter but the kind of uncontrolled Black laughter that results in tears or loss of breath. Rolling is not just the sound of laughter one hears on the laugh track of three-camera sitcoms but is the way laughter is mixed with screams, shrieks, and Black signifying practices. That Black laughter sonically differs from white laughter has long been "known" but was codified in the Black-cast sitcom production of the 1970s when laugh track pioneer Carroll Pratt developed a "Black laugh track" that included not just laughter but verbal expressions of delight and reactions that attempted to capture the Black practice of rolling.[1] But rolling is not just verbal; it is often visual. When a Black person is "rolling," they likely grab on to something or someone to avoid falling over (and sometimes that act is futile). Rolling is also often mobile. One who is rolling often walks (or more aptly stumbles around) as they attempt to seek relief from the joy of Black laughter. Thus, this collection is titled *Rolling* because I hope to examine and capture the myriad ways Black artists use humor to engage, revise, and subvert the intersections of Blackness, politics, culture, and comedy.

To return to the joke that opens this introduction, understanding it requires intimate knowledge of the scene in the made-for-TV movie *The Temptations* (NBC, 1998) in which David Ruffin (Leon Robinson) is confronted by bandmates Otis Williams (Charles Malik Whitfield) and Melvin "Blue" Franklin (D. B. Woodside) and told that he would have to clean up his act (and discontinue his drug use) to remain in the group. Ruffin, as the then-lead singer of the group retorts, "Ain't nobody coming to see you, Otis!" The line has been taken up in Black popular culture almost since it was uttered in 1998. TikTok videos abound that feature users reenacting and reappropriating the scene and its dialogue to discuss tensions between siblings (@ love.jaypee), zodiac signs (@asknikkibee), and even winter holidays (@jadacasity). Thus, while white folks might read the joke and (rightly) conclude that no one came to see Otis, it is the Black intertextual knowledges *and* the Black intonation and vernacular of "Ain't nobody coming to see you, Otis!" in which the joke's funny is found.

The aim in this collection is to treat Blackness and comedy as inextricably linked. As the joke that opens this introduction illuminates, the joke, in and of itself, might be funny across racial categories, but it carries a particular Black valence. Many times, otherwise excellent scholarship takes comedy for granted moving straight to the politics of Blackness and its cultural circulation within media. I suggest that rather than treating comedy and Blackness as dialectical, this work can be made more illuminating by the symbiotic relationship between Blackness and comedy.

My insistence on the "intersectionality" of Black comedy is partly because when Black folks began appearing as stars and subjects in film and television, it was often within comedy. For example, the 1898 short film *Watermelon Contest* was directed by James H. White—seriously, a man named James *White* directed a film that featured two Black men having a contest to see who can eat watermelon the fastest—and ultimately discursively helped visually craft the stereotype that Black people love watermelon. But more germane to this collection, IMdB categorizes the film as comedy. Thus, if the point of discussion is only *Watermelon Contest*'s engagement with/creation of stereotype, a key component of how *comedy* becomes a mode through which this stereotype gains purchase is missed.

With few exceptions, until the twenty-first century, Black-cast television meant Black-cast *sitcoms*. Television's *Amos n Andy* (CBS, 1951–1953) is one of the first times Black actors and characters took leading roles in a television series. It is no surprise that because the property began its life as a radio program that it starred two white actors adopting what Michele Hilmes identified as "Black voice," an oratory practice used by white performers that sonically linked Blackness to "improper" dialect.[2] When the program began anew on television, Black actors were hired to take on the roles that had already been established in its hit radio iteration. Thus, the Black actors, to ensure success of the program, mostly had to affect the same kinds of Black voice that had made the characters recognizable and "lovable" on radio. The NAACP began to pressure CBS because, in their purview, the series depicted all its Black characters as clowns or crooks. Ultimately, the NAACP filed a suit against CBS hoping to get the series canceled. The ensuing publicity was enough that the series' principal sponsor (television operated within a single-sponsor ad model in this period) Blatz Beer pulled its support, and the series was canceled. But again, the NAACP protest and lawsuit grappled with Black representation, not Black representation *and* the sitcom form. So, if television mediates the sign of Blackness almost exclusively within comedy, television and Blackness cannot be fully understood without a consideration of comedy. As I have demonstrated elsewhere, centering comedy alongside Blackness helps explain not only how comedy works but also for which audiences it is intended, which concomitantly illuminates why comedy is deployed as it is.[3]

I have frequently been in spaces at home (with my white husband) or in my office (among mostly white coworkers), rolling at something or other. And upon hearing my laughter, someone will stop by and ask, "What are you laughing at?" or "What is so funny?" That question evokes dread because in explaining the humor—the joke, gag, or situation—it ceases to be funny. Like some celebrities who have only a passing relationship to talent, often the things a particular person finds funny simply has the "it" factor. So, the answer to the question "What's so funny?" is that it depends on context: it depends on one's sense of humor, and oftentimes, it depends on one's social situation—gender identity, sexuality, class, and, most importantly for this collection of essays, race and, more specifically, Blackness.

The collection of essays that comprise *Rolling* is partly engaged in explaining how humor and Blackness converge across media. Because, as Brett Mills argues, "humor exists in discourse, and its meanings are inevitably affected by, and are a result of, that discourse," these essays are interested in the discursive formation of comedy as it intersects with the particularities of Blackness.[4] Blackness and comedy are often taken for granted. In other words, few studies explicitly engage with comedy alongside race. Within many scholarly investigations, comedy just *is*, and the object of the analysis is the focal point. The essays within *Rolling* seek to take comedy seriously by exploring what the intersections of comedy and Blackness can discursively mean. But before delving into what these intersections mean, it is useful to understand the broad ways humor and comedy have been theorized through the major theories of humor: superiority theory, incongruity theory, and relief theory.

Superiority theory dates to at least Plato and suggests "that people laugh when they feel a kind of superiority over other people."[5] The theory suggests that group laughter indicates how culture and people are uncivilized and, as a result, reveals the inner workings of humor. John Morreall suggests superiority theory is rooted in social, socioeconomic, and cultural hierarchies and can be useful in understanding humor rooted in differences of race, class, gender, and sexuality.[6] Supporting the idea that the superiority theory of humor is rooted in hegemony, Steve Neale and Frank Krutnik argue, "All instances of the comic involve a departure from the norm, whether the norm be one of action, appropriate behavior, conventional dress, or stereotypical features."[7] The superiority theory of humor is certainly concerned with the joke teller being perceived as better than the joke receiver—or an "in group" and "out group," respectively—but it is also rooted in the conduits through which one can be ridiculed for deviation from hegemonic normativity. Superiority theory can be observed in the use of humor with respect to a(n imagined) Black mainstream and Black queers. As I have argued elsewhere, the jokes within Black-cast sitcoms (often crafted by well-meaning Black heterosexual writers) make the Black gay body the abject object of jokes.[8] Because the Black-cast sitcom imagines a Black heterosexual viewer, the jokes about the gay "other's" expense are used to reify Black heterosexuality's superiority over the Black gay joke's target. In this way, the laughter on the laugh track, understood as "group laughter," creates an "in group" and an "out group," or, as Martina Kessell and Patrick Merzinger suggest, laughter and humor negotiates belonging and marks boundaries.[9]

Incongruity theory, widely regarded as having its roots in Kantian philosophy, hinges on the notion that "humor is seen to arise from the disparity between the ways in which things are expected to be and how they really are."[10] Incongruity theory is built on the assumption that as humans, we are somewhat like machines: we come to expect particular patterns and when things deviate from those patterns, they are inherently funny, mostly because they shock with their deviation, and that deviation is unexpected, but not dangerous. Michael Clarke succinctly demonstrates how incongruity theory works in three steps:

1. A person perceives (thinks, imagines) an object as being incongruous.
2. The person enjoys perceiving (thinking, imagining) the object.
3. The person enjoys the perceived (thought, imagined) incongruity at least partly for itself, rather than solely for some ulterior reason.[11]

Incongruity theory resides squarely within hegemonic constructions of the normative. Mills suggests that within this theory, "comedy only makes sense to viewers who understand and accept what is 'normal,' for without such norms any incongruity is not sufficiently marked."[12] In this way, the incongruity theory and superiority theory are related in that they are both used as a mechanism to separate normativity from deviance. For example, on the seventh season of *American Idol* (Fox, 2002–2016; ABC, 2018–) Arlington, Texas, resident Erick Mauldin, a fat Black man, auditioned for the show singing Boyz II Men's hit "A Song for Mama." The confluence of the stereotype of fat Black folks being able to sing (see the series' Ruben Studdard) and Mauldin's off-key rendition of the Boyz II Men hit results in the judges, Paula Abdul, Simon Cowell, and Randy Jackson, laughing at his effort. In other words, part of the humor, based on stereotypes as it is, is that the judges had one set of expectations and Mauldin delivered something different.

The third major humor theory, relief theory posits that laughter is a release. Consider the notion of "comic relief." In the very idea of comic relief, comedy is a release valve for pent-up energy. Therefore, the relief theory is about providing relief from any series of emotions from nervousness to discomfort, and destinations in between. Relief theory can be considered as not so much of a break from the superiority and incongruity theories as a companion to those theories. To return to the *American Idol* example noted previously, perhaps laced with the incongruity of a fat Black body and less-than-stellar vocal abilities, Abdul, Cowell, and Jackson may have also been laughing because they were uncomfortable when presented with Mauldin's vocal stylings. Taken together, these three theories help illuminate how humor functions, particularly within racialized instances of comedy. Of most importance here is how humor can be deployed to make an "Other" feel that otherness via ridicule and belittling.

Freud argues that jokes are the verbal manifestation of humor and theorizes tendentious and nontendentious jokes to center that understanding. As a deepening of relief theory, Freud suggests that tendentious jokes expose fears and inadequacies on the part of the person making the joke, while nontendentious jokes are considered "innocuous."[13] Tendentious jokes require three people to operate successfully. "Apart from the one who is telling the joke, it needs a second person who is taken as the object of the hostile or sexual aggression, and a third in whom the joke's intention of producing pleasure is fulfilled."[14] Put simply, Freud suggests that a producer, receiver, and object are necessary to produce tendentious jokes. For this reason, Freud posits "the activity of joking cannot be said to have no aim or purpose, for it has set itself the unmistakable aim of arousing pleasure in the listener."[15] Tendentious jokes create a communal link between the producer and the receiver of the joke at the expense of the object and work to uphold hegemonic ideals regarding who/what is funny. Mills complicates the simple link between producer, receiver, and object by noting that jokes have both insiders and outsiders. In other words, "people who knew each other well can find particular things funny which those outside of the group don't. Such 'in-jokes' rely more on the workings of that group dynamic than the specifics of the joke that was uttered."[16] Superiority, incongruity, and relief theories, alongside tendentious jokes, help shape the approach to humor and comedy *Rolling* undertakes while revising those theories to account for Blackness.

ROLLING: ON BLACK HUMOR

Christie Davies posits that racial jokes are told about groups who are in proximity to the joke teller and live at the margins of their culture.[17] In other words, there is often a familiarity within the marginalized group about whom racial jokes are told. In discussing the intersections of Blackness and comedy, then, the sheer proximity of Africans forced to immigrate to literally build what would become the United States folks and white slaveholders meant that racialized humor was all but inevitable. Put another way much earlier by Thomas Hobbes, jokes about race and ethnicity are a form of comic scapegoating wherein a person is found ridiculous and, as a powerless group, are laughed at by the powerful.[18] *Amos n Andy*'s radio iteration as well as minstrel shows provide an example of this type of humor. However, Hobbes, in centering whiteness as hegemonic, misses the combined power of Black humor and Black vernacular traditions to subvert the relationship between who is deemed laughable and who is not.

Simon Weaver identifies three types of humor regarding race: (1) humor *about* race often produced by "out groups" (like Davies's understanding of race and humor); (2) racialized satire, which is designed to transcode stereotypes; and (3) humor produced by raced bodies.[19] In Weaver's first taxonomical category, he centers whiteness within a discussion of the production of racialized humor. In the second instance, Weaver notes that humor's polysemic nature makes transcoding through comedy difficult because it requires the joke hearer to decode the joke within the joke teller's "dominant" code.[20] In the third instance, Weaver shifts to a discussion of the ways people of color use humor as an "in-group" set of knowledges. But in Weaver's discussions, he marks race as a broad and undifferentiated category.

Centering Blackness affords the opportunity to broaden the ways humor has been theorized. For example, while superiority, incongruity, and relief theories helpfully illuminate the inner workings of comedy generally, as Mel Watkins details, our ancestors utilized humor in ways that befuddled and, quite frankly, often enraged and irritated mainstream white culture.[21] Jelani Cobb notes that the brand of humor Black folks tend to use was developed out of necessity during slavery and frequently paranoid slave owners, who believed themselves to be the target of enslaved Black folks' laughter.[22] It was our African slave ancestors' and, by extension, our mastery of humor and comedy that at turns could offer biting social critique that spoke to the heart and soul of Black life during and after slavery *and* could be unintelligible to those outside Black interior spaces. Bambi Haggins adds that in the hands of Black folks, comedy "has always overtly *and* covertly explored the trials, tribulations and triumphs of African American communities."[23] Thus, successful humor generally, and successful Black humor specifically is predicated on decoding within what Stuart Hall calls the "dominant" mode in which the joke was encoded.[24]

As African Americans began seizing control of their mediated images, that Black comedic forms were subverting the white centric ways comedy had been understood could no longer be denied. Blackness and comedy took on a different tenor and began moving away from white folks adopting minstrelsy traditions to tell jokes using Black vernacular or Black folks having little to no agency in media productions to contest the comedy in which they were being asked to engage. The result was the creation of a brand of comedy that, like Black laughter, could often be vexing, mysterious, or a source of consternation for white America.[25]

While contemporary Black comedians might flippantly invite white folks with problems with their brand of comedy to "die mad," African American comedy during slavery did not have such latitude. Thus, a sense of double consciousness became enmeshed in Black comedic traditions. Or as put by W. E. B. Du Bois, a sense of knowing one's Black self *and* seeing that Black self through the eyes of a fundamentally racist culture.[26] In a period when Black folks (and especially men) could be arrested (and often lynched) for reckless eyeballing—the mere nonverbal *act* of the Black gaze—failing to understand the intersections of Blackness, politics, and humor could be deadly. Thus, double consciousness has colored African Americans' use of humor—humor that resonates with Black audiences but could perhaps still be legible, often on a different frequency for white and other raced audiences. Or, as Racquel Gates suggests, this twoness manifests in Black-cast media that functions dually—a text legible to Black viewers and one that attempts to appeal to white viewers.[27] This twoness recognizes that Black comedy (with Black here referring to race) could never be reliably sequestered within an "in group" of like-minded African Americans—to say nothing of other raced individuals.[28] As Black folks shifted from simply *performing* comedy to *producing* comedy, they could work "wholly inside their own racial constructions, only rarely allowing entry to crossover audiences."[29] As Black comedians began increasingly working in desegregated spaces (whether in comedy clubs, films, or television series), this double conscious humor became important for Black performers' financial well-being and, sometimes, literal safety.

Much of the contemporary work on Blackness and humor has centered the twoness inherent in how Black comedic artists use comedy in all its forms, but specifically satire.[30] Black uses of satire and humor can often be understood as what Danielle Fuentes Morgan calls "laughing to keep from dying": a "survival tactic that operates on two registers—the ability to inspire laughter in those who would cause harm becomes a form of protection in the plausible deniability of *just* jokes; the necessity of inspiring knowing in-group laughter opens up Black interior space that wards of psychic, or even physical, death."[31] In my own work, I extend and nuance Freud's theorization of tendentious jokes as "two-faced humor" suggesting that Black humor oftentimes functions covertly in its deployment "when the abject person is removed from the situation in which the joke is told."[32] Or, put another way, as Derek C. Maus argues, the "twoness" of Black comedy and satire is aimed at an "in group" of "African American readers [and] viewers" and an out group composed of "political institutions, social practices, and cultural discourses that arise outside the community and constrain, denigrate, or otherwise harm it in some way."[33] One of the important tenets of the twoness to which Gates, Morgan, Maus, and I refer is that African Americans use comedy *within* the culture industries. Even as comics like Moms Mabley, who initially performed in comedy clubs in Chicago's predominantly Black neighborhoods, could mostly imagine sequestering their humor (and critiques) to Black spaces and audiences, they still worked within the wider and whiter culture industries. Black folks became adept at using signifying practices, a Black oral practice Henry Louis Gates describes as communicating multiple levels of meaning simultaneously.[34] In other words, humor, as a Black signifying practice, could be used to convey a social critique that was legible to Black listeners and illegible to white listeners. Thus, Black comedic twoness and signifying practices remain a balancing act that is always mindful of the axiom that "bitches gotta eat."

At the same time, Black folks employ camp practices. Although camp is typically theorized as a raceless gay practice (which really means white), Pam Wojcik argues that not only are "race and sex . . . intertwined" but that "race discourse operates in camp generally."[35] Marlon Ross argues that camp is like the Black practice of playing "the Dozens." Ross defines the Dozens as entailing "both a playfully flaunting defiance of dominant norms, sexual and otherwise, and tolerated survival at the margins of a hostile world."[36] In Ross's configuration of the Dozens and camp, it is simultaneously a Black interior practice that playfully uses insults and barbs against another Black "opponent" *and* a way to use Black humor to critique dominant white hegemonies in white people's faces (as our slave ancestors did). Black camp, like all Black humor practices, employs a twoness by considering, to varying degrees, interior and exterior audiences. Taken together, the "classical" humor theories, Freud, Black satire, Black camp, and double consciousness help explain and perhaps even work toward new knowledges about Black comedy.

Part I of *Rolling* is interested in how Black comedy and Black comics navigate(d) the color line and, in some ways, also the wider and whiter culture industries. Gerald Butters opens this collection with a chapter on three Black comics negotiating Chicago's stand-up comedy scene between 1955 and 1970. He separates these comics into (1) traditional (Moms Mabley), (2) transitional (Nipsey Russell), and (3) contemporary (Bill Cosby) categories to help understand how these comics, and their comedy, played with/to Black and white audiences. Next, Josh Truelove engages how the postmodernist proliferation of television networks and the global rise of hip-hop converged to make "risky material" profitable for the media industries and attractive to a wide swath of audience segments. Using Martin Lawrence as a case study, Truelove details how Lawrence's use of "blue" comedy made him a hot commodity within the media industries. Lisa Guerrero contributes the final chapter in this section and turns to Eddie Murphy's work in the *Beverly Hills Cop* and *48 Hrs* franchises to illuminate what she calls "double conscious law and order," a Black-led comedy genre that takes as its central premise that Black characters are positioned as outside the law because of the semiotic connection to lawlessness in mainstream imaginations of Blackness.

The second part of this collection continues its focus on Black performers, but specifically examines how they use(d) their talents on television. The first two chapters, by Phillip Cunningham and Jacqueline Johnson, center racial performativity. Instead of engaging with how biracial comics Keegan-Michael Key and Jordan Peele use comedy and whiteface to critique whiteness, Cunningham argues that they instead demonstrate that race is fluid within their brand of comedy on *Key & Peele* (Comedy Central, 2012–2015). Next, Johnson examines the juxtaposition between how some Black people questioned Donald Glover's "authentic" Blackness before his series *Atlanta* (FX, 2016–) and the reception among some pockets of Black viewers after its premiere. Specifically, Johnson focuses on how Glover draws himself into a lineage of Black comics throughout *Atlanta*'s "Robbin' Season." Picking up on Johnson's use of the Black nerd archetype, Tim Havens engages with the "Blerd" and a case study of Steve Urkel on the long-running, Black-cast sitcom *Family Matters* (ABC, 1989–1997; CBS, 1997–1998). Havens calls Urkle a satirical character and suggests that because he is part of a conventional Black-cast sitcom, he opens a space for a "cultural reimagination" of Blackness. In the last chapter in part II of this collection, Scott Poulson-Bryant turns to musician Prince and his engagement with his "signifying, ironic humor" that can be observed in his song lyrics, music videos, and 2014 guest spot on the mostly white-cast comedy *New Girl* (Fox, 2011–2018) to argue that Prince is often constructed as a creative genius but his ironic humor and signifying practices are rarely considered.

Part III centers the liberations and limits of Blackness and comedy. Anshare Antoine and Mel Stanfill open this section with a chapter that examines Black Twitter, political humor, and COVID-19 to reveal what is specifically Black about online political humor and what is specifically political about online Black humor. Thus, they speak to how Black Twitter has been partly liberating to/for Black users. Kelly Cole turns to the limits of satire in her examination of the failure of *The Secret Diary of Desmond Pfeiffer* (UPN, 1998). Specifically, Cole draws a historical sketch of its production to argue the series ineffectively used satirical humor and overused the laugh track to try to downplay its more offensive attempts at comedy.

The final section of this collection focuses on production and production practices. The section opens with an autoethnographic essay in which *Saturday Night Live* (NBC, 1975–) alum turned academic Ellen Cleghorne discusses how seeing Flip Wilson's drag persona "Geraldine" convinced her that she wanted to be a sketch comedy performer. Next, television writer and showrunner Felicia Henderson details the long history of *The Game* (The CW, 2006–2009; BET, 2011–2015; Paramount+, 2021–), a series that moved from "traditional" sitcom on UPN to dramedy on BET and to drama on Paramount+. In detailing this history, Henderson explores and exposes the generic conventions that shape television production based on her own knowledges and interviews with *The Game's* creator Mara Brock Akil. In the final essay, Ken Feil and I use the made-for-TV film *Jackie's Back* (Lifetime, 1999) to discuss how camp, a reading practice most often associated with audience reception, was, indeed, encoded in production. Using interviews with *Jackie's Back* writers Mark Alton Brown and Dee La Duke and series star Jenifer Lewis, we argue that the telefilm produced Black camp, a slightly different register than white camp practices and referents.

The authors in *Rolling* are interested in understanding Blackness and comedy through examinations of industrial, production, cultural, and generic contexts. This scholarly trek through stand-up comedy, music, digital spaces, television, and film ultimately attempts to answer the question: What is so funny about Black comedy?

Alfred L. Martin, Jr. is Associate Professor of Cinematic Arts at the University of Miami. He is author of *The Generic Closet: Black Gayness and the Black-Cast Sitcom* (IUP, 2021).

Notes

1. Robert Kubey, *Creating Television: Conversations with the People behind 50 Years of American TV* (New York: Routledge, 2009), 115.

2. Michele Hilmes, "Invisible Men: *Amos 'n' Andy* and the Roots of Broadcast Discourse," *Critical Studies in Mass Communication* 10, no. 40(1993): 301–21.

3. Alfred L. Martin, Jr., *The Generic Closet: Black Gayness and the Black-Cast Sitcom* (Bloomington: Indiana University Press, 2021).

4. Brett Mills, *Television Sitcom* (London: Palgrave Macmillan, 2005), 16.

5. Brett Mills, *The Sitcom* (Edinburgh: Edinburgh University Press, 2009), 77.

6. John Morreall, *Comic Relief: A Comprehensive Philosophy of Humor* (Malden, MA: John Wiley & Sons, 2009), 7.

7. Steve Neale and Frank Krutnik, *Popular Film and Television Comedy* (New York: Routledge, 1990), 67.

8. Martin, *Generic Closet*.

9. Martina Kessell and Patrick Merzinger, Introduction to *The Politics of Humour: Laughter, Inclusion in the Twentieth Century* (Toronto: University of Toronto Press, 2012), 9.

10. Mills, *Sitcom*, 83.

11. Michael Clarke, "Humor and Incongruity," in *The Philosophy of Laughter and Humor*, ed. John Morreall (Albany: State University of New York Press, 1987).

12. Mills, *Sitcom*, 87.

13. Sigmund Freud, *The Joke and Its Relation to the Unconscious* (New York: Penguin Books, 2002), 87.

14. Ibid., 97

15. Ibid., 93.

16. Mills, *Sitcom*, 15.

17. Christie Davies, *Ethnic Humor around the World* (Bloomington: Indiana University Press, 1996).

18. Thomas Hobbes, *Human Nature*, vol. 4 of *The English Works of Thomas Hobbes of Malmesbury*, ed. William Molesworth (London: J. Bohn, 1841).

19. Simon Weaver, "Humor and Race," in *The Wiley Blackwell Encyclopedia of Race, Ethnicity, and Nationalism*, ed. A. D. Smith, X. Hou, J. Stone, R. Dennis, and P. Rizova (Hoboken, NJ: Wiley, 2015), 1–2.

20. See Stuart Hall, "Encoding/Decoding in the Television Discourse," in *Channeling Blackness: Studies on Television and Race in America*, ed. Darnell M. Hunt (New York: Oxford University Press, 2005).

21. Mel Watkins, *On the Real Side: A History of African American Comedy from Slavery to Chris Rock* (Chicago: Chicago Review Press, 1999), 16.

22. William Jelani Cobb, *The Devil and Dave Chappelle and Other Essays* (New York: Basic Books, 2007), 249.

23. Bambi Haggins, *Laughing Mad: The Black Comic Persona in Post-Soul America* (New Brunswick, NJ: Rutgers University Press, 2007), 3.

24. Hall, "Encoding/Decoding in the Television Discourse," 46.

25. Watkins, *History of African American Comedy*, 16.

26. W. E. B. Du Bois, *The Souls of Black Folk* (New York: Penguin, 1903).

27. Racquel Gates, *Double Negative: The Black Image and Popular Culture* (Durham, NC: Duke University Press, 2018), 58.

28. Alfred L. Martin, Jr., "The Tweet Has Two Faces: Two-Faced Humor, Black Masculinity, and RompHim," *Journal of Cinema and Media Studies*, 58, no. 3 (Spring 2019): 162.

29. Kristal Brent Zook, *Color by Fox: The Fox Network and the Revolution in Black Television* (New York: Oxford University Press, 1999), 37.

30. See Brandon J. Manning, *Played Out: The Race Man in Twenty-First-Century Satire* (New Brunswick, NJ: Rutgers University Press, 2022).

31. Danielle Fuentes Morgan, *Laughing to Keep from Dying: African American Satire in the Twenty-First Century* (Urbana: University of Illinois Press, 2020), 5.

32. Martin, " Tweet Has Two Faces," 161.

33. Derek C. Maus, Introduction to *Post-Soul Satire: Black Identity after Civil Rights* (Jackson: University Press of Mississippi, 2014), xiii–xiv.

34. Henry Louis Gates, Jr., *The Signifying Monkey: A Theory of African American Literary Criticism*, 25th anniversary ed. (New York: Oxford University Press, 2014).

35. Pamela Robertson Wocjik, *Guilty Pleasures: Feminist Camp from Mae West to Madonna* (Durham, NC: Duke University Press, 1996), 20.

36. Marlon B. Ross, "Camping the Dirty Dozens: The Queer Resources of Black Nationalist Invective," *Callaloo* 23, no. 1 (2000): 300.

PART I

BLACK COMEDY CROSSING OVER

1

BLACK STAND-UP COMICS IN CHICAGO

Navigating a Changing City (1955–1970)

Gerald R. Butters, Jr.

The relationship between desegregation and the stand-up comedy circuit in the mid-twentieth century is a complicated one. Community racial practices, venues available for Black performers, and generational breakout buzz led to historical patterns that were not necessarily linear. This chapter explores the careers of Black stand-up comics in Chicago from 1955 to 1970 who were attempting to navigate a rapidly changing industrial and social culture. In the mid-1950s, African American comic talent could only perform in "Black-only" venues on the South Side of the city. The cultural assumption was that these comics' work was so racially and culturally specific that only Black Chicago audiences would attend these shows. However, within fifteen years, Black comedians were playing clubs all over the city, appearing at the major cultural institutions of the Loop, plying their trade regularly on television, and making frequent public appearances at charity events. For Black comics who had begun under the strict racial segregation of the 1940s and 1950s, this meant quick, nimble adjustment to maintain career longevity and viability. As many of Chicago's "Black" venues closed, new desegregated ones opened. And Black comedians had to consider how they fit into the city's new comedic landscape, the demographic composition of their audiences, and the spaces in which they would perform.

Chicago earned an international reputation as a city that bred comedians.[1] African American comics had been publicly performing in Chicago since the beginning of the twentieth century. Black entertainers were mostly banned from white establishments; thus, a burgeoning entertainment industry that catered to Black Chicagoans emerged in the early part of the century. Theaters, including the Regal and the Savoy, and nightclubs throughout the South Side catered to a largely African American clientele. By the early 1950s, attendance figures at the Regal were as high as 125,000 per week.[2] Therefore, it is impossible to talk about the history of stand-up comedy in Chicago without centering African American comic traditions.

The Regal and Savoy were among the Chitlin' Circuit's stalwart establishments—a collection of venues throughout the upper Midwest, eastern, and southern parts of the United States that offered performance opportunities for African American comedians, musicians, and entertainers. The Chitlin' Circuit was key to African American entertainment in the early to mid-twentieth century. Segregation and racial discrimination prohibited Black entertainers from performing in many theaters throughout the nation; therefore, the circuit created performance spaces in which these performers could demonstrate their artistry. Black performers often played weekend or weekly stints at venues on "the circuit" before moving on to the next location. Tied into this circuit were several Chicago performance spaces, including well-established theaters, clubs, and lounges on the South Side. For Black comedians and performers, there was serious money to be made with Black Chicagoans. They were constantly on the road and had to be nimble and agile in determining what performance spaces would improve/shape their careers.

Black comedians could perform in several entertainment spaces in the post–World War II era, but the most prestigious—by far—was the Regal Theater at 4719 South Parkway.[3] American singer-songwriter Ruth Brown argued that a Black artist needed to play at four theaters to prove that they had "made it"—and one of those was the Regal in Chicago.[4] The Regal, which held over three thousand seats, was built in 1928 as part of a larger commercial center in the heart of Chicago's Black Belt—a series of Chicago South Side neighborhoods that contained 75 percent of Chicago's Black population. Originally part of the Balaban and Katz chain, the theater produced its own stage shows and hosted touring vaudevillian acts, musicians, comedians, and variety shows. By 1959, stage shows were coming back to life at the Regal as the management brought in big-name musicians. Many top Black comedians were added to the bill, creating a true variety act.[5]

The Regal's major competition was the Tivoli Theater in Chicago's Woodlawn neighborhood. The Tivoli was just as ornate as the Regal with a painted ceiling in the lobby meant to resemble the Sainte-Chapelle at Versailles. The Tivoli, at 3,250 seats, was even larger than the Regal but had largely become a movie house by 1955, although stage shows played the venue occasionally.[6] Both the Regal and the Tivoli were Chicago's top performance spaces for Black comedians through 1960. Always part of a variety act, comedians played before thousands of Black Chicagoans and created a relationship with their audience. The Regal and the Tivoli were segregated spaces where Black comedians could speak directly to Black audiences without the fear of "offending" white audience members.[7] The establishment of this relationship was crucial to the longevity of a career.

This study theorizes three patterns of geographically situated performance for comedians in Chicago from 1955 to 1970: traditional, transitional, and contemporary. Traditional entertainers, like Moms Mabley, performed at exclusively Black venues on the South Side during most of the period under study.[8] Their comedy spoke directly to Chicago's Black communities, and there was a distinct, emotional connection between comedian and audience. Transitional entertainers "cut their teeth" in Black venues in Chicago only to rapidly maneuver into white nightclubs in early 1960s. Examples include Dick Gregory and Nipsey Russell. Although they increasingly played to desegregated or white-dominant audiences, they were still known as "Black" comedians to club promoters and those who wanted to be entertained. Contemporary comedians include Bill Cosby, who had little to no experience playing Chicago's Black venues, although he was popular with Black Chicago audiences. After 1962, his comedy almost entirely avoided race, garnering him the reputation as a more "universal" comedian. His "safe" comedy endeared him to white audiences, but his rapid career projection also established him as a success to Black Chicagoans.[9]

TRADITIONAL COMICS AND THE SPECTATORSHIP OF BLACK AUDIENCES

Moms Mabley is considered the first great American Black comedienne. Born Loretta Mary Aiken but known primarily by her stage name Jackie "Moms" Mabley, she is known for the longevity of her career and because she was one of the few Black women who performed stand-up comedy in the early to mid-twentieth century. Mabley began her career on stage in the 1920s and became a veteran of the Chitlin' Circuit. One of the first openly queer comediennes, by the mid-1950s, Mabley had perfected her onstage persona: a toothless woman in a house dress and floppy hat. She used both vulgarity and frequent risqué references to critique sexuality, gender roles, and racism within American culture.[10] But Moms was no Black Mammy. The Mammy trope was brassy and large and catered to the white world. Moms, on the other hand, was sexualized, joking about her love for younger men,

Fig. 1.1 Moms Mabley is emblematic of the "traditional" categorization of Black comics because she began performing at a time when Black comedians could only perform in segregated venues.

and she was firmly in control of the stage. She was wildly popular with Black audiences; Terrence T. Tucker claims that "Mabley sought to go beyond mere entertainment. Her acts were equal part celebration, cultural sharing and elderly advice."[11] Moms spoke to her audiences in the vernacular of the neighborhood—equal parts loving and ribald and quintessentially "Black."

Moms Mabley is emblematic of the "traditional" categorization of Black comics who began performing in the early to mid-twentieth century, when opportunities for Black comedians were restricted to segregated spaces. Moms often opened her act by greeting audiences, "Thank you, children; thank you, darlings," illustrating a direct intimacy she had with her audience that connoted a familial connection.[12] She also spoke in a vernacular that was indicative of the Black working-class dialect. The following is an example from her 1948 routine "Don't Sit on My Bed," in which she explained her hearing loss:

> I ain't scared of no airplane. I'm no square. Is you young children said—
> it just never moved me,
> ridin no airplane, sho nuf. No sooner than I got in the plane, they strapped me down.
> The plane ain't got up no ways before something went, "Umpf" in my ear.
> I ain't heard nothin since.[13]

Traditional comics like Moms spoke directly to her Black audience and made no attempt to "cross over" until it was absolutely necessary in the 1960s. Due to the strict racial patterns of the era, these comics knew their audience was Black and spoke in a language and addressed issues that mattered to that audience.

As a "traditional" comic, Mabley appeared in several spaces that catered specifically to Black Chicago communities in the late 1950s and early 1960s. Theater historian Clovis E. Semmes suggests Mabley was "a favorite on the Regal stage."[14] She initially appeared at the Regal in the 1930s and maintained a close relationship with the theater. The Regal Theater and its direct competitor, the Tivoli Theater, each produced elaborate stage shows in 1959. In July, the Regal had a high-profile variety act with singers Tommy Edwards and Ernestine Anderson; vocal jazz group Lambert, Hendricks & Ross; a jazz orchestra; a magic act; and Moms Mabley. Theater management reported it had spent over $150,000 ($1.36 million in 2021 dollars) to produce two summer shows.[15] Mabley returned to the Regal for two weeklong shows with Ernestine Anderson in the spring and summer of 1961 (along with Aretha Franklin and multiple singing groups). After Mabley's April performance, the *Chicago Defender* claimed that "Mabley as always, stole the show with her down to earth act."[16] Semmes argues that Mabley used her stage persona to impart her vision of truth while entertaining and lovingly connecting with her audiences, whom she began to greet as her "children."[17] The unnamed *Defender* writer picked up on this audience response in his column. While Mabley was either fourth- or fifth-billed in Regal advertising, she was a familiar stalwart and beloved by Black Chicago audiences. Increasingly, the Regal tied its fortunes to rhythm and blues music, including shows with multiple singers of the era like Bobby Lewis, Jerry Butler, Maxine Brown, the Wanderers, the Spinners, and the Blue Notes. Moms was often the only nonmusical act on the bill. Mabley was firmly entrenched in the Black entertainment world in the late 1950s and early 1960s and was considered a staple in variety shows.

When Moms wasn't performing at the Regal, she found other Chicago-based opportunities for her act. Shortly before her first 1961 Regal appearance, she headlined at the Roberts Show Lounge for a weekend.[18] The Roberts Show Lounge was the largest Black nightclub in the nation.[19] Thus, she maneuvered between theaters and nightclubs in Chicago in performing her act.

Mabley was a savvy entertainer, knowing when to transform opportunities into continued success. Two other essential factors, besides her live performances, played into Mabley's long-lasting relationship with Black Chicago audiences. First, she recorded five comedy records between 1960 and 1961. A relatively new phenomenon in the early 1960s, her first album, *Moms Mabley Onstage*, released by Chess Records, earned the comedienne a gold record and further boosted her national prominence. Second, in August 1961,

Moms appeared at Chicago's Bud Billiken Parade, the largest African American parade in the United States. Driving in a convertible, Moms waved to the more than twenty-five thousand patrons who lined the parade route. The parade, held annually since 1929, is both a type of back-to-school celebration and a celebration of Black Chicago culture with celebrities, sports figures, and entertainers often participating in the more than three-hour-long event. Mabley, appearing at the Roberts Show Lounge at the time of the parade, solidified her relationship with the Black Chicago community.[20]

Moms Mabley's career skyrocketed with her television appearance on the ABC show *A Time for Laughter: A Look at Negro Humor in America*. Produced by Harry Belafonte, the program featured Mabley at her best, and she was much in demand for the rest of the decade. *The Smothers Brothers Comedy Hour* and *The Merv Griffin Show*, among many other television shows, featured Mabley. As a result, her performance venues became larger and were distinctly outside of Black Chicago neighborhoods. In November 1967, she appeared at the Civic Opera House as part of a Thanksgiving eve jazz festival. She followed this with shows at the Memorial Hall in Gary, Indiana, in 1967 and the Auditorium Theater in June 1968.

During the 1960s, Moms Mabley made the transition to mainstream notoriety and began performing at integrated or white-dominant performance spaces. Three major societal shifts made this national trajectory possible for Mabley. First, society caught up with her material. While white stand-up comic Lenny Bruce was arrested on obscenity charges in Chicago in 1962, what was acceptable on the stage dramatically increased in scope during the 1960s, as the judicial system increasingly supported First Amendment freedom of speech rights on stage. Moms Mabley's stand-up for much of her career in the 1950s and early 1960s had been considered raunchy but was looked on as cutting edge in the late 1960s. Because she performed at mostly Black venues, the Chicago Police Department was less interested in the content of her act in comparison to Bruce.

Second, the civil rights movement had pushed for integration in all aspects of American life. While it was almost impossible for Black comic stars to perform for integrated audiences prior to 1963, these venues opened later in the decade. The most prestigious performance space in Chicago for comics in the 1950s and 1960s was Mister Kelly's. It was a springboard to fame for many entertainers and comics. The restaurant/club sat on the corner of Rush Street and Bellevue Place on the city's North Side. Comedian Tom Dreeson argues that "Mister Kelly's was the place where all the big comedians and singers from all around the world whom you might see on *The Ed Sullivan Show* would perform; it was the ultimate place for those who wanted a career in show business."[21] The venue was also surprisingly open in regard to race; Della Reese, Ella Fitzgerald, and Sarah Vaughn had all recorded live albums there by 1958. In 1959, Mister Kelly's began a new policy of combining a musical act with a comedic act; this paved the way for rising comics to get fast notoriety. Moms Mabley didn't make her Mister Kelly's debut until 1970. Much can be read into this fact—that an elderly Black woman wasn't the "image" of a "normal" stand-up comic in the 1960s, that she was too connected to the Black community and largely unknown to white powers-that-be, or that white-dominant audiences simply wouldn't be interested in coming to her show.

The third factor that impacted the "traditional" comedians was the demise of Black performance spaces. The Tivoli Theater closed on September 19, 1963, and was razed to make way for a parking lot and supermarket in August 1966.[22] The last stage shows for the Regal Theater took place in 1968; it was heavily damaged by a suspicious fire in 1971 and razed in 1973. The performing spaces that had been the mainstays of Moms Mabley's and other Black entertainers' careers simply ceased to exist, forcing Black comedians to adjust if their careers were to survive.

TRANSITIONAL COMICS AND THE RACIAL TIGHTROPE

Transitional comedians are those Black comics who got their start in Black venues but quickly shifted to performing in primarily integrated performance spaces. Nipsey Russell is exemplary of "transitional" comedians. Russell began a stage act with film comedian Mantan Moreland in 1952. He played the Black Chicago club circuit for the rest of the decade but got his big break at the Robert's Show Lounge in 1959 when he was the comic relief for Sammy Davis, Jr., who was a huge star at the time. The popularity of Davis changed the demographics of the Lounge; during his booking, they were playing to 90 percent white audiences who seldom, if ever, went to the South Side. Comedian Dick Gregory reported that the club was "packed with white executives." Russell opened the show with a lot of racial comedy, and "they couldn't laugh hard enough." Russell stole the show from Davis and was called to play to a group of white club owners downtown the following Monday. Gregory said that "it was the same routine he had killed the customers with at Roberts, but that night Nipsey just sat up there and died." Gregory came to conclusion that at the Robert's, which had a reputation as being a Black club, the white customer is "filled with guilt and filled with fear." Downtown, though, it was "the white man's house, and the white man felt comfortable and secure. He didn't have to laugh at racial material that he didn't want to hear."[23] Russell was obviously stunned by this development and had to instantly reconsider

Fig. 1.2 Nipsey Russell, a transitional comedian, benefited from being able to perform in integrated spaces after he got his start in Black venues.

his material if he was going to play integrated audiences. Many Black comedians of the early 1960s who attempted racialized humor found themselves negotiating their material for an ever-changing audience.

An example of this balancing act is Russell's performance on the *Ed Sullivan Show* on June 17, 1962. First, Russell used language that almost directly countered the down-home feel of Mabley's routine. Russell showed off his linguistic knowledge. One such example was in describing his book on dating. He explained, "I have judiciously omitted any autobiographical sketches because all of my encounters in the romantic realm have been catastrophic." Second, Russell proclaimed that he has "foreseen my proclivity to indulge in personal commentary." Whether this was because of his direct experience or simply a shtick, he followed with a nonpartisan safe political joke explaining that "Washington is a rat race and it looks like the rats are winning." Third, when Russell finally addressed race, he did so in a nonthreatening manner. He joked:

> [I advocate] friendship for all the white people who are using Man Tan [a tanning product].
> I am using a bleaching cream called Yellow Fellow (huge laugh ensues).

If you are decent enough to brown down, I can be decent enough to meet you halfway.

Transitional Black comics could not completely avoid issues of race during the civil rights era, but they had to strongly consider the racial makeup of their audiences in their routines if they wanted a successful career.

Nipsey Russell must have reconfigured his act shortly after his disastrous 1959 Loop routine because he appeared with Della Reese at the Cloister at 900 North Rush Street on the North Side, a very "white" section of Chicago in 1960.[24] Russell's television exposure on *The Tonight Show* with Jack Paar, a rarity for Black comedians in the early 1960s, led him to a run at the Regal. Appearing with bandleader Billy Eckstine, Russell told the *Defender* that the Regal "was one of the last outposts of live stage entertainment" and that he wanted to be part of it.[25]

Russell held well-deserved resentment that he had been hindered from comic success because of his Blackness. In a 1962 interview, columnist Morton Cooper claimed that "Russell did nothing to hide his bitterness having been passed over for so long." Russell complained, "They're still categorizing me as a Negro comedian. Damn it, I want to make it as a comedian period."[26] Darryl Littleton discusses the difficulty of Russell's "transitional" status. He explains that Russell would play white-only performance spaces "challenging his audience's intelligence with his casual use of an extensive vocabulary," yet he would also play at Black venues. Russell embodied an integrationist mode of thinking; he didn't want to be known exclusively as a Black comic, because he considered his material "too universal to be squeezed into such a limited category."[27] Russell finally gained crossover success in Chicago appearing at Mister Kelly's in 1964 and the Playboy Club in Lake Geneva, Wisconsin, and the Empire Room in downtown Chicago in 1969. While Dick Gregory gained international attention with his racially provocative material in the early 1960s, his civil rights activism hindered his career and largely determined that his audience would be Black in the 1970s. Nipsey's material could be considerably more adult when playing before Black audiences or on the nightclub circuit. In his 1959 album, *Confucius Told Me*, the comedian told an audience member that he "picked up more tramps than the Salvation Army." He also joked that he loved bringing home chicken from the club and that he woke up in his room in the morning with a "breast in my mouth and a leg in each hand."[28]

Russell eventually went mainstream, though, appearing on countless talk shows and in fifteen episodes of *Car 54, Where Are You?* as well as three episodes of children's program *Captain Kangaroo* in the 1960s and 1970s. He also became a staple on 1970s daytime television, often appearing as the lone

Black face on game and quiz shows, including *Match Game*, where he became known for his limericks. He appeared on celebrity roasts, and while his material teetered on the verge of adult humor, his mainstream success was dependent on "safe" material, particularly because it came from a Black male comic.

Russell had clearly developed his comic skills playing to Black audiences for over a decade. But for him to go "mainstream" he had to adjust his material accordingly. As he attempted to transition to more universal appeal, he told a reporter that he felt most similar in style and delivery to Bob Hope.[29] Hope was anything but controversial. After Russell's 1959 fiasco at the downtown comedy club, he realized that white audience members were not comfortable being confronted with contemporary racial issues within white-dominant spaces. Russell explained in 1962, after doing twenty radio guest shots with Arthur Godfrey, "There was not one 'Negro' joke spoken or alluded to, nor was my color mentioned once."[30] For Russell, race was to be avoided, if possible.

Transitional Black comics of the early 1960s honed their craft in front of Black Chicago audiences in Black-dominant venues. Their initial primary audience was Black Chicagoans, and they sharpened their stage presence, relationships with audiences, and content in front of this demographic. But as the civil rights movement preached integration, and as Black performance spaces closed while other venues became open for the first time to Black comics, they had to adjust their acts. Comics like Nipsey Russell attempted to go mainstream, appearing on television programs that catered to white America. As white venues became open to him, he excised confrontational racial material from his act in hopes of having a longer, more lucrative career. Other comedians, like Dick Gregory, didn't adjust their racial material. While Gregory got the notoriety, he did not maintain the long career of Russell, who worked until 2001, four years before his death. This was a difficult period for Black comedians and conscious decisions that reflected both material and potential audiences had to be made.

CONTEMPORARY BLACK COMEDIANS:
THE UNIVERSAL AUDIENCE

Bill Cosby is emblematic of the "contemporary" comedian. Born in 1937, Cosby was tied more closely with East Coast clubs in New York City than the other comedians. His career quickly catapulted after playing the Gaslight Lounge in New York. However, in Chicago, Cosby played the Gate of Horn, a one-hundred-seat folk music club, located in the basement of the Rice Hotel at 755 North Dearborn in 1962. He then appeared on *The Tonight*

Fig. 1.3 Bill Cosby was a contemporary comedian because he immediately sought integrated audiences with his brand of comedy.

Show, and the Gate management asked him for a return engagement immediately afterward. He signed with the William Morris Agency and was already playing Mister Kelly's later that year.[31] Unlike his contemporary Redd Foxx who developed his material for a Black audience, Cosby told *Newsweek*, "I am trying to reach all the people." Cosby came to the same conclusion as Nipsey Russell—to have a successful career that did not rely on the dying Chitlin' Circuit, he had to create material that had universal appeal. Cosby originally told racial jokes, but in 1962, his manager Roy Silver told him to change his act, and thereafter, Cosby mainly told humorous tales involving "universal" topics such as childhood and family.[32] In 1964, Cosby told writer Lillian Calhoun, "There is nothing funny in the world about . . . the rioting in Harlem. It's difficult for me to get up on the stage and make fun of the problem. The rioting in Harlem, three guys lost in Mississippi."[33] Cosby opted to tell jokes about running for the bus or being married—universal themes. One of Cosby's 1964 television stand-up routines is indicative of this. In the six-minute performance, Cosby riffs on movie monsters and westerns and reimagines the Revolutionary War being fought using a football motif.

Nothing remotely resembling race, the civil rights movement, or any contemporary concerns was in this routine. The twenty-seven-year-old successfully appealed to a wide demographic who perhaps wanted to forget political assassinations, race riots, and Birmingham bombings.[34]

Bill Cosby was younger than Nipsey Russell, and his youthful good looks and charisma attracted television executives who had developed programming in the early 1960s that reflected a white-only world. Under pressure from the NAACP and other civil rights organizations, television took small steps to become integrated. In a 1965 television appearance before an all-white teenage crowd on a beach in an unnamed show on YouTube, Cosby jokes about being the worst possible student in shop class during high school where everything he attempted to make turned into an ashtray.[35] Cosby was more of a storyteller than a jokester like Nipsey Russell, and his stories of school friends, his family, and the neighborhood were about as innocuous as they could get.

Cosby was at the right place at the right time; his noncontroversial image was appealing to these executives, so they took a chance with him. Cosby became a major television star with *I Spy* (NBC, 1965–1968) and could choose his venues after this achievement. He played four concerts at Chicago's Civic Opera House in 1967. In 1968 and 1969, he returned for multiple shows at the Auditorium Theater. Cosby was the first Black comic in Chicago to have major television success and his path significantly differed from his predecessors who perfected their acts in front of Black Chicago audiences. He never played Black venues; he only performed in front of majority-Black audiences that were benefits for civil rights organizations or charities in Chicago. He simply did not have to perform in Black clubs due to his enormous popularity and widespread exposure. That doesn't mean Cosby didn't have appeal among Black audiences. Rather, as *Defender* columnist Doris E. Saunders wrote in 1967 "high on the agenda [this weekend] is the Bill Cosby happening at the Civic Opera House Saturday and Sunday. I know that I will personally have to find new arrangements for peaceful living if my children don't get to see him."[36] In the late 1960s and throughout the 1970s, a Cosby performance was an "event," and one traveled to major integrated cultural institutions to hear him.

CONCLUSION

For most Black comedians in the 1950s and early 1960s, Black performance venues were instrumental. Without those spaces to try out new material, play before appreciative (or unappreciative) audiences, make valuable career connections, and become comfortable on stage, most Black comedians would have never have had careers that took off. What changed in the 1960s was the relationship between audiences and how they helped create new Black comic stars. Traditional, transitional, and contemporary Black comics each embraced and negotiated their relationship to audiences differently. Traditional comic Moms embraced Black audiences as "home," while transitional comic Russell played to Black audiences but considered white, "crossover" audiences his bread and butter. On the other hand, from the start of his career, Cosby treated Black audiences as a desirable audience in so far as his white audience remained robust.

Dick Gregory is perhaps the embodiment of the comedian who could have found mainstream popularity in the 1960s, but his activism and racially toned humor largely relegated his routine to Black audiences in the 1970s and 1980s. His provocatively titled autobiography *Nigger* shocked the public in 1964 and further cemented his reputation as a controversial performer. In an *Audible* blog, his son Dr. Christian Gregory argues that his father walked away at the height of his success and fame because he believed that activism was far more important than entertainment. As a result, Gregory had more control over the trajectory of his career; he sacrificed mainstream success and compensation for activism, but it meant that he was freer to explore his material and his noncomedic projects.

As television slowly became integrated, Black comedians found that success could come far more rapidly with this mass medium. Cosby's meteoric rise was a prime example of this. Moms Mabley became a hit on the talk show circuit, Nipsey Russell became a staple on game shows, and Redd Foxx gained national notoriety with *Sanford and Son*. One went to a comedy club or performance venue to see one of these comedians *after* laughing with them on television. While Mister Kelly's was considered the epitome of stand-up comic success in Chicago, the nexus of Black entertainment venues in the city served as a nurturing and training ground for generations of comic geniuses and are fundamental to the history of popular culture in the city. One simply cannot discuss the history of stand-up comics in the city of Chicago without recognizing these important spaces at which Black audiences laughed.

Gerald R. Butters, Jr. is Professor of History at Aurora University and Faculty in the Graduate Liberal Studies Program at Northwestern University. He is author of *Black Manhood on the Silent Screen*; *From Sweetback to Super Fly: Race and Film Audiences in Chicago's Loop*; and *Banned in Kansas: Motion Picture Censorship, 1915–1966*. He is editor (with Novotny Lawrence) of *Beyond Blaxploitation*.

Notes

1. The popularity of Second City, which became a feeder for shows like *Saturday Night Live*, and the explosion of stand-up comedy clubs on the North Side of the city in the 1970s cemented this reputation. Unfortunately, this has erroneously been considered the period in which stand-up comedy "begins" in Chicago in the popular imagination. One such example of this is the writing of Brian Posen, former director and producer at Second City. He argues in a December 4, 2019, post that "comedy in Chicago began as early as 1955, when modern improv was born at the University of Chicago." What follows is a white-washed history that completely ignores African American comedians prior to Second City and during the explosion of Black comedy in Chicago during the 1960s. This is lazy and incorrect history.

2. Norman Spaulding, *History of Black-Oriented Radio in Chicago, 1929–1963* (Urbana: University of Illinois Press, 1981), 80.

3. The Regal was simultaneously a motion picture house and theater for stage shows.

4. "Why We Should Build the R&B Music Hall of Fame Museum," YouTube, accessed December 14, 2020, https://www.youtube.com/watch?v=voHveKbg6ZU.

5. Clovis E. Semmes, *The Regal Theater and Black Culture* (New York: Palgrave Macmillan, 2006), 156–59.

6. "Tivoli Theater," Cinema Treasures, accessed December 14, 2022, http://cinematreasures.org/theaters/943.

7. See Simon Critchley's book *On Humor* (New York: Routledge, 2002) or Alfred L. Martin, Jr.'s essay "The Tweet Has Two Faces," *Journal of Cinema and Media Studies* 58, no. 3 (Spring 2019): 160–65, for a discussion on the curation of comic audiences.

8. Redd Foxx would also fit this mode.

9. Cosby was often asked to play at Black fundraisers in Chicago.

10. Terrence Tucker, *Furiously Funny: Comic Rage from Ralph Ellison to Chris Rock* (Gainesville: University Press of Florida, 2018), 72.

11. Ibid., 79.

12. Moms Mabley, "Don't Sit on My Bed, 1948," YouTube, accessed December 19, 2022, https://www.youtube.com/watch?v=4hot_teqE_E.

13. Ibid.

14. Semmes, *Regal Theater*, 100.

15. "Regal Spends $150,000 for Live Summer Shows," *Chicago Defender*, July 1, 1959, 18.

16. *Chicago Defender*, May 6, 1961, 16

17. Semmes, *Regal Theater*, 100.

18. *Chicago Tribune*, April 19, 1962, a15.

19. Stephen A. Duncan, *The Rebel Café: Sex, Race and Politics in Cold War America's Nightclub Underground* (Baltimore: John Hopkins University Press, 2018), 185.

20. "Bud Billiken Talent Show Thrills 25,000 Patrons at Annual Parade," *Chicago Defender*, August 15, 1961, 16.

21. Megan McKinney, "When Chicago Was a World-Famous Party Town," *Classic Chicago Magazine*, July 1, 2018, accessed December 28, 2022, https://www.classicchicagomagazine.com/mister-kellys-london-house-and-all-that-jazz/.

22. "Tivoli Theater."

23. Dick Gregory, *Nigger* (New York: Plume), 130–31.

24. Advertisement, *Chicago Defender*, March 24, 1960, A21.

25. "Nipsey Views the Regal," *Chicago Defender*, August 1, 1962, 16.

26. "Nipsey Reaches Main Event," *Chicago Defender*, November 15, 1962, 20.

27. Daryll Littleton, *Black Comedians on Black Comedy* (New York: Applause Theatre and Books, 2006), 95.

28. Nipsey Russell, *Confucius Told Me*, 1959, YouTube, accessed December 28, 2022, https://www.youtube.com/watch?v=tS_bR-ePWIc&t=347s.

29. "Nipsey Reaches Main Event," 20.

30. Ibid.

31. Mark Whitaker, *Cosby: His Life and Times* (New York: Simon & Schuster, 2014), 117.

32. Stanley Karnow, "Bill Cosby: Variety Is the Life of Spies," *Saturday Evening Post* 238, no. 19 (1965): 86–88.

33. Lillian S. Calhoun, "Fast-Rising Comedian Bill Cosby Talks about His Different Approach to Comedy," *Chicago Defender*, August 1, 1963, 4.

34. "Bill Cosby 1964 Standup Comedy 2," YouTube, accessed December 19, 2022, https://www.youtube.com/watch?v=cyyE-q33kGY.

35. "Bill Cosby with Teens 1965 Comedy Routine," YouTube, accessed December 28, 2022, https://www.youtube.com/watch?v=Lfe9MCGsYP4&t=47s.

36. Doris E. Saunders, "Confetti," *Chicago Defender*, August 23, 1967, 14.

2

BLUE IS THE NEW GREEN

Martin Lawrence and the Mainstream
Appeal of Vulgarity

Joshua Truelove

"Hurry up!" an audience member yelled at comedian Martin Lawrence while he was taking a sip of water during his 2002 stand-up comedy special *Martin Lawrence Live: Runteldat*. Responding to the heckler, Lawrence fired back, "Somebody put something in his mouth. My zipper is stuck, y'all." The audience roared as Lawrence continued to make fun of the audience member who dared to challenge him. "I'll warn you, watch your mouth now. Don't forget who the original *Def Jam* host was, mother fucker."[1] The audience continued to laugh as Lawrence pointed out that although he was the original *Def Comedy Jam* (HBO, 1992–1997) host and biggest comedy star of the 1990s, he was no longer either. However, the comedian of the hip-hop generation and the heir apparent to Eddie Murphy and Richard Pryor had not changed his brand of comedy.

In the 1990s, Lawrence was inarguably the biggest comedy star. *Def Comedy Jam* and his eponymous sitcom, *Martin* (FOX, 1992–1997), were massive hits, and Lawrence starred in comedy film classics like *Nothing to Lose* (1997, dir. Steve Oedekerk), *Blue Streak* (1999, dir. Les Mayfield), *Life* (1999, dir. Ted Demme), and *Bad Boys* (1995, dir. Michael Bay). After years of being berated for his vulgarity by detractors, and admittedly being burned out from working so much, Lawrence's comedy and film career waned. However, at the height of his career—from about 1992 to 2003—Lawrence proved through *Def Comedy Jam*, stand-up specials, and rated-R comedy films that blue humor is a profitable mainstream brand. This chapter argues that despite his controversies, Lawrence's ability to blend hip-hop culture and blue humor—vulgarity used to talk about explicit scenarios and topics—into the mainstream not only illustrated the agency of the comedian but also showed vulgarity was profitable. It is important to note, though, that Lawrence was not a hack who simply used profanity to get cheap laughs. Rather, he was a master at physical comedy, crowd work, and the use of blue language for comedic emphasis. Nor did he originate the use of profanity in the mainstream. Comedians like Lenny Bruce, Redd Foxx, George Carlin, Richard Pyror, and Eddie Murphy had popularized the use of blue humor. While they all faced varying levels of repercussion, the backlash to Lawrence's comedy in the 1990s was odd, since popular culture in the 1990s encouraged edgy content. Lawrence, though, was able to bring blue comedy into the mainstream more than other comics before him.

I argue that Lawrence harnessed a particular brand of vulgarity through his stand-up comedy, sitcom, and films that was not only profitable but also surprisingly mainstream. The first section focuses on Lawrence's rise to fame from 1992 to 1993. Lawrence became a breakout star as the host of *Def Comedy Jam* and the star of *Martin*. Lawrence's brand of comedy was malleable enough not only to attract different audience segments at FOX and HBO but also to work within the constraints of each network. The second section focuses on the backlash Lawrence received for his language in 1994, which found Lawrence briefly banned from NBC for telling a blue joke in his opening monologue on *Saturday Night Live* (*SNL*) and battling with the Motion Picture Association of America (MPAA) over an NC-17 rating for his comedy special *You So Crazy*. The third section examines how the backlash in 1994 had little impact on Lawrence's career, as he took blue humor into mainstream films for the rest of the decade and more, even during and after television networks and cable stations were cutting Black-cast shows from their programs. Ultimately, these three sections coalesce to show how Lawrence's blue comedy helped him rise to fame and how he eventually took that same brand of comedy into mainstream films even with a year of critical and industry backlash.

This chapter builds on scholarship about Black comedians and their mainstream appeal. In "Branding Blackness on US Cable Television," Jennifer Fuller explores Blackness as a branding strategy and argues that cable networks not only needed Black viewers to succeed but also used Blackness as a brand to appeal to a transracial audience through "riskiness" as a signifier for Blackness.[2] Tying into the manipulation of Blackness as a brand to gain mainstream appeal, I use Kristal Brent Zook's work on the FOX network's use of dual casting to demonstrate how networks used Blackness to build large audiences, get sports broadcasting rights, and then cut the shows from their programming.[3] While networks often claim they cut Black-led shows due to poor ratings, Zook argued that networks often simply want to target more lucrative viewers. As Alfred Martin details, reaching Black eighteen- to forty-nine-year-old viewers is simply cheaper than reaching white eighteen- to forty-nine-year-old viewers.[4] Thus, regardless of viewership numbers, networks can make more money from programming that reaches white eighteen- to forty-nine-year-old viewers. Finally, this chapter builds on Herman Gray's arguments about networks and cable stations targeting Black and youth audiences with Black-cast TV shows and Black culture.[5] Throughout this chapter, I demonstrate how FOX and HBO used Lawrence's comedic talent to gain transracial and mainstream appeal to a wide age range of audiences in the hip-hop generation. It also illustrates Lawrence's ability to work inside multiple production constraints while maintaining his blue brand of humor. This chapter is chiefly concerned with asserting Lawrence's agency as he achieved mainstream success and stardom even as networks and cable channels were cutting Black-cast programs.

MARTIN LAWRENCE AS A BRAND:
BLUE HUMOR AND DUAL CASTING

In 1992, HBO premiered Russell Simmons's *Def Comedy Jam*. The monthly comedy showcase provided a platform for up-and-coming Black comedians. Hosted by Lawrence, who often introduced the show by making fun of audience members and doing small bits from his own work, *Def Comedy Jam* developed a reputation for being raw, offensive, and vulgar. More importantly, it was *the* comedy showcase of the hip-hop generation. Simmons himself was a hip-hop producer with his record label *Def Jam*, deejay Kid Capri spun hip-hop music between comics, and the comics themselves, from their jokes to their attire, were hip-hop inspired.[6] More significantly, the show was unabashedly vulgar. Not every use of four-letter-words was tasteful or even necessary, but the use of the language in itself and refusal to apologize for it was not only a powerful statement but also a prime example of vulgarity as a key component of the edgy content central to HBO's quality brand.[7]

Def Comedy Jam was not without its critics. White *New York Times* writer John O'Connor frequently wrote about the showcase, acknowledging its significance but also lambasting its vulgarity. He argued that the show was defined by its language and referred to it as "street talk."[8] He referred to the "foul language" and "foul attitude" on *Def Comedy Jam* "with its routines about 'bitches and ho's,' genitalia and sexual dexterity" as "reprehensible."

O'Connor, trying not to make his critique about a racial barrier, argued that the imagined and monolithic Black middle class were also fed up with the show. He continued to criticize *Def Comedy Jam* by mentioning examples of Black comedians who did not curse, like Bill Cosby. O'Connor expressed his disappointment in Lawrence on multiple occasions, including challenging Lawrence's take that Cheryl Underwood was undeniably funny, when he stated "so was Moms Mabley, and she did it without the thumping language, at least on television."[9] O'Connor also suggested that HBO censor the show due to the "consequences of verbal assault. In a society riddled with violence, the mere toning down of voices and moderating of language could prove incredibly helpful."[10] In all, O'Connor displayed an absurd gatekeeping mentality of Black culture as a white man, and his fundamental misunderstanding of HBO's brand and use of vulgarity to make quality television and that it was a subscription service not subject to the rules of the FCC. He also promoted a stereotype that Black men are aggressive. This racist stereotype dates back to slavery but was modernized through John F. Kennedy's juvenile delinquent program in the 1960s which targeted and profiled young Black men as aggressive.[11] O'Connor's pearl-clutching over the dirty words he heard on *Def Jam* is an extension of this decades-old trope.

Unfortunately for opponents of the show, *Def Comedy Jam* was popular among viewers during the Lawrence-hosted years. And although Lawrence only hosted the first two seasons before leaving to focus on his television and film career, the original iteration of *Def Comedy Jam* lasted seven seasons on HBO.[12] *New York Times* critic Jonathan Hicks acknowledged that "virtually every joke is unprintable"; however, he spent more time stressing the popularity of the show. According to Hicks's research, among homes with pay-cable stations, *Def Comedy Jam's* 1.7 million viewers were the most of any television program airing at midnight on Fridays. The showcase bested *The Arsenio Hall Show*, *The Dennis Miller Show*, and even *The Tonight Show*.[13] Clearly, the vulgarity of *Def Comedy Jam* was not hurting the show. Its ratings along with the explosion of the careers of Lawrence and other comics who appeared on the show demonstrated that the blue material of *Def Comedy Jam* was not only welcomed but also profitable.

Lawrence was especially popular. His sitcom *Martin* debuted on FOX in 1992 and was a television hit throughout its five-year run. The show starred Lawrence as Martin Payne, a Detroit-area radio disk jockey trying to make ends meet, and focused on his relationship with his girlfriend, Gina (Tisha Campbell), and their friends. The show was a clear example of FOX's continued use of hip-hop culture and Black comedians to appeal to Black and young audiences.[14] Although a success, *Martin* was not without its critics. Some argued that *Martin* was perpetrating Black stereotypes and that although Lawrence was working inside the constraints of network television, he was still offensive. Cosby was particularly harsh on Lawrence and his sitcom as well, saying that *Martin* presented a bad example for Black Americans.[15] Lawrence fired back at Cosby, suggesting that Cosby was "missing the point." He pointed out that *The Cosby Show* portrayed an upper-middle-class family, while he was portraying himself on *Martin*. Lawrence explained, "I'm portraying me, my personal experience. Young Black men struggling to be the head of their households. Not always doing it right."[16] He further critiqued Cosby and other critics of the sitcom, asking "Sam Malone wants to bone every woman that comes into *Cheers*, and he's a national hero. . . . Why is it they only expect Black characters to act like role models?" On Cosby, Lawrence stated "For all his clean, wholesome, Jell-O pudding, I-ain't-never-done-no-wrong image, they still didn't let his ass buy NBC, now, did they?"[17] The irony of Cosby's constant pestering of Black comedians over their image is not lost.

Martin may have had its critics, but the sitcom's appeal reached far beyond the older *Def Comedy Jam* audience. Multiple reviews of *Martin* mentioned its appeal to younger viewers, and critic Bill Carter referred to it as a "teenage trend" and that *Martin*'s key demographic was "about 22" years old.[18] In fact, according to the *New York Times*'s Mark Stuart Gill, *Martin* ranked in the top five among viewers age twelve to seventeen and in the top ten among ages two to eleven in the Nielsen ratings. Lawrence acknowledged his younger audience and joked, "I'm huge with the under-5 crowd."[19] While other critics worried about Lawrence's cross-generational and multiracial appeal due to the possibility of children hearing his raunchier material, Gill instead praised Lawrence's ability to work inside different constraints and gave credit to his unique lovable masculinity. John Bowman, *Martin*'s executive producer, told Gill that Lawrence stands out because "Martin is a Black man in his own world. He does hard, physical comedy. But he can be silly and gentle and romantic. His persona is about trying to find a place in society and a loving relationship that works." In the same article, Gill interviewed Stan Lathan, the executive producer of *Def Comedy Jam*, who explained that Lawrence is "like a mirror of the current hip-hop generation. The kids are all trying to maintain this macho exterior even though they have a lot of inner sensitivity and insecurities."[20] In a 1994 interview with *Entertainment Weekly*, Lawrence addressed those concerned about his vulgarity reaching children by saying, "Hey, people know Martin. They ain't surprised by this shit."[21] Lawrence's blue work was not a secret, and it had little negative impact on his appeal as FOX used him in their attempts at dual casting—reaching Black viewers as well as primarily white, young adult males.

In addition to Gill's praise of Lawrence's ability to balance a sensitive masculinity and appeal to a wide range of audiences, others, particularly fellow comedians, raved about Lawrence's comedic skill. Controversial comedian and podcast host Joe Rogan frequently tells his audience that he was often asked to perform after Lawrence in the 1990s and found it immensely difficult. He dramatically emphasized that he has never heard a comedian "murder" a room like Lawrence did.[22] Legendary comic Chris Rock also emphasized Lawrence's stand-up skill. Rock told a story of the time he had to follow Lawrence and that he peeked from the side of the stage because the room was so loud that he thought there was a fight in the crowd. "When I got there I realized it wasn't a fight," he explained, "it was people laughing so hard that the building was shaking. People were crying, standing, stomping their feet—screaming laughter. I was terrified. It was like watching somebody fucking your wife with a bigger dick."[23] Rock argued that following Lawrence was one of the most humbling nights of his comedy career.

Lawrence released his first comedy album in 1993, *Talkin' Shit*. He joked about overweight women, his friend coming out as gay, penis sizes, women's orgasms, oral sex, women's hygiene, and farts.[24] *Talkin' Shit*, like its name, was vulgar, offensive, and sometimes homophobic and misogynistic. However, just like on *Def Comedy Jam* and *Martin*, Lawrence showed that his blue brand of humor was profitable in the entertainment industry. *Talkin' Shit* was in *Billboard*'s top two hundred records for nine weeks, reaching as high as seventy-six, and reached the top ten for weekly hip-hop and R&B albums.[25]

BACKLASH BLUES: THE LIMITS OF MARTIN'S BLUE MATERIAL

Lawrence's star continued its meteoric rise in 1994. But as his star rose, so did controversies surrounding his blue material. On February 19, 1994, he hosted *Saturday Night Live* for his first and final time. In his opening monologue, Lawrence did not shy away from his blue material. He opened by making fun of network censors following him around. "Wish they'd get off of my ass," Lawrence joked. "Oops, damn. Did I slip?" Lawrence continued, "It's just bothering me man. 'You can't say this, you can't say that!' And I'm like how am I going to talk about the world?"[26] He continued with his monologue, and one joke in particular, where he stated that women need to "wash their ass," "douche," and "put a Tic-Tac in your ass," caused uproar among network executives.[27] This bit of his opening monologue was removed before the West Coast airing of *SNL* and is still absent from the monologue in NBC's footage from the episode. Lawrence was never invited back to *SNL* and was temporarily banned from NBC.

John O'Connor returned to gloat about Lawrence's *SNL* folly. He explained that "what is accepted in the relatively tight, enclosed world of *Def*

Fig. 2.1 Screenshot from Lawrence's 1994 appearance on *Saturday Night Live*, which resulted in his getting banned from both the series and NBC, the network on which the series aired.

Comedy Jam won't necessarily translate to a larger context." He continued, saying Lawrence "learned the hard way" that he should stick to the "amiable persona he developed for *Martin*" rather than his "four-lettered *Def Comedy Jam*" act.[28] O'Connor was not alone in his offense to Lawrence, as NBC received over 177 complaints filed by viewers of the broadcast.[29]

Lawrence responded to the backlash and explained that he did not think *SNL*, NBC, or the audience wanted a clean monologue due to its 11:30 p.m. ET timeslot. He also claimed that he ran the same monologue through rehearsals, and no one complained about it. The comic believed what he said was no worse than some of the show's other edgier content, referring to a skit with actor Alec Baldwin as a pedophile camp counselor, and asked for clarity about bad taste. Lawrence explained, though, that he was not mad about NBC's decision. "They made the decision they thought they had to, and I'll live with it," he said.[30] In a 2020 interview on the radio show *The Breakfast Club*, Lawrence replied "I don't give a damn!" when asked about being banned from *SNL* and NBC. He then clarified that he was never banned from *SNL*, only briefly NBC, and NBC executives wrote him a letter shortly after the incident apologizing for their overreaction.[31]

The *SNL* monologue was not the only controversy Lawrence caused with his blue material in 1994. That same year, *You So Crazy* debuted. The eighty-five-minute filmed comedy special featured jokes about his potential of getting raped in prison, masturbation, oral sex, having sex with Dorothy from *The Wizard of Oz*, farting, ejaculation, and another version of the "wash your ass" joke he got in trouble for on *SNL*.[32] "Stand-up allows the most freedom, but TV gives the most exposure. Movies mean a lot of money," explained Lawrence.[33] The film was a defining moment in Lawrence's career, as he saw stand-up as the most freeing platform for him to perform his comedy.

While *You So Crazy* enabled Lawrence more freedom to perform his comedy, the MPAA found its material too vulgar. Lawrence intended for an R-rated theatrical release of the special, but the MPAA felt an NC-17 rating was more appropriate until Lawrence edited it to make it suitable for an R rating. The comedian was frustrated over feeling unfairly censored. "I'm not inciting violence or racism or anything negative," Lawrence explained, "I'm just making you laugh."[34] The comedian stated that he did nothing wrong and challenged the legitimacy of the First Amendment when he said, "If talking about ourselves gets me in trouble, then so be it. I'll continue to say what I want to say because this is America, the land of the free. The land of free speech. Or that's what they keep telling us."[35] Eventually, Lawrence and lawyers for Miramax, who planned to distribute the special, appealed the MPAA's rating on the basis of free speech, arguing that it was the first time an NC-17 rating was given solely on the basis of language. Lawrence also argued that his comedy was not any more vulgar than the previous theatrical releases of Pryor's and Murphy's stand-up specials, which received R ratings.[36] Lawrence and Miramax lost the appeal, and the film was handed an official NC-17 rating.

Beyond artistic agency, Lawrence fought to receive an R rating because an NC-17 rating meant it would limit the distribution of *You So Crazy* to theaters, shrinking its box office potential. His fears were legitimate, and Miramax dropped distribution for the film. It was picked up by the Samuel Goldwyn Company and released without a rating. The damage over the rating controversy had been done. *You So Crazy* opened in 417 theaters nationwide with a $2.5 million weekend and finished with $10 million total at the domestic box office.[37] Comparatively, Eddie Murphy's 1987 special *Raw* finished with over $50 million and Richard Pryor's 1982 special *Live on the Sunset Strip* finished with over $36 million at the domestic box office, $65 million and $55 million, respectively, in 1994 dollars.[38] *You So Crazy* received mixed reviews, some praising the comedian's talent and energy, while others expressed their disgust with his language.[39] Despite the setback, Lawrence moved on to record a new comedy album, continued filming *Martin*, and starred in more movies. In his 1995 comedy album, *Funk It!*, Lawrence opened with a bit about his censorship battles over the past year with particular focus on *SNL*. Doing an impression of the media's overreaction to his language, Lawrence joked, "'Oh, you're going to get banned from NBC!

You'll never go on TV again!' and I'm like 'Why? Because I talked about washing your ass?'"[40] The comedian repeatedly expressed his confusion over the negative backlash he received because he felt it was in line with his blue comic persona.

Martin Goes to Hollywood:
Blue Humor in the Mainstream

While continuing to work on *Martin* until 1997, Lawrence's film career sky-rocketed. Even with backlash about his language, the comedian continued to illustrate his bankability at the box office. The success of rated-R comedies like *Bad Boys* (1995), *Nothing to Lose* (1997), and *Life* (1998) proved that the brand of blue humor Lawrence made famous on *Def Comedy Jam* was profitable. *Bad Boys* grossed over $140 million at the worldwide box office.[41] *Nothing to Lose* made $44 million and *Life* made over $73 million at the worldwide box office.[42] Lawrence also demonstrated that he could still make profitable comedy inside PG-13 constraints, as both *Blue Streak* (1999) and *Big Momma's House* (2000) made $117 million and $173 million, respectively, at the worldwide box office.[43]

In 2002, Lawrence produced a new comedy special: *Runteldat*. On stage, Lawrence was his old self. He joked about crawling into his wife's vagina to yell at his unborn baby, vaginas after child birth, descriptions of different types of women's breasts, descriptions of deformed penises, having sex with women during menstruation, and "weird sex." Sometimes xenophobic and misogynistic, Lawrence continued his unapologetic brand of blue comedy and the special grossed $19 million at the US box office, and he even sent a message to critics of his language in the special when he said "If there is any critics here tonight, fuck you and kiss my ass. I don't give a shit about you. They're like the scum of the earth to me. Fuck them. I can't stand a critic."[44] Lawrence's message was loud and clear: he was back after a brief hiatus, and he did not care if critics did not like his brand of comedy, as they are not his intended consumer.

In 2003, Lawrence teamed up with Will Smith again for a sequel to the 1995 hit *Bad Boys*. The duo verified their rated-R action-comedy was still financially viable, as *Bad Boys II* grossed $273 million at the worldwide box office. That same year, he starred in *National Security*, which also performed well at the box office, although not as well as *Bad Boys II*. Lawrence's career began to slow, although he starred in two *Big Momma's House* sequels (2006 and 2011) and joined ensemble casts for *Death at a Funeral* (2010) and *Wild Hogs* (2007). He worked periodically, but mostly, the biggest comedy star of the 1990s was now an aging comedian who stepped out of the spotlight.

Fig. 2.2 *Nothing to Lose* was one of Lawrence's R-rated film successes that demonstrated his appeal across film and television with his blue brand of comedy.

CONCLUSION

Although Lawrence never again reached the heights he achieved in the 1990s, his most recent work attested to the appeal of his blue brand of comedy. In 2016, he released a new comedy special, *Doin' Time*, in which he was as unapologetically dirty and offensive as ever, as he joked about menstruation, impressions of Cosby having sex, masturbating on Skype, Viagra's side effects, defecating his pants, and defecating with an erection.[45] A few years later, Lawrence and Will Smith reteamed for a long-awaited *Bad Boys* sequel. *Bad Boys for Life* released in January 2020 with an R rating, earned $426 million at the worldwide box office, and was the highest-grossing film of 2020.[46] With *Doin' Time* and *Bad Boys for Life*, Lawrence again displayed his blue style of humor was profitable.

There is no exact answer for why Lawrence's language caused such uproar in the 1990s, but it is telling that the most popular comedian of the 1990s, a Black man, was so heavily criticized for vulgarity during the "sex sells" culture of the decade while Howard Stern's radio show was on public radio airwaves and *The Jerry Springer Show* aired on network television. Both of those programs were more or at least as offensive as Lawrence's jokes and were easily accessible on morning public radio and daytime network television. Critics of Lawrence tended to use his appeal to younger audiences, including children, as a reason his blue material was problematic, but all they proved was Lawrence's ability to make profitable comedy inside any constraints placed on him. Due to an increase in the number of platforms, and his ability to act and do physical comedy in addition to his joke writing, Lawrence illustrated that vulgarity is profitable and has mainstream appeal.

Joshua Truelove is a PhD candidate in History at Boston College and Affiliated Faculty at Emerson College. His work appears in *Afrofuturism in Black Panther: Gender, Identity, and the Re-Making of Blackness.*

NOTES

1. Martin Lawrence, *Martin Lawrence Live: Runteldat*, dir. David Raynr (New York: Viacom, 2002).
2. Jennifer Fuller, "Branding Blackness on US Cable Television," *Media Culture & Society* 32, no. 2 (2010): 285–305.
3. Kristal Brent Zook, *Color by Fox: The Fox Network and the Revolution in Black Television* (New York: Oxford University Press, 1999).
4. Alfred L. Martin Jr., *The Generic Closet: Black Gayness and the Black-Cast Sitcom* (Bloomington: Indiana University Press, 2021), 34.
5. Herman Gray, *Watching Race: Television and the Struggle for Blackness* (Minneapolis: University of Minnesota Press, 1995).
6. Bakari Kitwana, *The Hip Hop Generation: Young Blacks and the Crisis in African American Culture* (New York: Basic Civitas Books, 2002); Jeff Chang, *Can't Stop Won't Stop: A History of the Hip-Hop Generation* (New York: Picador, 2005).
7. Fuller, "Branding Blackness on US Cable Television."
8. John J. O'Connor, "The Curse of Incessant Cursing," *New York Times*, July 31 1994.
9. John J. O'Connor, "Onstage at the Outer Limits of the Outrageous: Russell Simmons's Def Comedy Jam," *New York Times*, July 8, 1993.
10. O'Connor, "Curse of Incessant Cursing."
11. Kennedy's juvenile delinquent program is best described in Elizabeth Hinton, *From the War on Poverty to the War on Crime: The Making of Mass Incarceration in America* (Cambridge, MA: Harvard University Press, 2016).
12. Howard Rosenberg, "Where Are Critics of 'Def Comedy'?," *Los Angeles Times*, April 15, 1994.
13. Jonathan Hicks, "Russell Simmons Taps Street Culture to Build an Empire in Entertainment," *New York Times*, June 14, 1992.
14. Zook, *Color by Fox.*
15. Barry Koltnow, "Crazy Like a Fox: Martin Lawrence Puts a Positive Spin on Criticism," *Chicago Tribune*, March 27, 1994; Isabel Wilkerson, "Black Life on TV: Realism or Stereotypes?," *New York Times*, August 15, 1993.
16. Mark Stuart Gill, "He's Half Macho Man, Half Teddy Bear," *New York Times*, August 1, 1993.
17. Martin Lawrence, "Got to Be Real," *VIBE*, April 1994.
18. Bill Carter, "Fall Network Schedules Offer Plenty of Choices (At Least for the Young)," *New York Times*, May 27, 1992; Carter, "This Fall, the Barely Adult Set Is the Object of Network Desire: Networks Court the Barely Adult Set," *New York Times*, September 10, 1992.
19. Gill, "He's Half Macho Man, Half Teddy Bear."
20. Ibid.
21. Martin Lawrence, "Martin Lawrence Makes the Jump from TV to Film," *Entertainment Weekly*, February 4, 1994, https://ew.com/article/1994/02/04/martin-lawrence-makes-jump-tv-film.

22. Joe Rogan, *The Joe Rogan Experience*, episode 1712, "Bert Kreischer (Part 2)," podcast audio, September 2021.

23. Judd Apatow, "Chris Rock: The E-mail Interview," *Vanity Fair*, December 5, 2012.

24. Martin Lawrence, *Martin Lawrence Live: Talkin' Shit*, East West Records, 1993.

25. "Chart History: Martin Lawrence," Billboard, https://www.billboard.com/music /Martin-Lawrence/chart-history/BLP; "Talkin' Shit," Billboard, https://www.billboard.com /music/martin-lawrence/chart-history/TSL/song/177370.

26. *Saturday Night Live*, season 19, episode 14, dir. Lorne Michaels, aired February 19, 1994, on NBC, https://www.nbc.com/saturday-night-live/video/martin-lawrence-monologue/n10550.

27. Don Roy King, "Martin Lawrence's Monologue," SNL Transcripts Tonight, updated October 8, 2018, 1993, https://snltranscripts.jt.org/93/93nmono.phtml; *Tampa Bay Times*, "SNL Went Too Far, Viewers, Censor Agree," *Tampa Bay Times*, March 22, 1994, https://www .tampabay.com/archive/1994/02/22/snl-went-too-far-viewers-censor-agree/?outputType=audit.

28. O'Connor, "Curse of Incessant Cursing."

29. *Tampa Bay Times*, "SNL Went Too Far, Viewers, Censor Agree."

30. Chuck Crisafulli, "Martin Lawrence: Dr. Dirt or Mr. Clean? Barred by NBC, He's Generally Blue on Stage but Not on TV," *Los Angeles Times*, March 8, 1994.

31. Breakfast Club Power 105.1 FM, "Will Smith & Martin Lawrence Talk 'Bad Boys' Trilogy, Growth, Regrets + More," podcast audio, 2020, https://www.youtube.com /watch?v=wACxobztaXk.

32. Martin Lawrence, *Martin Lawrence: You So Crazy*, dir. Thomas Schlamme (New York: HBO Independent Productions, 1994).

33. Gill, "He's Half Macho Man, Half Teddy Bear."

34. Crisafulli, "Martin Lawrence."

35. Koltnow, "Crazy Like a Fox."

36. Esther Iverem, "Lawrence to Appeal MPAA Rating of 'You So Crazy,'" *Los Angeles Times*, February 16, 1994.

37. "Martin Lawrence: You So Crazy," Box Office Mojo, accessed January 10, 2020, https:// www.boxofficemojo.com/release/rl1836090881/weekend/.

38. "Eddie Murphy: Raw," Box Office Mojo, accessed January 10, 2020, https://www .boxofficemojo.com/title/tt0092948/?ref_=bo_se_r_1; "Richard Pryor: Live on the Sunset Strip," Box Office Mojo, accessed January 10, 2020, https://www.boxofficemojo.com/title /tt0084597/?ref_=bo_se_r_2.

39. Caryn James, "A Corrosive Comedy of Hip-Hop Manners: Aiming Gags about Prison Rape and Feminine Hygiene at the Mainstream," *New York Times*, April 27, 1994; Kenneth Turan, "Martin Lawrence's Family Values," *Los Angeles Times*, April 27, 1994.

40. Martin Lawrence, *Funk It!*, East West, 1995.

41. "Bad Boys," Box Office Mojo, accessed January 10, 2020, https://www.boxofficemojo .com/title/tt0112442/?ref_=bo_se_r_1.

42. "Nothing to Lose," Box Office Mojo, accessed January 10, 2020, https://www .boxofficemojo.com/title/tt0119807/?ref_=bo_se_r_1; "Life," Box Office Mojo, accessed January 10, 2020, https://www.boxofficemojo.com/title/tt0123964/?ref_=bo_se_r_3.

43. "Blue Streak," Box Office Mojo, accessed January 10, 2020, https://www .boxofficemojo.com/title/tt0181316/?ref_=bo_se_r_1; "Big Momma's House," Box Office Mojo, accessed January 10, 2020, https://www.boxofficemojo.com/title/tt0208003/?ref_=bo_se_r_1.

44. Lawrence, *Martin Lawrence Live: Runteldat*; "Martin Lawrence Live: Runteldat," Box Office Mojo, accessed January 10, 2020, https://www.boxofficemojo.com/title /tt0327036/?ref_=bo_se_r_1.

45. Martin Lawrence, *Martin Lawrence Live: Doin' Time: Uncut*, dir. David Raynr (New York: Showtime Networks, 2016).

46. "Bad Boys for Life," Box Office Mojo, accessed January 10, 2020, https://www .boxofficemojo.com/release/rl1182631425/?ref_=bo_yl_table_2.

3

"THERE'S A NEW SHERIFF IN TOWN"

Eddie Murphy and the Comedy of Double Conscious Law and Order

Lisa Guerrero

COMEDY THROUGH THE VEIL

In 1982, at the height of his popularity on NBC's *Saturday Night Live* (NBC, 1975–), and at the age of twenty-one, Eddie Murphy starred in his first feature film, *48 Hrs.* (1982, dir. Walter Hill). Sharing top billing alongside well-known actor Nick Nolte, Murphy would test his star power with the film as well as his ability to transition from television sketch comedy to film comedy. Murphy did not waste his shot; he was nominated for a Golden Globe for his performance in the film, solidifying him as a bankable star and launching him into a film career that is arguably unmatched by any other successful Black comedian in the twentieth century. In *48 Hrs.*, Murphy plays Reggie Hammond, a streetwise criminal who is furloughed from prison for forty-eight hours by San Francisco police detective Jack Cates to help catch a killer. Only two years later, Murphy was given top billing in *Beverly Hills Cop* (1984, dir. Martin Brest) as Detroit detective Axel Foley, searching for his friend's killer in glamorous Beverly Hills, California. The success of the movie spawned two *Beverly Hills Cop* sequels and turned Murphy into a 1980s icon.[1]

Interestingly, these iconic Murphy roles were never initially intended for the actor who would go on to make them famous: *48 Hrs.* was originally meant to be made in the 1970s with Clint Eastwood and Richard Pryor in the roles that ultimately ended up going to Nick Nolte and Eddie Murphy, respectively. Before Nolte and Murphy were eventually cast, Sylvester Stallone, Mickey Rourke, and Burt Reynolds were considered for the role of Jack Cates, and Gregory Hines and Denzel Washington were considered for the role of Reggie Hammond. And in the case of *Beverly Hills Cop*, Sylvester Stallone was slated to play Axel Foley up until two weeks prior to filming. As reported in Screen Rant, "As difficult as it is to imagine anyone other than Murphy bringing his comedic chops to *Beverly Hills Cop*, there were several other actors considered before him. Mickey Rourke, Richard Pryor, Al Pacino, and James Caan were all linked to the project at one time, but it was Sylvester Stallone who came the closest to starring in the film."[2]

Though it is a common occurrence in Hollywood for several different actors to be considered, or even cast, in a role that eventually goes to another actor, I think it is worth considering the significance of that trend in the case of Murphy and the two roles that set the stage for his meteoric rise. The fact that neither Reggie Hammond nor Axel Foley were imagined with Eddie Murphy in mind makes Murphy's ineluctable embodiment of both characters even more notable. In the first case of *48 Hrs.*, Murphy was a virtual unknown so that his interpretation of Hammond was relatively untainted by audiences' cultural associations of him in other roles. I say "relatively" as he was enjoying success as a member of the cast of *Saturday Night Live*, and we do see some of that residual characterization in the scene where Murphy's character is introduced. In this scene, Murphy's Hammond is sitting in his cell belting out The Police's classic song "Roxanne" while wearing headphones and sunglasses. His stylization of that moment strongly echoes the actor's impersonation of Stevie Wonder on *SNL*. However, aside from this momentary flash of recognition, Murphy's portrayal of Reggie is something completely new—to Murphy, to audiences, and to film genealogy. Since Murphy wasn't part of the filmmakers' imaginary before filming, it meant that Murphy himself created that imaginary for them. We can't imagine Reggie Hammond *not* being played by Eddie Murphy because Reggie Hammond *can't* be played without Eddie Murphy. Reggie Hammond doesn't exist as a character, or eventually as a blueprint, until Murphy brings him into existence. If we think about this origin story in hindsight, it may seem unsurprising considering what we know now about Murphy's humongous talent. However, when we view it without this knowledge, what we see when we watch *48 Hrs.* is Eddie Murphy creating what would become one of the most recognizable and lucrative film archetypes in contemporary film: the wise and wise-cracking crime fighter of color.

The case of Murphy's casting in *Beverly Hills Cop* can be seen as a variation on a casting theme. The fact that Murphy was not seriously considered for the role of Axel Foley until filmmakers had two weeks to replace Sylvester Stallone before filming began is slightly different than his casting experience in *48 Hrs.* for two reasons. The first is that Murphy was a more known quantity by the time *Beverly Hills Cop* was cast, with a proven, if short, track record. In other words, filmmakers had a sense of what casting Murphy in the role meant for the role. The second, and more interesting, reason is that aside from Pryor, only white, dramatic actors were being imagined in this role. The solo cop who doesn't play by the rules was created as a vehicle for white hypermasculinity. Even so, Stallone apparently leaned into the white, hypermasculine frame a bit too much. In fact, the primary reason why Stallone didn't end up in the role was because he had completely rewritten the script to be a classic action film with *his* Axel Foley, or Axel Cobretti, as he renamed the character, out for vengeance over the murder of his brother. Because the revamped script removed the comedy the filmmakers imagined for the film, and because the new budget would cost too much, Stallone was replaced with Murphy in the eleventh hour.[3]

Murphy's Axel Foley is a clear palimpsest of Reggie Hammond. The racial and class signifiers that distinguish Murphy's Axel Foley are clearly being supported by the house that Reggie Hammond built, in particular in the ways in which Hammond occupied white spaces, both literal and imagined. Neither Foley nor Hammond before him feels compelled to assimilate to white spaces. Murphy's portrayals demand that presumed spaces of whiteness are deliberately disrupted by Blackness, from Torchy's in *48 Hrs.* to the Beverly Palm Hotel and the Harrow Club in *Beverly Hills Cop*. The undeniability of Blackness in the way Murphy plays both Hammond and Foley directly relates to the subgenre at the center of this essay, which relies on the layering of racial and class dimensions that deliberately and unapologetically resist the white racial frame. This subgenre originates with Eddie Murphy.

Despite his introduction of this racial reframing with his roles in *48 Hrs.* and *Beverly Hills Cop*, Murphy's body of work is largely considered as mainstream fare and is rarely discussed in terms of Black cultural resistance. That is not to say that scholars don't acknowledge his importance in the legacy of Black comedy, but it is apparent that his domination of mainstream cinema in the 1980s, as well as his transformation in the twenty-first century into a beloved animated sidekick (his character Donkey from the *Shrek* franchise is likely more recognizable to younger audiences than Murphy himself), has contracted the critical lens through which his work is most frequently considered.[4] However, there is both space and need to reconsider Murphy's earliest film work through Black consciousness and counternarrative.

This chapter examines how Eddie Murphy's work in *48 Hrs.* and *Beverly Hills Cop* created a new template for Black comedic film that I am calling "double conscious law and order." W. E. B. Du Bois's concept of double consciousness wherein he identifies the state of Black subjecthood as "always looking at one's self through the eyes of others," describes how Black Americans experience their lives as a constant twoness between how they perceive themselves and how they are perceived by white society.[5] This state of Black consciousness in America is a direct result of a white supremacist capitalist frame that indulges a racialized social order where people of color, in particular Black people, are at the bottom. This order, while artificial, is not unreal, and it creates a material and ideological power around whiteness and wealth that directly shapes the meanings of Blackness, Black identity, and Black humanity. And though these meanings have great impact on the American social world and Black people's place in it, Du Bois is also clear in his assessment that double consciousness presents Black people with a unique power to understand white people as well as white people do—maybe even better. I think it is important to note that Du Bois doesn't refer to this state as a "split" consciousness, which would imply two halves of a whole. He is deliberate in naming this state "double" consciousness: *two whole* consciousnesses. In this way, double consciousness is not only the idea that Black people are constantly straddling their perceptions of themselves and the perceptions white society has of them but also the idea that in order to live a life that is divided in that way, Black people must know white people as well as they know themselves. This power, while taking a heavy toll, does allow Black people to disrupt the white supremacist capitalist model in very unique ways, often without white society even noticing, so busy is it believing in its own power. This is the starting point of double conscious law and order. This template builds on the notion that the Black characters, be they criminal or cop, are always already outside of the law because of the way the Black body is generally attached to concepts of lawlessness in the white public imagination.

In *48 Hrs.*, Murphy plays a criminal; in *Beverly Hills Cop*, he plays a detective. However, regardless of their different positions in the imagined law-and-order taxonomy, both characters are essentially the same character due to their relationship to double conscious law and order. At the heart of double conscious law and order is the Black characters' understanding not only of how both sides of the law work but also of how Blackness and whiteness are positioned differently in relationship to dominant imaginations of lawfulness. The humor of the films is derived from watching how white law and order and Black law and order run parallel to each other, not necessarily working at cross purposes but definitely *not* working together. This formula draws on the incongruity theory of comedy where laughter stems from our expectations being disrupted and our actual enjoyment of the incongruous. Typical white audience expectations of cop films are based in the assumption that the act of solving crime is absent of race. People of color know that those expectations aren't supported by reality. Murphy's cop films rely on this template of double conscious law and order to introduce these incongruous notions of crime and crime solving that are based in Black racial realities that disrupt the expected white racial frame. Even as "their goal" is allegedly the same as that of their white counterparts, the Black characters' approaches to achieving their goals make it clear that they are working toward different ideological ends. In Hammond's and Foley's cases, each character goes against colorblind social expectations and breaks the rules endlessly to achieve their goals. From their double conscious point of view, they see how the barriers between law and order are permeable and fluid. They are pursuing *justice*, not law and order, which makes rule- (and law-) breaking both incidental and instrumental in achieving their goal.

When we consider the template of double conscious law and order within the genre of comedy, it highlights how closely related comedy is to drama in the human experience and how the generic categories of comedy and drama are determined largely by the discursive frames in which they circulate. Social and cultural phenomena aren't inherently comedic or dramatic or tragic, to use the common juxtaposition. Our reactions to social and cultural phenomena are just one element of the discursive frame that helps categorize those phenomena as either comic or tragic. When we think specifically about television or film genres, our responses are largely informed by anxiety, either the dissolution of it or the creation of it. Thinking about comedy in particular, Lauren Berlant and Sianne Ngai have stated, "Comedy's pleasure comes in part from its ability to dispel anxiety . . . but it doesn't simply do that. As both an aesthetic mode and a form of life, its action just as likely produces anxiety."[6] In the case of *48 Hrs.* and *Beverly Hills Cop* and other comedies that rely on race, either explicitly or implicitly as a basis of laughter and pleasure, racial anxiety is ever present. This anxiety manifests differently for white audiences and audiences of color, where white audiences generally will rely on laughter to defuse the anxiety while audiences of color generally will rely on laughter as a validation of experiences they are familiar with. In either case, the racial anxiety demands a response, and when it comes to race, the response could quickly and easily be one of tragedy. In fact, in both *48 Hrs.* and the *Beverly Hills Cop* series, there are many moments where the blurring between what is comic and what is tragic becomes noticeably uncomfortable. Despite this fact, both are readily identified as comedies, though marked as particular kinds of comedies because of the discursive signs and practices used to mark them as unique.

As Jason Mittell has stated about genre, "Genres emerge only from intertextual relations between multiple texts, resulting in a common category.... Texts cannot interact on their own; they come together only through cultural practices such as production and reception." He goes further to say, "Processes of genre reproduction ... occur only through the actions of industries and audiences, not through any action of the text themselves."[7] As we consider the creation of the comedic subgenre of double conscious law and order, *48 Hrs.* and *Beverly Hills Cop* serve as origin texts. These texts, coupled with Eddie Murphy himself as a sign of both Blackness and comedy and the industry's marketing of these films, lead audiences toward particular racial incongruities and create certain assumptions and expectations that then reaffirm the existence of this particular subgenre.[8] Interestingly, even in its generic contours, double conscious law and order spans the double terrains of racial comedy and racial drama. And it is a subgenre that has proved both popular with audiences and lucrative to movie studios. Double conscious law and order and Murphy's Hammond and Foley have spawned the likes of Chris Tucker in the *Rush Hour* trilogy, Damon Wayans in *The Last Boy Scout,* and Will Smith and Martin Lawrence in the *Bad Boys* trilogy, as well as Murphy himself in other films and many other double conscious law-and-order characters and plots. Once audiences came to recognize the formula and embrace the particularities of racial incongruities, the sky was the limit.

THE COLOR OF LAW AND ORDER

Another important element to consider about the emergence of double conscious law and order in these two movies are the ideas around the actual policing and crime fighting based in race. Formalized policing in the United States has its roots partly in the slave patrols of the South beginning in the 1700s. These origins created an enduring connection between social control and protection of property, as well as the codified idea of the function of police in American society. Moreover, both of the primary functions of social control and protection of property were originally predicated on the containment of Black bodies, which has endured as a problematic defining feature of modern policing and criminal justice to this day. At its heart, law and order in the United States is organized around an implicit (though, oftentimes, explicit) racial "logic" that refuses the possibility of a noncriminal Black body. Regardless of a Black person's actual status as cop or criminal, law-abiding or law-breaking, that person remains unable to participate in the system of law and order on any terms other than those of white supremacy that deem

Black people as inherently "against the law." This reality is one that has taken center stage in an explosive and tragic way in the second and third decades of the twenty-first century with the overwhelming number of Black deaths in America at the hands of police officers and the impassioned and sustained resistance that followed these extralegal killings of Black men, women, and children. And it is one reality that has always necessitated that Black Americans operate with a doubled understanding of how law and order works not only generally in US society but also specifically *on* and *against* its Black citizens. In other words, it requires that Black Americans be able to, as W. E. B. DuBois stated, "See [themselves] through the revelation of the other world."[9] Thus, double conscious law and order plays out in film when Black characters are paradoxically positioned as both *solving* a crime and *being* a crime.

Eddie Murphy's Criminal Acts

While my focus here is on Eddie Murphy's introduction of the frame of double conscious law and order to the comedy genre and its impact, his films *48 Hrs.* and the *Beverly Hills Cop* trilogy are also notable for introducing two other significant innovations to contemporary Hollywood filmmaking: the action-comedy genre and the buddy cop movie.[10] In the twenty-first century, the action-comedy genre is common moviegoing fare, making it hard to imagine a time when it did not exist. However, prior to Nolte and Murphy's escapades in *48 Hrs.*, movies were either action *or* comedy. The genre distinctions between the two were stark. Charles Bronson and Dirty Harry were not throwing out humorous one-liners, and Mel Brooks, Woody Allen, and the crew from Monty Python were not writing elaborate car chase scenes or taut fight scenes. It was presumed that never the twain shall meet. Enter Reggie Hammond and Jack Cates to spawn the likes of *Bad Boys, Men in Black, Rush Hour, The Kingsmen*, and pretty much everything from the latter part of Ryan Reynolds's career.

    48 Hrs. is also considered the archetype for the modern buddy cop movie, in particular the formula of the grizzled, veteran cop partnered with the new young upstart; the two are most often from different racial backgrounds. In this formula, the procedures and perspectives on both crime solving and race from each partner are at odds and the clashing between the two provides the central comedy, while their ultimate solving of the crime along with their "unexpected" friendship provides the satisfying and predictable denouement and usually paves the way for a sequel. As Ed Guerrero notes, these buddy cop movies perform ideological work.[11] "Black critics Warrington Hudlin and Donald Bogle astutely observe that contemporary biracial buddy films present the audience with escapist fantasy narratives and resolutions, which in some instances articulate allegorical or metaphorical dimensions that mediate America's very real and intractable racial problems."[12] While these innovations are responsible for a large transformation of the mainstream movies that came out during the late part of the twentieth century and into the twenty-first century, I argue that Murphy's use of double conscious law and order is equally significant for the impact it had on contemporary Black comedy in film. Reggie Hammond and Axel Foley are not only the comedic counterparts of the white cops but also comedic Black counternarratives to the dysfunctional logic of American law and order.

48 Hrs.

The premise of the movie is that San Francisco detective Jack Cates needs help catching a cop-killing escaped convict, Albert Ganz. In an attempt to get a sense of where Ganz may be headed in the city, Cates pays a visit to Ganz's former colleague, Reggie Hammond, who is finishing a three-year sentence in federal prison. Cates gets Hammond released on a pass for "forty-eight hours" to help him catch Ganz and his partner, Billy Bear. During the pursuit of Ganz, there are car chases, fistfights, and shoot-outs, all of which reflect the last vestiges of '70s action filmmaking. Cates also finds out that Hammond's investment in helping him find Ganz is the $500,000 that Hammond heisted with Ganz and a crew and is now safely squirreled away in the trunk of Hammond's car in a long-term parking garage in downtown San Francisco. As they trail Ganz there are endless sharp comedic exchanges between Nolte and Murphy, which were, in large part, the result of improvisation between the two actors, a practice that would become common for Murphy in his subsequent films. There are also several Murphy moments that have now become part of classic comedy history. The unlikely duo of Cates and Hammond ultimately take down Ganz and Billy Bear, having become "partners" in the process.

Double conscious law and order is inherent in the film's narrative framing. Even as Cates's is drawn as a risk-taking, rule-breaking cop, Hammond's status as a "criminal" and Black dictates that Cates's whiteness makes him more respectable and more capable of restoring order. However, it is Hammond's criminality, both literally, as a thief, and ideologically, as a Black man, that gives him the particular doubled knowledge of race necessary to solve this crime. He knows how the system works for white people and also how it works differently for Black people. This insight, inaccessible to Cates as a white cop, makes Hammond crucial to making the case, and he knows it. So despite Cates's reminders that he "owns" Hammond and his attempts to keep him "in his place," verbally through berating and racial epithets and

Fig. 3.1 Screenshot from Murphy as Reggie Hammond in *48 Hrs.* pretends to be a cop in Torchy's bar and exemplifies double consciousness law and order.

physically by continually handcuffing Reggie and, at one point, fighting him in the street, Hammond unflaggingly asserts both his humanity and his equality to Cates.[13] Ultimately, it isn't that Hammond is familiar with Ganz that is useful to Cates; it is that Hammond is familiar with white supremacy that makes him invaluable to Cates. Hammond's double conscious dexterity, coupled with Murphy's comedic command is on full display in one of the most memorable scenes in comedy film, the bar scene at Torchy's.

REGGIE: You said bullshit and experience is all it takes, right?
JACK: Right.
REGGIE: Come on in and experience some of my bullshit.

Jack and Reggie have come to Torchy's looking for a lead. Jack suspects that the patrons will recognize him as a cop and suggests that Reggie should back up whatever play he makes and act like he has a gun. When Reggie balks at that idea, the two make a bet about Reggie's ability to go into the bar, put on a good enough act, and come away with a lead. Jack even gives Reggie his badge to help with the act, which is an interesting moment within the double conscious frame, seemingly confirming that law and order is performative, as Reggie is arguing, advanced by attitude and convincing props like badges and guns.

As they enter what is clearly a white country bar, complete with cowboy hats and Confederate flags, Reggie notes matter-of-factly, "Not a very popular place with the brothers." Reggie, in his "$957" Giorgio Armani suit, proceeds to stride purposefully into the bar amid not-so-friendly stares from the all-white patrons. After the bartender tells him "maybe [he] should have a black Russian," Reggie puts a halt to the action in the bar by throwing his shot glass to break a mirror behind the bar, immediately and authoritatively commanding the attention of patrons. He begins to question the crowd about information on Billy Bear. As noted by film scholars and popular culture commentators, this scene is almost an exact inverted version of the bar scene in *The French Connection* when Popeye Doyle and his partner, Buddy Russo, roust the patrons of an all-Black bar. In Murphy's version, however, he is expertly playing with the positioning of Du Bois's veil that typically prevents white society from seeing beyond itself, by showing white people, especially those assumed to be racist, how they are seen by Black people, perhaps for the first time.[14] In his discussion of "the cool pose," Herman Beavers explains this aspect of Murphy's comedy as "center[ing] [Murphy] within a popular culture milieu that arranges his subject matter around him, as if he were engaged in a kind of social spectatorship where society is the object of the gaze. This means that he is positioned to look at people looking at him."[15] The act of Reggie's "oppositional gaze," as bell hooks refers to it, the audacity of looking back at white people, is a double conscious power play on Reggie's part that Murphy plays expertly.[16]

He starts his group interrogation by saying "I've never seen so many backwards-ass, country fucks in my life." He shifts the racial hierarchy in the all-white bar by putting his Blackness on top because of its tacit legitimation through his assumed class superiority (his suit) and presumed lawfulness (his/Cates's badge). This shift sets the tone for the rest of the scene and is also extremely funny because of how incongruent it is with audience expectations of how law and order should look. In any other context, Hammond's Blackness in an all-white, semiotically racist bar would put him in a vulnerable position, even a dangerous one. But here, Hammond advantageously uses his double conscious insight. He knows his Blackness is being interpreted by the white patrons as "not belonging" and not just in the bar but socially. But instead of being intimidated by the white hostility in a bar whose name blatantly recalls the KKK and the racial terror of Black bodies and Black property being "torched," he counters it with a Black hostility that is so rarely given attention, especially such a direct and white one. As a "cop," though, his Black hostility is given space and traction, as he seems to know it will. Accordingly, a few minutes later he becomes more explicit in his disdain when he says, "All right, listen up. I don't like white people. I hate rednecks. You people are rednecks. That means I'm enjoying this shit." He says this as he's patting down several of the patrons while surreptitiously stealing weapons from them, existing simultaneously as cop and con. This criminal behavior from a cop pushes one of the patrons to ask, "What the hell kind of cop are you?" While holding a switchblade on the patron, Reggie responds in a threatening way, again playing with the perceived lawlessness attached to Blackness. "You know what I am? I'm your worst fucking nightmare. I'm a nigger with a badge. That means I've got permission to kick your fucking ass whenever I feel like it." This indelible moment is powerful because Reggie isn't kidding. The inherent lawlessness attached to the Black body coupled with the inherent lawfulness attached to the police creates a cognitive dissonance for white people in America that Reggie comprehends and exploits for the purposes of both getting a lead and indulging in some Black joy.

The scene ends with Reggie donning the suggestive black hat of the bartender and telling him in a country drawl, "Well, look, Hoss, you start running a respectable bidness, and I won't have to come in here and hassle you every night. Know what I mean?" flipping the notion of racial surveillance. He then turns to the rapt patrons, saying, "And I want the rest of you cowboys to know something. There's a new sheriff in town [taking off the cowboy hat and shifting into African American Vernacular English tone and intonation]. And his name is Reggie Hammond. Y'all be cool. Right on." Reggie's double conscious script flip gets them a lead, wins him the bet, and demonstrates how double conscious law and order plays with the veil in the pursuit of justice.

As the film moves toward its climax and finale, an important shift occurs that is a distinct characteristic of the frame of double conscious law and order. Cates comes to both trust and rely on Hammond's instincts and approaches that are both completely different from his own (white racialized) instincts and approaches and are, in most cases, more effective than standard (white) instincts and approaches to law and order. This shift, while often portrayed as progress and growth for white characters, is more complicated because it is informed by a white supremacist racial frame. The seeming change of heart of the white character relies on the Black character being the one to play the role of deviant, allowing for the white character to maintain social superiority. The white character is often shown as eventually "following the lead" of the Black character in breaking the rules. In reality, the white character indulges in a kind of criminal Blackface by using the Black character as a social extension to distance himself from any rule breaking he does while also having a ready defense for his behavior: it was the Black guy's idea. The Black subject as the canvas on which white racial anxieties and white social deviance is projected is at the heart of the definition of double consciousness.

As it plays out in buddy cop films, Black characters are always the bad influence, even as they are also the best cop.

Beverly Hills Cop

Two years after the success of *48 Hrs.*, Eddie Murphy was top billed in *Beverly Hills Cop*. As Detroit cop Axel Foley, Murphy's use of the double conscious law-and-order frame is in full effect. After Axel's friend Michael Tandino is murdered during an unexpected visit to Detroit, the young police detective (Murphy/Axel was twenty-four years old at the time) travels to Beverly Hills, California, to solve his murder against the wishes of his captain, whom he tells he's taking vacation. Since he has no official sanction from his own department or any official jurisdiction from the Beverly Hills Police Department, Foley is literally outside the law. Upon arriving in Beverly Hills, Foley eventually comes into contact with Sergeant Taggart and Detective Rosewood (after getting arrested for being thrown out of a window), ultimately "working" with the two detectives to solve the crime.

Foley focuses on a rich art dealer (also drug smuggler) named Victor Maitlin. His investigation of the well-known Beverly Hills citizen continually places him in tony locations in and around white Beverly Hills, visually reiterating his outsider status. While the "fish out of water" scenario is typical for comedy, the class and racial dynamics of the formula in this film accentuate the double consciousness of Foley's character. Upon his arrival in Beverly Hills, Foley is immediately marked by both race and class by his car, a "crappy blue Chevy Nova," and his attire, blue jeans and his now iconic Mumford Phys. Ed. Dept. T-shirt, as well as by his demeanor and "one of these things is not like the other" interactions with the citizens of Beverly Hills. Foley's outsider status is shaped wholly by his race and working-class background. This outsider theme, recurring in many of Murphy's movies, "is predicated upon the Black penetration of clearly demarcated White cultural, social or physical space. Moreover, the expression of this penetration is tinted with class concerns and tensions."[17] However, instead of being tentative because of how he is being perceived through his race and class, Foley indulges his positionality and subverts the expectations of inferiority of the white upper class. The comedy comes out of Foley's boldness in these spaces that clearly were never imagined with Black working-class bodies in mind (or, as discussed earlier, with Murphy in mind). Moreover, the effect of these interactions put the power of double consciousness on full display in its ability, as mentioned previously, to disrupt white supremacist capitalist models, in this case by reducing the ideological power of whiteness and wealth.

This also extends to reducing the ideological assumptions around the relationship of whiteness to law and order once Axel begins to engage the detectives in the Beverly Hills Police Department. His first interaction is with Sergeant Taggart. The scene highlights how white perceptions of crime and criminality follow class and race-based logics that obscure the ability to solve crimes.

FOLEY [*to Taggart*]: You always treat visitors from out of town like this?

TAGGART [*ignoring his question*]: Why didn't you identify yourself as a police officer when you were arrested?

FOLEY: 'Cuz I was minding my own business. And where the fuck do you guys get off arresting somebody for getting thrown out of a window?

TAGGART: We have six witnesses that say you broke in and started tearing up the place and then *jumped* out the window.

FOLEY: And you guys believe that. What the fuck are you, cops or doormen?

TAGGART: We're more likely to believe an important local businessman than a foul-mouthed jerk from out of town.

FOLEY: Foul-mouthed? [*Taggart nods confirmation*] Fuck you, man.

TAGGART [*rising from his chair*]: You watch your mouth.

FOLEY: Hey, man. Don't square off on me with some bullshit. You want to start some static [*pushing Taggart*]?

TAGGART: Hey, don't push me [*pushing Foley back*].

FOLEY: Fuck you, man [*pushing Taggart*].

[*Taggart punches Foley in the stomach garnering the attention of Lieutenant Bogomil*]

The exchange between the two cops demonstrates how the Black body communicates criminality to white people. For Taggart, because of Maitlin's station in Beverly Hills, it is easier to believe that Foley is the transgressor. Foley's expletive-laden responses only further Taggart's assumption of his subversiveness until the point where he confronts Foley like a criminal and punches him. The subsequent exchange is equally telling with Lieutenant Bogomil reprimanding Taggart and forcing him to issue an apology to Foley, like a scolded child. Bogomil further asks Foley if he would like to press charges against Taggart. Foley states that "where [he's] from cops don't file charges against other cops," to which Bogomil replies "Well, in Beverly Hills we go strictly by the book." The brief moment reveals the two sides of the law-and-order veil: what the rules are (whiteness) versus what is right (Blackness). Throughout the film, Foley flouts the rules not simply to be funny and contrarian but also because, in all senses, *the rules don't apply to him*. He's aware that regardless of what he does, as a Black man in society, specifically

Fig. 3.2 As Axel Foley in *Beverly Hills Cop*, Murphy is aware that regardless of what he does, as a Black man in society, he is always already rule breaking, so he uses white supremacist logic against itself and breaks as many rules as he can in order to bring justice to his friend.

in Beverly Hills, he is always already rule breaking, so he uses white supremacist logic against itself and breaks as many rules as he can in order to bring justice to his friend.

Later, after an earlier incident where Foley thwarted Taggart and Rosewood's tail of him by putting bananas in their car's tailpipe so the car wouldn't accelerate, emphasizing his role as trickster, Foley attempts to connect with them as fellow police officers. The two detectives, especially Taggart, continue to react to him as if he were a criminal who needs to be surveilled. Foley gives up and says if they want to follow him, he's going to go get a drink. He leads them to a strip club.

In the strip club scene, the split between the priority of procedure for white law and order and the reliance on instinct for Black law and order is further highlighted. The three men sit at a table near the dancers. While Foley admonishes the server to make sure that the drinks are right because "I'll throw up if I drink club soda," he shows coffee grounds to Taggart (used frequently to traffic drugs because it throws off the scent of the detection dogs) that he discovered in a shipment in Maitlin's warehouse, to which Taggart responds, "So?" Mocking their lack of crime-solving skills, Foley comments, "You guys don't know nothin' about nothin', do you? You just got your badges and your guns and you're on the job." Like in *48 Hrs.*, the idea that for whiteness, law and order is performative and without much substance plays out throughout this scene, including its twist ending. As Rosewood gives money to the dancer and Taggart wonders about the coffee grounds, Foley notices two men who appear ready to commit a crime. He alerts Taggart and then proceeds to approach one of the men as a drunken long-lost friend. Foley's act opens up the opportunity for him and Taggart to foil the crime. Once they have controlled the situation and disarmed the criminals, Rosewood rushes over, brandishing his gun, and yells at the man Foley has on the ground, "Don't move! Roll over!," to which Foley replies, much as one would reply to a child, "Way to go, Rosewood. You're some kind of cop, you know that?" Foley's ability to see much that is unseen is based in the double consciousness of the Black subject. Meanwhile, Taggart and Rosewood are portrayed as being largely ineffectual and childlike as they are only able to see things singularly through the lens of their assumptions, which is largely determined by white supremacy.

At the end of the film, the detectives, especially Rosewood, have come to trust and rely on Foley's instinct and approaches, just like Jack Cates came to trust Reggie Hammond, and they are able to bring Victor Maitlin down. Though this reconciliatory move within buddy cop genre is meant to engender feelings of progress and acceptance, it is a conditional reconciliation that exists *despite* the Black character being a rule breaker. Like in *48 Hrs.*, the white detectives in *Beverly Hills Cop* don't use Foley as a model for how they can more effectively solve crimes or as a motivation to change their perspectives and approaches to crimes and criminals. They remain as they were. Foley serves as a convenient conduit through which they can break rules and still remain untainted by notions of lawlessness, especially since Foley returns to Detroit (where "he belongs").

LAW AND ORDER IN BLACK AND WHITE

One of the key elements of double conscious law and order, especially in the way Murphy introduces it to Black comedy is that the crime-fighting plot has the Black character being placed in all- or mostly white environments. It is a curious requirement that the Black character is not only solving crimes that are committed by and perpetrated against white people but also that he does so without having any Black community or Black cultural anchors around him as he does so. It is the epitome of white assumptions around Blackness that it only exists as white people see it and at their pleasure. Blackness through the lens of white supremacy is not individuated. That this single Black person exists primarily in spaces uninhabited by other Black people or Black references does not register as extraordinary for both the white people in the movie or the white people in the audience. It also, ostensibly, doesn't register as extraordinary to the Black character because double conscious-ness provides the knowledge that white society views Black people through the singularity of race, not the individuality of subjectivity. Racquel Gates reads Murphy's use of his position in these spaces through her concept of "formal negativity" and as inherently subversive. "Finally, Murphy himself, as arguably the biggest movie star of the 1980s with success primarily in white-cast films, exemplifies formal negativity as he constantly works within the very structures that Hollywood typically uses to ensure white privilege and black marginalization in order to ultimately subvert them and destabi-lize whiteness in his film and television projects."[18]

What the double conscious law-and-order frame helps us understand is that even as the Black actor may be the star, the character he or she plays re-mains in service to whiteness and its notions of Blackness. It also makes clear that crime is relative to which side of the veil you are on. The comedy formula built by Murphy in these films is one that plays both sides of not only the law but also the veil as a way of countering the dominant ways that systems of law and order contain the Black body and the Black consciousness. The frame of double conscious law and order teaches the viewers again and again that Blackness is always attached to disorder while whiteness is always attached to order making. For Murphy, and the Black actors who have followed his blue-print, the comedy is derived both from indulging in the disorder and allow-ing white society to believe in the goodness of its order making but also from knowing that white order making has no meaning without the presumed existence of Black disorder. Reggie Hammond and Axel Foley lifted the veil for many moviegoing audiences, and Eddie Murphy showed that for Black comedians, crime pays.

Lisa Guerrero is Vice Chancellor for Equity and Inclusive Excellence and Professor of Comparative Ethnic Studies and American Studies and Culture at Washington State University. She is author of *Crazy Funny: Popular Black Satire and the Method of Madness*.

1. As of the writing of this essay, a third sequel is in production, *Beverly Hills Cop: Axel Foley*, with an anticipated release date in 2023.

2. Cooper Hood, "Beverly Hills Cop: Why Eddie Murphy Replaced Sylvester Stallone," *Screen Rant*, October 24, 2020, https://screenrant.com/beverly-hills-cop-eddie-murphy -replaced-sylvester-stallone/.

3. Ibid.

4. One recent notable exception is Racquel J. Gates's *Double Negative: The Black Image and Popular Culture* (Durham, NC: Duke University Press, 2018). Her chapter on Murphy

discusses his work, as well as the actor himself, in her terms of "formal negativity." It is one of the few, perhaps only, pieces of critical scholarship on Murphy that recasts his work and career in a critical frame that at once amplifies the Black cultural, aesthetic, and material significance of the various texts of his career, as well as his position within the Hollywood industry.

5. W. E. B. Du Bois, *The Souls of Black Folk* (New York: Penguin, 1903), 3.

6. Lauren Berlant and Sianne Ngai, "Comedy Has Issues," *Critical Inquiry* 43, no. 2 (2017): 233, https://doi.org/10.1086/689666.

7. Jason Mittell, "A Cultural Approach to Television Genre Theory," *Cinema Journal* 40, no. 3 (2001): 6.

8. The tagline on the marketing poster for *48 Hrs.* is: "The Boys are back in town. Nick Nolte is a cop. Eddie Murphy is a convict. They couldn't have liked each other less . . . they couldn't have needed each other more. And the last place they expected to be was on the same side. Even for . . . 48 Hrs." The tagline on the marketing poster for *Beverly Hills Cop* is: "He's been chased, thrown through a window, and arrested. Eddie Murphy is a Detroit cop on vacation in Beverly Hills." In both cases the incongruities, implicitly based in race and class, are foregrounded to create audience expectations of the kind of comedy these two films will present.

9. Du Bois, *Souls of Black Folk*, 3.

10. Some movie fans and scholars take exception to designating this film as the blueprint for the buddy cop film, noting *Freebie and the Bean* (1974) as the first instance of a film about buddy cops. Many also note that Murphy is not a cop in this film; although, to the point of my argument, it doesn't matter whether he's a cop or a criminal. What is important is how he is positioned in relation to the white cop toward the goal of solving a crime.

11. Ed Guerrero, "The Black Image in Protective Custody," in *Black American Cinema*, ed. Manthia Diawara, 237–46 (New York: Routledge, 1993), 240.

12. Ibid.

13. An interesting parallel to Hammond asserting his humanity in the film is the way Murphy asserted his power to create humanity for Hammond in the first place. The main character was originally named Willie Biggs. Murphy thought the name was too stereotypically "Black sounding" and suggested the character's name be changed to Reggie Hammond.

14. This, too, is an inverted moment that recalls Murphy's "White Like Me" sketch on *Saturday Night Live*, where Murphy dons whiteface so he can experience the world as a white man and see, among other things, how white people *really* view people of color.

15. Herman Beavers, "The Cool Pose: Intersectionality, Masculinity, and Quiescence in the Comedy and Film of Richard Pryor and Eddie Murphy," in *Race and the Subject of Masculinities*, edited by Harry Stecopoulos and Michael Uebel, 253–85 (Durham, NC: Duke University Press, 1997), 263.

16. bell hooks, "The Oppositional Gaze: Black Female Spectators," in *Black Looks: Race and Representation*, 115–31 (Boston: South End Press, 1992).

17. Guerrero, "Black Image," 243.

18. Gates, *Double Negative*, 39.

PART II

BLACK COMEDY/BLACK PERFORMANCES

4

"WHAT CAN WE DO THAT NO ONE ELSE CAN DO?"

On *Key & Peele*, Comedy, and Performing Race

Phillip Lamarr Cunningham

In her critique of the Comedy Central sketch comedy series *Key & Peele* (2012–2015), *Salon* writer Kartina Richardson chides the show's creators—Keegan-Michael Key and Jordan Peele—for kowtowing to white liberal sensibilities and avoiding serious critiques of racism. Richardson—like several African American critics—argues that the show fell short of its predecessor, *Chappelle's Show* (Comedy Central, 2003–2006), which Richardson contends was less willing to subject Blackness to ridicule.[1] Filmmaker and critic Dylan Valley agreed, noting, "While Key and Peele frame themselves as 'bi-racial' and thus able to occupy both Black and white spaces and identities, Black people bear the brunt of their humor in all of their skits. White supremacy isn't questioned at all, while Black masculinity is fair game."[2] Indeed, Chappelle refused to continue his series after filming his infamous "Stereotype Pixies" sketch, which he felt was socially irresponsible as it highlighted racial stereotypes.[3]

However, this chapter contends that critics like Richardson—while fair in their critiques that *Key & Peele* frequently lampooned Blackness generally and Black masculinity specifically—miss the mark in ignoring the show's fervent embrace of racial performativity and, to paraphrase E. Patrick Johnson, its cognizance of authenticity's arbitrariness.[4] As this chapter evidences through an examination of performances of whiteness during the series' five-season run, *Key & Peele* was committed to an ethos that suggested race is performative and fluid, which is exemplified by the actors' refusal to don whiteface (as Chappelle occasionally did) when playing ostensibly white characters. This essay argues that it is this approach—and not a capitulation to white liberal sensibilities—that allowed *Key & Peele* to endure and not succumb to the pressures that undermined *Chappelle's Show*.

KEY & PEELE AS POSTPOLITICS/POSTSOUL

Key & Peele (2012–2015) emerged as Black-helmed comedy series appeared to be in a state of decline. *Chappelle's Show*, the show to which *Key & Peele* is most often compared, had been off the air for six years. Three years prior to the series' debut, The CW—the merger of the fledgling UPN and The WB networks—wiped its slate clean of the bevy of Black-cast sitcoms on which its predecessors once relied.[5] Moreover, *MadTV* (FOX, 1995–2009), the late-night sketch comedy series on which Keegan-Michael Key and Jordan Peele broke into the mainstream, had been canceled in 2009, and *Saturday Night Live* only had one Black repertory member, Kenan Thompson (though Jay Pharoah also was a cast member). As such, a void certainly existed that *Key & Peele* filled.

Comedy Central was a natural fit for *Key & Peele*, for the series aligned well with the network's previous efforts. Nick Marx categorizes the show as one that espouses a "post-politics" ethos that "satirizes televisual representations of race/ethnicity, gender, and sexuality without positioning any one identity as dominant over another."[6] Marx argues that Comedy Central series featuring people of color and women like *Key & Peele*, *Broad City*, and *Inside Amy Schumer* allowed the network to target diverse audiences without alienating the young white male demographic on which it has relied.[7]

However, to claim that *Key & Peele* is apolitical or even wholly postracial—as it often is framed—is erroneous. While the series generally refrains from advancing a particular ideology, it certainly has tackled racial issues in sketches such as "Hoodie," in which Jordan Peele portrays a young Black man wearing a hooded sweatshirt while walking through a predominantly white neighborhood. A white mother brings her frightened children inside; a white homeowner mowing his lawn stares menacingly at Peele's character. Tension builds as a police car looms in the distance. However, as it approaches, he pulls his hood—which features a lifelike picture of a young white man's head—over his head, and the police car passes by. The sketch appeared in the season following the murder of Trayvon Martin.[8] "Hoodie" and other sketches—for instance, "Black Republicans," which lampoons Black conservative rhetoric and appearance—evidenced the duo's willingness to engage with contemporary politics.

Other scholars have positioned *Key & Peele* as "postsoul." In *Laughing Mad: The Black Comic Persona in Post-Soul America*, Bambi Haggins utilizes the term *postsoul*—borrowed from music critic Nelson George—to refer to those comedians who emerge after the Black Power movements.[9] The hallmark of these postsoul comedians is greater access to the mainstream and increased potential for crossover success.[10] Haggins contends that Eddie Murphy and Chris Rock epitomize the first and second waves of postsoul Black comedy, respectively.[11] She argues that Chappelle represents a point of convergence—one in which conflict exists between his comedic persona and his crossover success.[12] However, Lisa Guerrero suggests that—unlike *Chappelle's Show*—*Key & Peele* complicates the postsoul aesthetic and is grounded in the "paradox of post-racial blackness."[13]

Though often compared to each other due to their commonalities in format (comedic sketches preceded by stand-up interludes), network (Comedy Central), and temporality (postmillennium), *Key & Peele* and *Chappelle's Show* differ dramatically, particularly regarding their respective treatments of race. Of Chappelle, Haggins writes, "[He] enjoys a sort of dual credibility—his comic persona is inflected by both the Afrocentrism of the Black hip-hop intelligentsia and the skater/slacker/stoner ethos of suburban life. . . . Chappelle is simultaneously a part of and at odds with integrationist mythologies, overtly political and involved in established notions of social action yet wary of the machinations of the political process."[14] Chappelle's strong ties to Afrocentric hip-hop are evidenced by his frequent interactions with performers such as Common, The Roots, Talib Kweli, and Yaasin Bey (formerly known as Mos Def) and his hosting of *Dave Chappelle's Block Party*, a 2005 documentary film chronicling Chappelle's efforts to organize a street concert in Brooklyn.

The Afrocentrism to which Haggins binds Chappelle comes with the burden of essentialism. In short, *Chappelle's Show* proved unable to negotiate the paradox of postsoul, for it often conceded that race is transfixed. The series, to be sure, often parodied this essentialism. Sketches such as "The Racial Draft," in which representatives from various racial and ethnic groups draft (in the manner of professional sports leagues) celebrities whose racial makeup is fluid—such as Tiger Woods, who publicly identified himself as "Cablasian"—or who have otherwise expressed some affinity for another culture, like the Wu-Tang Clan.[15] While the sketch acknowledges that identities often are in flux, it also suggests that sides eventually must be chosen.

One must also consider the sketches that seemingly brought about the end of *Chappelle's Show*. As the third season began taping, Chappelle withdrew from his series after filming "Stereotype Pixies," a series of sketches in which four men—Asian, Black, Latinx, and white—are visited by "racial pixies," the embodiment of their respective consciousness, as they face crucial decisions that force them to confront their stereotypes. For instance, the Black man (played by Chappelle himself) is offered his choice of either fish or fried chicken for dinner during a flight. As he ponders his decision, a racial pixie—Chappelle wearing Blackface and a train porter's uniform—appears, encouraging Chappelle to select the fried chicken. Chappelle does everything to avoid selecting the dinner even as he is chided by the pixie.[16] In a *Time* interview, he revealed that, during the taping of this sketch, a white crew member laughed loudly enough to make him reconsider not only the sketch itself but the very nature of his comedy.[17] He lamented to Oprah Winfrey, "I know the difference of people laughing with me and people laughing at me," which implies that a dissonance exists between Black humor and white reception.[18] This dissonance exemplifies what Alfred Martin refers to as "two-faced humor," that being humor in which "the abject object is removed from the situation in which the joke is told."[19] In this instance, the two-facedness of "Stereotype Pixies" created a "moral dilemma" for Chappelle, who, in the post–*Chappelle's Show* stage of his career, has wrestled publicly with the notion of social responsibility in ways that Key and Peele have not.

David Gillotta argues Key and Peele—along with comedic writer and hip-hop artist Donald Glover—exemplify a humor that is not necessarily apolitical but also is not entrenched in the style of their predecessors. Gillotta writes, "Rather than interrogating broad social and systemic inequalities, Glover, Key, and Peele approach race . . . through the lens of personal experience. . . . This seemingly idiosyncratic and apolitical approach to race, however, ultimately challenges the rigid and essentialized visions of Blackness that are often perpetuated by mainstream media, including most African American humor. The humor of these 'Black nerds' thus points to a small yet increasing diversification of the ways in which Blackness can be represented and explored in mass culture."[20]

Though the aforementioned comedians share a similar upbringing with Dave Chappelle in that they are all products of middle class, suburban families, their comedy—unlike Chappelle's—often focuses on the tension that come with being an outsider within Black and white worlds. Key and Peele operate as outsiders to Black comedic traditions in two important ways. First, unlike Chappelle who worked his way through the stand-up circuit, Key and Peele's origins are in improvisational comedy. Key and Peele both emerged from the famed Second City improv troupe before transitioning to television via *MadTV* in 2003–2004. Second, Key and Peele are both biracial, the sons of Black fathers and white mothers. While neither eschews their Blackness, they also revel in their biracial identities. Paul Easterling notes that the duo effectively utilizes their biracial status to interrogate racial essentialism and treat Blackness—and whiteness—as performative.[21] He further argues that their comedic approach rejects the Black-white binary and undermines the signifiers and codes of "Blackness."[22] Jordan Peele highlights the liberating capacity of rejecting the binary. In a *New York Times* interview, Peele says, "For me playing as many different races as possible, it's liberating . . . and it makes the show a safer place to come in some way. . . . Warmth is a hallmark of this show, and one of the things that sets it apart from what preceded it. We recognized early on that we would be compared to 'Chappelle's Show' a lot, and that did happen. . . . So we did ask ourselves that question: 'What can we do that no one else can do?'"[23]

Key envisioned the series less as multiracial and more as "universal": "So, 'This is a funny scene about vanity' or, 'This is a scene about trying to impress a girl. But let's make that happen with a bunch of Cholos.' So it's not about Cholos, it's about trying to impress, being nervous around my friend. It can be like a Cyrano de Bergerac scene, just do it in East LA."[24]

The aforementioned scholarship on *Key & Peele* justifiably highlights how the series uses comedy to satirize Blackness—to varying degrees of effectiveness. However, scant attention has been given to how the show does the same for whiteness.

Whiting Up on *Key & Peele*

Marvin McAllister defines *whiteface* as "extra-theatrical, social performance in which people of African descent appropriate white-identified gestures, vocabulary, dialects, dress, or social entitlements. Attuned to class as much as race, whiteface minstrels often satirize, parody, and interrogate privileged or authoritative representations of whiteness."[25] McAllister's *Whiting Up* articulates four functions of whiteface performance that are useful for exploring whiting up on *Key & Peele*:

1. Satirical and parodical—both subtle and aggressive—representations of whiteness intent on undermining racial hierarchies;
2. Imitation based on building interconnections or personal identifications with "white aesthetic practices, artists, and histories";
3. The exposure of white terror as warning to African Americans; and
4. The restructuring of personal identity within established hierarchies of difference, which allows for the identification and creation of new Black styles.[26]

He notes that these acts can be performed simultaneously.

Key & Peele features only one instance of literal whiteface (at least in the traditional sense), which occurs in season 1, episode 3's "Das Negros" sketch.

Set in Germany in 1942, "Das Negros" focuses on two Black men who have escaped detention (for unspecified reasons) but live covertly in a small village. They are visited one evening by Colonel Hans Mueller (Ty Burrell), who reports that he had received word that "two Negroes" were seen in the area. The camera cuts to Key and Peele, both who appear in poorly applied whiteface. The escapees barely maintain their disguises, as Peele's character immediately introduces himself as "Leroy" in a heavily affected Black southern accent before "correcting" himself to say, "Leroy . . . heimer. Leroyheimer is my last name, and my first name is very German, and that is because it is Heinrich." Key's character also stumbles as he introduces himself as "Baron Helmut . . . Schnitzelnazi." Colonel Mueller enters their home and reveals that the Germans have perfected a series of tests to determine if someone is Black. Mueller removes Leroy's hat and, with a nod to phrenology, measures Leroy's head as he notes that "the Negro's head only comes in half sizes." After the duo passes this initial test, Mueller suddenly conjures a plate of beets and waves it underneath their noses. Key and Peele stare awkwardly as Mueller reveals that "the Negro cannot resist the beet." Mueller apologizes for wasting their time, but as he starts to leave, he suddenly unveils a dangling cat toy as the last test, to which neither Key nor Peele respond. Mueller concedes that they have passed his tests despite an awkward exchange in which neither character is able to refrain from speaking in a dialect. As Key cautiously watches him leave, the camera pans to reveal Peele playing with the cat toy. "Das Negros," much in the vein of traditional whiteface performance, ridicules the most extreme form of racial bigotry as it satirizes racial pseudoscience and white understanding of Blackness.[27]

Burrell reprises his role as Colonel Mueller in season 4, episode 2's "Awesome Hitler Story." Key plays an African American soldier who, along with two white soldiers, is separated from their unit. The soldiers take shelter in an abandoned hotel only to find that it is not as safe as they originally believed. Shots are fired from behind a closed door, killing the two white soldiers. Key panics as he hears the Nazi soldiers approach before deciding to play dead alongside his fallen comrades. Colonel Mueller enters with two infantrymen and Peele—who is not in whiteface but is playing a Nazi soldier—as his second-in-command. Mueller orders the infantrymen to search the rest of the building as he and Peele talk before the fallen Americans. Mueller recounts a chance encounter with Adolph Hitler; however, Peele notices that Key has inched away from a broad swath of bright sunlight. Mueller is mortified whenever Peele tries to interrupt his story, which Peele has to do several times as Key continues to move to swat away a fly and to eat rations. Finally, Peele convinces Mueller to inspect the dead bodies. Mueller stabs at the two

Fig. 4.1 Jordan Peele (*left*) and Keegan-Michael Key (*right*) don whiteface in "Das Negros." *Key & Peele* (2012) © Comedy Central.

white soldiers with a bayonet; however, as he attempts to stab Key's body, he dodges even as he continues feigning dead. Mueller remarks, "I'll never get used to those final death throes" to Peele, who is stunned at his superior's stupidity. After Peele's character calls him "an idiot," Mueller shoots him, and Peele's body falls next to Key's. The camera pulls in for a two-shot on Key and Peele, revealing that Peele's wallet has blocked the bullet. As Key—still feigning dead—looks over at Peele, Peele knowingly winks at him. Given the reoccurrence of Colonel Mueller in this sketch, the wink suggests that Peele perhaps has been passing as German during his tenure as an SS officer.[28]

Both "Das Negros" and "Awesome Hitler Story" harken to other sketches—namely, Eddie Murphy's "White Like Me" mockumentary from *Saturday Night Live*, in which a comedic whiteface performance is used to poke fun at racial essentialism and white knowledge (or subsequent lack thereof). As is the case with "White Like Me," in which Murphy dons whiteface and traverses through the world as a white man, both sketches involve characters who undermine the white gaze through trickery, or what Henry Louis Gates refers to as *signifyin'*. In writing about "White Like Me," Racquel Gates notes how it calls back to a 1975 *Saturday Night Live* sketch with a similar premise that featured Richard Pryor and enacts a form of "coded communication"—that is, signifyin'—that has the twofold effect of criticizing white hegemony and privileging Black cultural texts.[29] While not as explicit or sophisticated as "White Like Me," "Das Negros" and "Awesome Hitler Story" do so, as well.

The Season 4, Episode 1 sketch "Someone's Gotta Say It" also relies on misdirection. Key and Peele play a pair of bargoers whose accoutrements—camouflage clothing, flannel shirts, and trucker hats (one of which bears a Confederate logo)—and dialect suggest that they are working-class southern white men. As they sip beer, a Mexican dishwasher nods at them as he gathers glasses from the bar. They stare at him, seemingly in judgment, before beginning this exchange:

PEELE: Fuckin' Mexicans.
KEY: Oh, man, do not get me started on the Mexicans.
[A pause.]
PEELE: Hey, I was just saying. They hold the goddamn economy together.
KEY: You know what, man? Damn straight. If 12 percent of the Mexicans in this country stopped working, just 12 percent, the USA would shut down.
PEELE: I don't even care who hears me. . . . They work their asses off, and they got strong family values.
KEY: Essential immigrants.[30]

In this instance, Key and Peele's misdirection plays on our expectations—based on the actors' appearances, their "straight talking" nature, and the sketch's dive bar setting—that these patrons will be racist. To be sure, the Confederate flag hat and the nature of their comments—which frame Mexicans, African Americans, Asians, and Native Americans as "model minorities"—are problematic. However, the sketch forces its viewers to wrestle with stereotypes, especially after the sketch reveals that Peele's Confederate hat–wearing character happens to be a librarian who laments being paid more than his librarian wife.

However, not all of Key and Peele's performance of whiteness are geared toward exposing bigotry. Several sketches are straightforward parodies of popular culture figures and tropes. For example, in sketches "Gideon's Kitchen," "Undercover Boss," and "Who Thinks They Can Dance?" Key and Peele play white characters to poke fun at reality television conventions. In "Gideon's Kitchen," the duo play on the misleading compliments often made by Chef Gordon Ramsey on Hell's Kitchen. Key plays Chef Gideon, a British chef whose backhanded and confusing compliments frustrate Peele's contestant character. The duo also parodies the musical Les Misérables in the season 3, episode 1 sketch "Les Mis." The sketch draws attention to the distracting

Fig. 4.2 Keegan-Michael Key (*left*) and Jordan Peele (*right*) portray southern white men in "Someone's Gotta Say It." *Key & Peele* (2014) © Comedy Central.

nature of overlapping vocals and interrogates whether a musical is really fitting for an adaptation of Victor Hugo's novel about injustice and inequality in early nineteenth-century France.

Much of Key and Peele's whiting up is situated in the series postracial ethos. This ethos aligns with Key's contention that the duo's thoughts about the race and ethnicity of their characters usually were secondary to a sketch's premise. As a result, most of the series' characters—particularly its recurring ones—are coincidentally white. "Hot mess" couple Meegan and Andre, for example, appear throughout the series. Meegan is a vain, self-absorbed, and often cruel young woman who forces the easygoing and more emotionally intelligent Andre to chase after her or defend her honor. Key attests to basing Meegan and Andre on couples they saw at Chicago Cubs games during their time at Second City and ImprovOlympics.[31] Another recurring character, Wendell Sanders, serves as a vessel for the social ineptitude of comic book geeks. Wendell is a veritable recluse who often lies to get out of awkward situations or, in the "Sex-Addict Wendell" sketch, to pick up women at a sex addicts recovery meeting. He is so ensconced in his fantasy world that he spends $15,000 for a music video for his hard rock song "The Power of Wings," in which he plays a chivalrous knight who comes to rescue a captive princess. The sketch features a running tally of his budget, and as it decreases, so does the video's aesthetics. By the video's end, Wendell has

Fig. 4.3 Keegan-Michael Key as Andre (*left*) and Jordan Peele (*right*) as Meegan are a "hot mess" couple in "Andre and Meegan's First Date." *Key & Peele* (2015) © Comedy Central.

resorted to home video, and the actress hired to play the princess has been replaced by a doll.[32]

Conclusion

New York Times critic Wesley Morris argues that *Key & Peele* eventually suffered the same fate as *Chappelle's Show*. "The show started as a commentary on the hilarious absurdity of race, but it never fully escaped the pernicious reality of racism. The longer it ran, the more melancholy it became, the more it seethed. In the final episode, its anger caught up with its fancifulness and cheek, exploding in an old-timey musical number called 'Negrotown.'"[33] "Negrotown," an overt nod to 1940s Black musicals, certainly is a haunting sketch and a somber note on which to end the series.

However, *Key & Peele*'s last episode also features a sketch, "These Nuts," that is in line with much of their work throughout the series. In "These Nuts," Key plays a coincidentally white businessman who tries to stop his friend Vince (Peele) from his continuous string of "These nuts on your chin" jokes.[34] Additionally, in "The Morty Jebsen Show Goes Off the Rails," Key plays Morty Jebsen, a parody of CNN stalwart Larry King, as he probes into rapper Yung Bidness's personal life. Unhappy with the personal questions, Yung Bidness attempts to leave the set but is unable to because he is still attached to the microphone cord. Morty and Yung Bidness fumble around to free Yung Bidness, who after nearly disrobing completely is knocked unconscious by a boom microphone. As such, even as the show grew more acerbic, *Key & Peele* maintained its fidelity to race as performance.

Phillip Lamarr Cunningham is Assistant Professor of Media Studies at Wake Forest University. His work appears in *Journal of Graphic Novels and Comics, Journal of Popular Music Studies, Journal of Sport and Social Issues,* and *Popular Culture Studies Journal.*

NOTES

1. Kartina Richardson, "'Key & Peele's Edge-Less, Post-Racial Lie," *Salon*, February 21, 2012, https://www.salon.com/2012/02/21/key_peeles_toothless_post_racial_lie.

2. Dylan Valley, "Key and Peele Unchained," *Africa Is a Country*, January 17, 2013, https://africasacountry.com/2013/01/key-and-peele-unchained/.

3. Bambi Haggins, *Laughing Mad: The Black Comic Persona in Post-Soul America* (New Brunswick, NJ: Rutgers University Press, 2007), 229.

4. E. Patrick Johnson, *Appropriating Blackness: Performance and the Politics of Authenticity* (Durham, NC: Duke University Press, 2008), 3.

5. Alfred Martin Jr., *The Generic Closet: Black Gayness and the Black-Cast Sitcom* (Bloomington: Indiana University Press, 2021), 184.

6. Nick Marx, "Expanding the Brand: Race, Gender, and the Post-Politics of Representation on Comedy Central," *Television & New Media* 17, no. 3 (March 2016): 273, https://doi.org/10.1177/1527476415577212.

7. Ibid.

8. *Key & Peele*, season 3, episode 1, "Les Mis," dir. Peter Atencio, aired September 18, 2013, on Comedy Central, https://www.cc.com/video/4pocoy/key-peele-hoodie.

9. Haggins, *Laughing Mad*, 4.

10. Ibid., 4.

11. Ibid., 11.

12. Ibid., 12.

13. Lisa Guerrero, "Can I Live? Contemporary Black Satire and the State of Postmodern Double Consciousness," *Studies in American Humor* 2, no. 2 (2016): 270.

14. Haggins, *Laughing Mad*, 179.

15. *Chappelle's Show*, season 2, episode 1, "Sam Jackson Beer & Racial Draft," dir. Neal Brennan and Rusty Cundieff, aired January 21, 2004, on Comedy Central, https://www.cc.com/episodes/3d8tr2/chappelle-s-show-samuel-jackson-beer-racial-draft-season-2-ep-1.

16. *Chappelle's Show*, season 3, episode 2, "Black Howard Dean & Stereotype Pixies," dir. Rusty Cundieff, aired July 16, 2006, on Comedy Central, https://www.cc.com/episodes/ynn1mr/chappelle-s-show-black-howard-dean-stereotype-pixies-ep-2.

17. Christopher John Farley, "Dave Speaks," *Time*, May 14, 2005. http://content.time.com/time/magazine/article/0,9171,1061512,00.html.

18. "Chappelle's Story," Oprah, last modified February 3, 2006, https://www.oprah.com/oprahshow/chappelles-story.

19. Alfred Martin Jr., "The Tweet Has Two Faces: Two-Faced Humor, Black Masculinity, and RompHim," *Journal of Cinema and Media Studies* 58, no. 3 (2019): 161, https://doi.org/10.1353/cj.2019.0031.

20. David Gillota, "Black Nerds: New Directions in African American Humor," *Studies in African American Humor* 3, no. 28 (2013): 18, JSTOR.

21. Paul Easterling, "Biracial Butterflies: 21st Century Racial Identity in Popular Culture," in *Color Struck: Teaching Race and Ethnicity*, ed. Lori Latrice Martin et al. (Rotterdam: Sense Publishers, 2017), 25–26.

22. Ibid., 26.

23. Jon Caramanica, "'Key & Peele,' with Keegan-Michael Key and Jordan Peele," *New York Times*, December 26, 2013, https://www.nytimes.com/2013/12/29/arts/television/key-peele -with-keegan-michael-key-and-jordan-peele.html.

24. Hunter Daniels, "Comic-Con: Keegan-Michael Key, Jordan Peele and Director/Producer Peter Atencio Talk 'Key and Peele' Season 4, Animated Spinoffs, FARGO, and More," *Collider*, July 26, 2014, http://collider.com/key-and-peele-season-4-keegan-michael-key -jordan-peele-interview/.

25. Marvin McAllister, *Whiting Up: Whiteface Minstrels and Stage Europeans in African American Performance* (Chapel Hill: University of North Carolina Press, 2011), 1.

26. Ibid., 12–14.

27. *Key & Peele*, season 1, episode 3, "Das Negros," dir. Peter Atencio, aired February 14, 2012, on Comedy Central, https://www.cc.com/episodes/eytrvv/key-peele-das-negros -season-1-ep-3.

28. *Key & Peele*, season 4, episode 2, "Little Homie," dir. Peter Atencio, aired October 1, 2014, on Comedy Central, https://www.cc.com/episodes/lgsnos/key-peele-little-homie -season-4-ep-2.

29. Racquel J. Gates, "Bringing the Black: Eddie Murphy and African American Humor on Saturday Night Live," in *Saturday Night Live & American TV*, ed. Nick Marx, Matt Sienkiwicz, and Ron Becker (Bloomington: University of Indiana Press, 2013), 164.

30. *Key & Peele*, season 4, episode 1, "Alien Imposters," dir. Peter Atencio, aired September 24, 2014, on Comedy Central, https://www.cc.com/episodes/apyii9/key-peele-alien -imposters-season-4-ep-1.

31. Tracy Swartz, "Hot Mess Cubs Inspired Two Iconic 'Key and Peele' Characters," *Chicago Tribune*, August 5, 2016, https://www.chicagotribune.com/entertainment/ct-key-peele -meegan-andre-20160805-story.html.

32. *Key & Peele*, season 3, episode 11, "The Power of Wings," dir. Peter Atencio, aired December 4, 2013, on Comedy Central, https://www.cc.com/episodes/ho3vr3/key-peele-the -power-of-wings-season-3-ep-11.

33. Wesley Morris, "The Year We Obsessed over Identity," *New York Times*, October 6, 2015, http://nyti.ms/1j2L3uC.

34. *Key & Peele*, season 5, episode 11, "The End," dir. Peter Atencio, aired September 9, 2015, on Comedy Central, https://www.cc.com/episodes/ho3vr3/key-peele-the-power-of-wings -season-3-ep-11.

5

"THESE BLACK KIDS WANT SOMETHING NEW. I SWEAR IT"

Donald Glover's Racial Performance, *Atlanta*, and the New Quality Comedy

Jacqueline E. Johnson

In 2017, Donald Glover was seemingly at the height of his career. In a *Wired* profile that followed the release of *Atlanta*'s (FX, 2016–2022) first season, Glover's album *Awaken, My Love!*, and Glover's casting as a young Lando Calrissian in *Solo: A Star Wars Story* (dir. Ron Howard, 2018), journalist Allison Samuels chronicled Glover's ever-increasing number of projects and the ways his creative production, going all the way back to his early days in sketch comedy, relies on intertextuality.[1] Since the publication of the *Wired* profile, Glover has remained busy. He has released another Childish Gambino album, written and starred in the independent film *Guava Island* (dir. Hiro Murai, 2019), and starred opposite Beyoncé in the "live-action" remake of Disney's *The Lion King* (dir. Jon Favreau, 2019). The FX series *Atlanta*, however, remained one of his key creative projects where he was cocreator, executive producer, writer, and star until its series finale in 2022. In making *Atlanta*, Glover has said he wanted to "show people what it feels like to be Black."[2] To do so, he did something relatively unprecedented on a prestige cable network like FX; he hired an all-Black writing staff, of which several members had no television experience.[3] In this chapter, I use *Atlanta*'s "Robbin' Season" and Donald Glover's star text to examine shifts in the Black comic persona in the 2000s and the relationship between racial and ethnic performance, television, and discourses of quality.[4]

Building on scholarship on post–civil rights African American humor, cable network's branding strategies, and "quality" television, I argue that through *Atlanta*, and specifically its second season, Glover moves away from the Black nerd whose surreal and absurdist commentary on Blackness is located within his personal position on the periphery of African American communities. Instead, he uses local specificity and intertextuality to construct comedy that resonates with the experiences of African Americans while maintaining crossover appeal.

While the term *quality television* has frequently elided Black-cast shows, both critics and viewers have firmly positioned *Atlanta*, a Black-cast series with an all-Black writing staff, within this discourse.[5] I position this categorization within the history of cable television's relationship to Blackness and Black comedians, who networks have used to present themselves as hip, edgy risk takers.[6] Additionally, I examine how the distinct formal and narrative choices of *Atlanta*'s second season—and their critical reception—are also in line with mainstream, white notions of quality.

AFRICAN AMERICAN HUMOR:
FROM POSTSOUL TO POST-OBAMA

American ethnic humor scholars have traditionally marked two periods: the first, spanning from colonization to the mid-twentieth century, is dominated by the white majority making jokes at the expense of racialized and ethnicized others. The second emerges around the civil rights movements when marginalized comics had more power and control within media culture and the opportunity to craft jokes by and for their own groups to speak back to white, mainstream culture.[7] However, throughout the first wave of American ethnic humor, marginalized groups had their own comedic enclaves and forms of in-group humor.[8] For example, as Christine Acham explains, comedian Redd Foxx toured the Chitlin' Circuit in the late 1940s and early 1950s with routines that were explicitly for African American audiences and imbued with African American linguistic and comedic traditions, including signifyin' and the adoption of the "Bad Nigger" of African American folklore.[9] While Foxx's racy style of comedy played well in underground clubs with Black audiences, as what Gerald Butters in this volume calls a "traditional comic," his stand-up comedy could not crossover to mainstream audiences. The African American comics that got their starts after Foxx have been associated with the cultural and temporal framework of postsoul, first coined by Nelson George. *Postsoul* refers to the period after the Black Power and civil rights movements but also is used to distinguish a set of aesthetics and Black creators having more influence and control over dominant American culture.[10]

Bambi Haggins has used George's formulation of postsoul and the work of Mark Anthony Neal to articulate what differentiates comics she

studies—Eddie Murphy, Whoopi Goldberg, Chris Rock, and Dave Chappelle—
from their predecessors Dick Gregory, Bill Cosby, Flip Wilson, and Richard
Pryor. Haggins explains that the personae of postsoul Black comedians are
"inflected by complex tastes and cultural practices . . . [which] are based on
individual and communal experiences of the African American condition"
as well as imbued with a "hopeful cynicism."[11] Haggins's focus on the crossover appeal of postsoul comics as well as how they move across mediums is
especially resonant for my work, specifically her analysis of Dave Chappelle
who Glover cites as an influence alongside Bernie Mac. Speaking of Chappelle's multiracial appeal Haggins writes, "Chappelle enjoys a sort of dual
credibility—his comic persona is inflected by both the Afrocentrism of the
black hip-hop intelligentsia and the skater/slacker/stoner ethos of suburban
life."[12] In a similar vein, *Atlanta* builds its own form of dual credibility and
cross-racial appeal through its use of the city as part of the narrative, humor
that relies on Black American experience, and guest stars in conjunction
with Glover's established appeal to white, mainstream audiences through his
work in sitcoms and his music persona Childish Gambino.

Drawing on the work of Haggins and Watkins, American humor scholar
David Gillota argues that Donald Glover and Keegan-Michael Key and Jordan Peele of *Key & Peele* (Comedy Central, 2012–2015) are at the forefront
of a new wave of African American comedy that discusses race in ways that
differ from the traditions of African American humor prevalent since the
1970s.[13] Designating this as "black nerd humor," Gillotta places this new turn
within a diversification of images of Black men that also includes former president Barack Obama. Gillota argues that Glover, Peele, and Key explore the
boundaries of Blackness, in line with their postsoul predecessors; however,
these three comics use an ironic distance and speak about their Blackness
in ways that highlight the personal and individual rather than the communal. Further, these comedians didn't get their starts in Black ethnic enclaves
and then achieve crossover appeal (as Butters, in this volume, details about
transitional comics); rather, their comic beginnings were through the white
networks of United Citizens Brigade, NBC writer's rooms, and MadTV. In
his analysis of Glover's stand-up specials and his role as Troy on *Community*
(NBC, 2009–2014, Yahoo! Screen 2015), Gillota illustrates how Glover "deliberately constructs a 'black nerd' persona, which contrasts sharply with the
hip, loose, and stylish visions of black masculinity that are most often represented in popular culture."[14] In both his stand-up specials and his music,
Glover continually referenced his long-standing failure at appropriate racial
performance; persistent comments from peers and audiences that Glover
"wasn't Black enough" hinge on a stereotypic conceptualization of Blackness

that Glover himself (re)presented in his own works. So then, how did Donald Glover go from a preoccupation with not fitting into Blackness to making what has been regarded as the Blackest show on television?[15]

Donald Glover from NBC to FX

Glover has a dynamic and productive career, especially given that at the time of writing he is still under forty. Glover's performances and work span mediums—stand-up, music, television, film, and now virtual reality—and within various works, he negotiates a particular performance of Black masculinity. As Gillotta argues, Glover used his stand-up performances and recorded specials to adopt an adolescent persona where he could demonstrate his consistent failure at appropriate Black masculinity, a trend that extends into his Childish Gambino projects.

Glover began making sketch comedy videos with the group Derrick Comedy while a student at NYU, and in 2006, a spec script he wrote landed him a job writing for *30 Rock* (NBC, 2006–2013). Both his writing on *30 Rock* and his role as Troy on *Community* cemented Glover as a reliable comedic voice within "quality" television comedy. The early 2000s were marked by television criticism that became disenchanted with the "hackneyed" sitcom plots that had fueled television comedy for decades. Michael Z. Newman and Elana Levine trace cultural, industrial, and textual shifts that have led to television's most recent "Golden Age" of "elevated" half-hour comedies and male antihero cable dramas.[16] Specifically, they note NBC's stylistic abandonment of the hallmarks of television sitcoms—the multicamera set up, the live studio audience, and the laugh track—before other networks. NBC's critically acclaimed comedies of the 2000s found new ways to "upgrade" and diversify the sitcom. Unlike the "segregated sitcoms" of earlier years described by scholars like Amanda Lotz, *Community* boasted a racially diverse cast that included Glover, Yvette Nicole Brown, Ken Jeong, and Danny Pudi.[17] In their work on gay characters and network television, Ron Becker and Alfred L. Martin have argued that the gay viewers being represented by marginalized characters are not actually the target audience for such programs.[18] Rather, as Becker states, in the 1990s networks, now more concerned with narrowcasting than the mass audience of prior decades, "envisioned the audience to be 'hip,' 'sophisticated,' urban-minded, white and educated 18-to-49 year olds (perhaps even 18-to-34) with liberal attitudes, disposable income, and a distinctively edgy and ironic sensibility," and critically, these gay series were crafted for straight audiences.[19] This same group that Becker outlines is the imagined audience for series like *Community*, where diversity on-screen becomes a way to appeal to "sophisticated" white viewers. This new wave of broadcast comedies, which also includes shows like *Parks and Recreation* (NBC, 2009–2015) and *Brooklyn Nine-Nine* (FOX 2013–2018, NBC 2019–2022), integrate nonwhite characters in ways that demonstrate a version of multiculturalism that does not challenge white hegemony.[20] Through his work on *30 Rock* and *Community*, Glover illustrated his ease moving within white, hegemonic frameworks of humor.

Glover's work as a rapper overlaps with his time on *Community* and explicitly engages how others always read him as not quite Black enough. On his debut extended play, titled *EP*, Glover negotiates his position on the margins of Black masculinity. On the final track, Glover raps:

> Black dudes assume I'm closeted or kinda gay
> White people confused like girl on *Glee* and Gabourey
> IAmDonald is a full-time job
> These niggas want me to fail so they can write me off[21]

This engagement with the ways he is racially read continues on the album *Camp*, released the same year. The song "Fire Fly" references Glover being called "Oreo" and "F*gg*t" throughout his life and that some thought his rap career was a joke.[22] Taken together, these insults demonstrate how Glover's performance of self was perceived by both Black and white audiences as inauthentically raced and gendered. That Glover returns to these themes on multiple albums and mixtapes suggests that this was a persistent thread throughout his life. Later on "Fire Fly," he mimics naysayers who have told him that he can't possibly speak to the hood, but Glover responds that he actually thinks he could if he had the chance.

Enter: *Atlanta*. In his early career, Donald Glover used his position on the periphery of Blackness to lament the performativity of race and the narrow constructions and standards of Blackness his peers held him up against. At the same time, he leveraged this positionality for crossover appeal to build an audience across mediums; on "Bonfire" he raps, "Black and white music, now nigga that's a mixtape."[23] *Atlanta's* narrative is loosely framed around the broke Ivy League dropout Earn (Donald Glover), who sees a potentially lucrative possibility in managing his cousin Alfred's (known as Paper Boi, played by Brian Tyree Henry) burgeoning rap career. Hip-hop music, both diegetic and nondiegetic, is a crucial component of the series. Writing in the 1990s about the success of FOX's *In Living Color* (1990–1994), Herman Gray argued, "Rap and hip-hop are used deliberately but quite strategically in the program to generate identifications across racial lines."[24] Jennifer Fuller extends this argument in her analysis of the use of hip-hop in *Chappelle's Show* (Comedy Central, 2003–2006) and *Def Comedy Jam* (HBO, 1992–1997;

2006–2008).[25] In addition to Donald Glover's star text and the show's use of hip-hop, *Atlanta*'s placement on the cable network FX is in line with the series' cross-racial appeal and its location within discourses of quality television.

FX has cultivated a particular brand identity. Michael L. Wayne argues, "Previously known as 'Fox on cable,' FX reinvented its brand with the complex, hypermasculine antihero drama *The Shield* (2002–2008) establishing itself as one of cable's premiere destinations for 'gritty,' 'risky,' and 'edgy' fare."[26] Further, Wayne notes, through this type of programming FX became the second-highest-rated cable network among white, male viewers ages eighteen to forty-nine, a prized audience demographic.[27] Since the premiere of *The Shield*, FX has relied on risk and edginess to also distinguish its comedy series. Jennifer Fuller's work demonstrates how cable networks have used Blackness, and its attendant associations with hipness or edginess, "as a method of cultivating brand identities with transracial appeal."[28] *Atlanta*'s riskiness is twofold: FX becomes narrativized as a brave risk taker for taking a chance on a series with a loosely structured, unconventional narrative, multiple writers with no television experience, and a frequent director (Hiro Murai) mostly known for music videos.[29] Second, the series' emphasis on hip-hop and Black life produce "edginess" in line with the FX brand. In the 2010s, FX made more concentrated efforts to appeal to viewers outside of its white, male core; this included Ryan Murphy's *American Horror Story* (2011–) anthology series and *The Bridge* (2013–2014) a crime drama adapted from the Swedish/Danish series Bron/Broen. Michael L. Wayne asserts that FX's decision to move the Scandi-noir adaptation from the US-Canada border to the southern one was not just about expanding narrative possibilities; rather, FX sought to attract Latino viewers while maintaining its white, male audience with a demonstrated investment in gritty crime dramas.[30] In a similar vein, *Atlanta* created the potential to attract more African American viewers to FX, and at the same time, the series' style and Glover's proven popularity with white audiences appealed to the channel's core base.

Stylistically, *Atlanta* uses a single-camera setup, natural lighting, and expressive cinematography, a clear step away from the formal conventions of many of the sitcoms starring Black, postsoul comedians on network television in the late 1990s and early 2000s. These elements, as well as the series' genre mixing and the framing of Glover as "auteur," are components of the most recent wave of series designated as "quality" by television critics and viewers.[31] In addition to noting aesthetic and narrative innovations, some critics have identified *Atlanta* as quality through comparing it to other media. In a review of the second season in *The Hollywood Reporter*, critic Tim Goodman equates *Atlanta* with several quality series but most critically *Louie* (FX,

2010–2015) and the FX brand.[32] Similarly, the *Guardian* likens *Atlanta* to *The Sopranos* (HBO, 1999–2007), which is referred to in the review as the *Citizen Kane* (1941) of television.[33] The comparison to a canonized film extends the quality discourse even further; *Atlanta* is so good, this framing suggests, that it can surpass the boundaries of a (supposedly) aesthetically, narratively, and culturally lesser medium. These reviews also effectively place *Atlanta* within a lineage of "great" white shows without acknowledging that *Atlanta* in many ways stems from traditions of African American humor with their own long histories.

ATLANTA AND AFRICAN AMERICAN HUMOR

On a panel to promote *Atlanta* before the start of its first season, Glover remarked that the show's central thesis "was to show people what it's like to be black, and you can't write that down. You have to feel it." He went on to state, "I want people to feel scared because that's what it feels like to be black. Amazing things can happen, but it can be taken away at any moment."[34] In this quote, Glover demonstrates his awareness of who FX sees as its core audience and, moreover, his own role in negotiating how to represent a specific, localized experience of Blackness to the predominantly white audience of prestige cable. Throughout the series, and especially in "Robbin' Season," Glover and the other writers balance the desire to make Blackness felt by constructing a heightened sense of precarity, while simultaneously speaking directly to Black viewers through culturally resonant material. The season premiere, "Alligator Man," begins with a drug deal that quickly turns into a robbery and shoot out, leaving one woman bleeding and screaming as the robbers flee the scene. The title card, positioned over aerial shots of the city of Atlanta, transitions to our main characters. Earn is being evicted from the storage unit where he has been squatting and his cousin Alfred is on house arrest. Trying to get on Alfred's good side, and hopefully secure a place to stay, Earn agrees to talk to his uncle Willy (Katt Williams guest starring) and resolve a domestic dispute. Since "Robbin' Season" alters the narrative structure of the show by following a single main character in each episode, the guest stars in the series' second season have more pronounced roles in their respective episodes. Katt Williams's casting as Earn's uncle, and its embedded intertextuality, position both *Atlanta* and Donald Glover as part of the genealogy of African American postsoul comedians.

Despite cultivating a fan base and following with African American audiences and his myriad roles in film and television, Williams, unlike Glover, never garnered crossover appeal or "mainstream" success. Comparing Williams to Chris Rock, Racquel Gates writes, "Whereas Rock's identity is buffered by a respectability conferred by his time in media with a mixed audience . . . Williams's celebrity is largely confined to the black community. . . . More broadly, Rock embodies a global cosmopolitanism with appeal to both black and nonblack audiences, while Williams more aesthetically and functionally invokes aspects from the history of black comedic traditions."[35]

For the Black viewers watching "Alligator Man," the inclusion of Williams, who is performing a version of his comic persona, may add additional layers of intertextuality.[36] Williams began his career doing stand-up locally in Ohio and, as he gained popularity, began to perform across the country. Williams went on to cable television and starred in multiple stand-up comedy specials, three produced by HBO, and appeared on Black comedy series like BET's *Comic View* (1992–2008; 2014) and HBO's *Def Comedy Jam*. As Bambi Haggins articulates, "the performers of *Def Comedy Jam* . . . embodied bawdy (often physical) humor that reaches back beyond the Chitlin' Circuit into the conventions of minstrelsy."[37] As I previously explained, Glover has a different career trajectory and comedic style than many Black postsoul comedians who came before him. However, Williams's casting works to collapse some of the distance between Glover's body of work and Black comedians who never garnered mainstream success. Moreover, having Williams play Earn's uncle firmly situates Glover within the direct lineage of the postsoul Black comic rather than outside of it or on the periphery. In one of the more serious and vulnerable moments of the episode, Earn tells Uncle Willy that he doesn't want to end up like him. After giving him a gold handgun, Willy remarks thus if Earn doesn't want to end up like him: "Get rid of the chip on your shoulder. It's not worth the time."[38] Critic Justin Tinsley frames this scene, stating, "It's an OG comedian/actor who had the world in his palms, but self-inflicted mistakes ruptured the potential he had in his hands—giving a current comedian/actor with nothing but green pastures ahead of him game he needs to survive not just the game but his own pitfalls."[39] Earlier in his career, Glover continually lamented his position on the margins of Black masculinity; with *Atlanta*, Glover seems to have gotten rid of the chip on his shoulder. Through culturally resonant elements, like the casting of Williams, "Robbin' Season" moves Glover further from his place on the periphery of Blackness to a position with dual credibility for both Black and non-Black audiences.

In a similar vein, "Barbershop" (season 2, ep. 5) follows Alfred trying to get a haircut from his regular barber, Bibby (comedian Robert S. Powell III).[40] As critic Bryan Washington notes in his episode review, the episode is really an extended bit.[41] What should be a fairly straightforward appointment is drawn out over the course of the day as barber Bibby keeps putting off the haircut so he can take care of something "real quick."[42] These "quick"

Fig. 5.1 Promotional image from *Atlanta*'s "Robbin' Season."

errands include going to his girlfriend's house to give her son a haircut because he technically had an appointment before Alfred, stealing lumber from a house under construction, reprimanding Bibby's son when they catch him and his friends skipping school, and fleeing the scene after a hit and run. Bibby's antics cause Alfred to lose his temper more than once, but the payoff comes when Bibby finally gets around to cutting Alfred's hair. Bibby gives Alfred "the usual" and the cinematography and Donald Glover's direction emphasize Bibby's craftsmanship in a way that makes clear why Alfred even bothered with such an unprofessional and absurd character in the first place.[43] In the last scene, Alfred comes back into the shop and smugly sits in another barber's chair. However, when the new barber asks Alfred which size razor he normally gets his hair cut with, Alfred comes to the realization that it's really only Bibby who can give him what he needs. The key to the comedy in this episode is twofold: it takes situations that could conceivably happen and dials up the absurdity for comedic effect, and second, it plays on a hyperspecific Black experience. In her analysis of the Black *Game of Thrones* (HBO, 2011–2019) fandom, Sarah Florini illustrates how through the use of African American Vernacular English and references to Black cult media, Black fans "engage in fandom in culturally resonant ways that eschew processes that make whiteness normative and instead tap into the symbolic energy of Black cultural commonplaces that resonate with Black audiences, invoking Black epistemologies and interpretive frames."[44] Similarly, this episode's humor relies on Black cultural commonplaces and forgoes white ways of knowing.

The Black barbershop is a social and communal space and scholars have theorized it in terms of an alternate or counter to the Habermasian public sphere and as a type of cultural forum.[45] Alfred and Bibby do not converse with the other barbers or clients in the shop; however, their own conversation, about the lack of Black people on movie posters, is representative of some of the key ideas in the scholarship about African Americans and the barbershop. Bibby has launched into rapid, circuitous chatter that touches on local news and the state of entertainment, with Alfred chiming in minimally in the hopes that Bibby will stop talking and start cutting. At one point, Bibby winds up at the poster for the 2016 film *Keanu* (dir. Peter Atencio). Bibby remarks, "Key and Peele put a movie out with a cat in it, [and] they put the cat on the poster! They dressed the cat up like a nigga instead of putting the two niggas that made the movie on the poster . . . shit's nuts out here."[46] This episode is yet another structural experiment in a series full of them. It revolves around Bibby and Alfred, and while the relationship between barber and client unfolds and is pushed near its limits, at no point is it explained for non-Black viewers. Akin to series like *One Day at a Time* (Netflix 2017–2019; Pop TV 2020) deciding not to translate its characters' use of Spanish, the lack of translation in "Barbershop" prioritizes viewers with the cultural competency to interpret the episode. Across "Robbin' Season" the four core characters are ensconced in increasingly absurd or precarious situations that illustrate the myriad conditions of African American life.

Whose Quality Is It Anyways?

Atlanta's "Robbin' Season" balances Black cultural resonance with transracial appeal, and the dual credibility Haggins identified in Dave Chappelle now also describes Donald Glover. After receiving acclaim and six Emmy nominations for its first season, many viewers and critics alike wondered how Glover and his creative team would shape the second season. If anything, critics were even more impressed with the series' sophomore effort. In his review, the *New York Times* television critic James Poniewozik wrote, "Robbin' Season is so good. It's almost criminal."[47] While the critical establishment's championing of a Black-cast show with a Black writer's room might suggest a diversification of what types of programs can be regarded as quality television, it is still important to note how *Atlanta* is buoyed by Glover's mutability and the FX brand. Further, my focus on how the discourse of quality television has been applied to *Atlanta* is not offered as a verdict about *Atlanta*'s cultural or aesthetic merit but rather to illustrate how the classification highlights how race and industrial formations inform the politics of taste and the critical assessment of cultural texts at a particular conjuncture. What I have aimed to do is illustrate both how *Atlanta* has come to be regarding as quality television while also being lauded for the specificity and care that informs its representation of Black American, and especially southern, experiences and how Donald Glover became the auteur behind such a show. My analysis of both Glover's star text and *Atlanta* illuminates new ties among the Black comic, Black creative production, and humor in the current television landscape.

Jacqueline Johnson is a PhD candidate in the Division of Cinema and Media Studies at the University of Southern California. Her work appears in *Sartorial Fandom: Fashion, Beauty Culture, and Identity* and *Watching While Black Rebooted!: The Television and Digitality of Black Audiences.*

Notes

1. Allison Samuels, "Inside the Weird, Industry-Shaking World of Donald Glover," *Wired*, January 19, 2017, https://www.wired.com/2017/01/childish-gambino-donald-glover/.
2. Liz Shannon Miller, "'Atlanta': Donald Glover Wants You to Feel What It's Like to Be Black," *Indie Wire* (blog), August 9, 2016, https://www.indiewire.com/2016/08/donald-glover-atlanta-fx-hiro-murai-trump-1201714877/.
3. Samuels, "Inside the Weird, Industry-Shaking World of Donald Glover."
4. Robbin' season refers to the increase in crime, especially robbery, that occurs in Atlanta before the holidays. The second season of the series makes a narrative departure from its predecessor through constructing episodic character studies. Rather than the whole main cast appearing across every episode in the season, most episodes revolve around one or two characters.
5. Alfred L. Martin Jr., "Notes from Underground: WGN's Black-Cast Quality TV Experiment," *Los Angeles Review of Books*, May 31, 2018, https://lareviewofbooks.org/article/notes-from-underground-wgns-black-cast-quality-tv-experiment/; Kristal Brent Zook, *Color by Fox: The Fox Network and the Revolution in Black Television* (New York: Oxford University Press, 1999).
6. Jennifer Fuller, "Branding Blackness on US Cable Television," *Media, Culture & Society* 32, no. 2 (March 1, 2010): 285–305. https://doi.org/10.1177/0163443709355611.
7. David Gillota, *Ethnic Humor in Multiethnic America* (New Brunswick, NJ: Rutgers University Press, 2013).
8. Ibid.; Watkins, *On the Real Side: A History of African American Comedy from Slavery to Chris Rock* (Chicago: Chicago Review Press, 1999).
9. Christine Acham, *Revolution Televised: Prime Time and the Struggle for Black Power* (Minneapolis: University of Minnesota Press, 2004), 87.
10. Mark Anthony Neal, *Soul Babies Black Popular Culture and the Post-Soul Aesthetic* (New York: Routledge, 2002).
11. Bambi Haggins, *Laughing Mad: The Black Comic Persona in Post-Soul America* (New Brunswick, NJ: Rutgers University Press, 2007), 11.
12. Ibid., 179.
13. David Gillota, "Black Nerds: New Directions in African American Humor," *Studies in American Humor*, no. 28 (2013): 17–30. JSTOR.
14. Ibid.

15. Soraya Nadia McDonald, "'Atlanta,' the Weirdest, Blackest Show on TV, Finally Gets a Return Date," *Undefeated* (blog), January 6, 2018, https://theundefeated.com/features/atlanta-the-weirdest-blackest-show-on-tv-finally-gets-a-return-date/.

16. Michael Z. Newman and Elana Levine, *Legitimating Television: Media Convergence and Cultural Status* (New York: Routledge, 2012).

17. Amanda D. Lotz, "Segregated Sitcoms: Institutional Causes of Disparity among Black and White Comedy Images and Audiences," in *The Sitcom Reader: America Viewed and Skewed*, ed. Mary M. Dalton and Laura R. Linder, 139–50 (New York: SUNY Press, 2005), https://www.sunypress.edu/p-4180-the-sitcom-reader.aspx.

18. Ron Becker, *Gay TV and Straight America* (Piscataway, NJ: Rutgers University Press, 2006), https://www.jstor.org/stable/j.ctt5hj2qo; Alfred L. Martin Jr., *The Generic Closet: Black Gayness and the Black-Cast Sitcom* (Bloomington: Indiana University Press, 2021).

19. Becker, *Gay TV and Straight America*, 95.

20. This trend, of course, is not exclusive to television comedy. See, Mary Beltrán, "Meaningful Diversity: Exploring Questions of Equitable Representation on Diverse Ensemble Cast Shows," *Flow* (blog), August 27, 2010, https://www.flowjournal.org/2010/08/meaningful-diversity.

21. Childish Gambino, "Not Going Back," recorded circa 2010–2011, track 5 on *EP*, Glassnote, digital.

22. Childish Gambino, "Fire Fly," recorded 2011, track 2 on *Camp*, Glassnote, digital.

23. Childish Gambino, "Bonfire," recorded 2011, Track 3 on *Camp*, Glassnote, digital.

24. Herman Gray, *Watching Race: Television and the Struggle for Blackness*, 2nd ed. (Minneapolis: University of Minnesota Press, 2004), 138.

25. Fuller, "Branding Blackness on US Cable Television."

26. Michael L. Wayne, "Ambivalent Anti-Heroes and Racist Rednecks on Basic Cable: Post-Race Ideology and White Masculinities on FX," *Journal of Popular Television* 2, no. 2 (October 1, 2014): 206, https://doi.org/10.1386/jptv.2.2.205_1.

27. Michael L. Wayne, "Critically Acclaimed and Cancelled: FX's *The Bridge*, Channel as Brand and the Adaptation of Scripted TV Formats," *VIEW Journal of European Television History and Culture* 5, no. 9 (August 1, 2016): 116–25, https://doi.org/10.18146/2213-0969.2016.jethc107.

28. Fuller, "Branding Blackness on US Cable Television," 287.

29. This narrative persists despite Glover initially lying to FX executives about what the series would be.

30. Wayne, "Critically Acclaimed and Cancelled."

31. Newman and Levine, *Legitimating Television*.

32. Tim Goodman, "'Atlanta Robbin' Season': TV Review," *Hollywood Reporter* (blog), February 28, 2018, https://www.hollywoodreporter.com/news/general-news/atlanta-robbin-season-review-1088898/.

33. Charles Bramesco, "Atlanta: Robbin' Season Review—The Best Show on TV Returns in Style," *Guardian*, February 28, 2018, http://www.theguardian.com/tv-and-radio/2018/feb/28/atlanta-robbin-season-review-the-best-show-on-tv-returns-in-style.

34. Miller, "Atlanta."

35. Racquel J. Gates, *Double Negative: The Black Image and Popular Culture* (Durham, NC: Duke University Press, 2018), 6.

36. Ibid.

37. Haggins, *Laughing Mad*, 187.

38. Donald Glover, writer, *Atlanta*, season 2, episode 1, "Alligator Man," dir. Hiro Murai, featuring Donald Glover, Brian Tyree Henry, and LaKeith Stanfield, aired March 1, 2018, FX.

39. Justin Tinsley, "'Atlanta' Recap: Season 2, Episode 1: The Family Scars That Bind," *Undefeated* (blog), March 2, 2018, https://theundefeated.com/features/atlanta-recap-season-2-episode-1-the-family-scars-that-bind/.

40. Despite not reaching the same notoriety among Black audiences as Katt Williams, Powell had appeared on *All Def Comedy* (HBO, 2016–2017) prior to appearing in *Atlanta*, placing him in the same lineage as popular Black postsoul comics.

41. Bryan Washington, "Atlanta Robbin' Season Recap: A Good Day," *Vulture*, March 30, 2018, https://www.vulture.com/2018/03/atlanta-recap-season-2-episode-5-barbershop.html.

42. Stefani Robinson, writer, *Atlanta*, season 2, episode 5, "Barbershop," dir. Donald Glover, featuring Brian Tyree Henry and Robert S. Powell III, aired March 29, 2018, FX.

43. Washington, "Atlanta Robbin' Season Recap."

44. Sarah Florini, "Enclaving and Cultural Resonance in Black 'Game of Thrones' Fandom," *Transformative Works and Cultures* 29 (March 15, 2019), https://doi.org/10.3983/twc.2019.1498.

45. Melissa Victoria Harris-Lacewell, *Barbershops, Bibles, and BET* (Princeton, NJ: Princeton University Press, 2010), https://www.degruyter.com/document/doi/10.1515/9781400836604/html; Catherine Knight Steele, "The Digital Barbershop: Blogs and Online Oral Culture within the African American Community," *Social Media + Society* 2, no. 4 (October 1, 2016), https://doi.org/10.1177/2056305116683205.

46. Robinson, "Barbershop."

47. James Poniewozik, "Review: 'Atlanta' and the Surreal Larceny of Life," *New York Times*, February 28, 2018, Arts, https://www.nytimes.com/2018/02/28/arts/television/atlanta-robbin-season-review.html.

6

STEVE URKEL AND THE CONTINUING RESONANCE OF THE "BLERD"

Satirical Television Characters and Cultural Change

Timothy Havens

From Andre Meadows's YouTube channel, "Black Nerd Comedy" to William Jackson Harper's character in *The Good Place* (NBC, 2016–2020), Chidi Anagonye, the Black nerd character, or "Blerd," has become a mainstay of American popular culture. Ten years ago, CNN heralded "the rise of the black nerd in pop culture," and any current Google search will confirm the widening discussion of Black nerdiness and the range of people who identify with the term.[1]

Meadows claims the Blerd exists at the narrow intersections between African American culture and nerd culture. If he is correct, it is also true that those intersections have been actively built, not simply found. Not long ago, popular culture could barely imagine the Blerd as a unique character. In the 1984 movie *Revenge of the Nerds*, for instance, the lone Black member of the nerd fraternity, Lamar, mainly served as an example of "compound otherness," who stood in for a range of nonnerdy social outcasts, particularly queers and Blacks.[2] In 2001, Buchholz found that self-identified high school nerds defined nerdiness as a "hyper-white" identity category—the antithesis of Black youth identity.[3] While Buchholz studied people rather than popular representations, her subjects' attitudes were undoubtedly shaped by and consistent with popular portrayals of nerds.

As a controlling image, the white nerd functions to maintain the articulation of white men with intelligence and Black men with physicality, helping suture intellectual capacity with race.[4] Attempts to deconstruct the race, gender, and class of nerd characters, then, are simultaneously efforts to expand the range of people who can imagine and express themselves as intelligent beings.

The process of articulating nerd culture and African American culture has been no small feat. As the first—and perhaps still the best known—Blerd in popular culture, Jaleel White's Steve Urkel in the Black-cast sitcom *Family Matters* (ABC, 1989–1998) was central to beginning the disarticulation of nerdiness and whiteness. Although he did little to deconstruct the racial identity of the nerd character, instead trading on the humorous incongruity of white cultural values in a Black male body, Urkel nevertheless opened a discursive space to begin deconstructing and reimagining nerd culture.

The case of Urkel requires a theorization of how satirical television characters function as popular figures. While scholarship on television satire focuses almost entirely on whole series that work as satires, I argue that individual satirical characters such as Urkel, who appear in otherwise conventional series, possess the capacity to enable significant cultural reimaginations. Through their persistent repetition across episodes and years and their one-dimensionality, popular figures like Urkel help deconstruct dominant cultural categories by persistently revealing them as arbitrary and ridiculous. As satirical characters are repeatedly taken up in subsequent cultural expressions, these figures can help collapse cultural categories altogether, including those between racial identity and intellectual capacity. The fact that someone like Meadows must continue to clear space for Blerd culture suggests that those categories have not yet collapsed. Nevertheless, Urkel was central to beginning the process.

To theorize how Urkel opened a discursive space for the sustained cultural politics of Black nerd culture, this chapter develops a medium- and genre-specific argument about satirical characters in television sitcoms, with specific attention to the unique functions and sensitivities surrounding satire in sitcoms with predominantly Black casts. With Urkel, *Family Matters* developed an innovative approach to managing satirical Black characters that subsequent situation comedies copied. Specifically, by overendowing Urkel with identifiably white character traits, the series short-circuited the likelihood that viewers would read him as offensive. Several of Urkel's character traits identified him as a nerd: his frequent donning of a lab coat and briefcase, his famous bragging that he "knows Wayne Newton," and his love of the accordion and polka music all align Urkel with decidedly white cultural tastes. He becomes ridiculous because of this overendowment of white cultural tastes and expressions in a Black male body. This strategy of creating ridiculous Black characters by overendowing them with white cultural traits became common in Black-cast television series in the 1990s, and continues today. More importantly, the character innovations that Urkel inaugurated became central to expanding the overlapping space between nerd culture and African American culture that identifies the figure of the Blerd.

URKEL, PLASTIC REPRESENTATION,
AND SATIRICAL FIGURATION

Steve Urkel first appeared in 1989 and quickly became a national sensation. With his trademark high-water jeans pulled up to his waste, suspenders, oversized glasses, stoop-shouldered gait, and popular catch phrase, "Did I do that?" spoken in a high nasally voice, Urkel appeared for years across the American media landscape. The contradiction at the heart of Urkel—at once a ridiculous buffoon *and* a "positive" image in comparison with the Black gangsta figure—offers a textbook case of what Kristin Warner calls "plastic representation," in which a demeaning Black stereotype is written over with white, heteronormative, middle-class traits.[5] The resulting character thus becomes inoffensive for many viewers and critics, even as it does little to deconstruct the original stereotype or complicate Black media representations. Nevertheless, as I hope to show, the contradictions at the heart of these plastic representations can open a cultural space where the deconstruction of racial stereotypes can occur.

The plastic nature of Urkel's representation led to wildly divergent interpretations of the character among critics at the time. Dr. Alvin Poussaint, a noted psychologist, consultant for *The Cosby Show*, and television personality of the day, said of Urkel, "He's not up on street talk, not a dancing, bopping kind of kid. . . . The fact that he's a nerd and very bright may be a step forward—accepting that a Black kid can be bright and precocious and might end up in an Ivy League school."[6] On the other end of the spectrum, noted journalist and television critic, John O'Connor, complained that Urkel's "broadly caricatured antics uneasily smack of a modern Stepin' Fetchit in the making."[7]

Both Poussaint and O'Connor fall into the trap of assessing popular television characters as textual phenomena that reproduce either positive or negative attitudes in viewers rather than as cultural figures that focalize, circulate, and participate in major social debates of the day.[8] Reading popular television characters as figures, rather than attitudinal stimuli, allows an assessment of how they function socially, the kinds of social and political impact they have, and the reasons for their often-sudden appearances and disappearances within popular culture. To read the cultural work of Urkel, and the Blerd figure in general, in a manner that goes beyond dichotomous, cognitive models of positive and negative characterizations, it is necessary to fully account for African American satire, television satire, and the role popular characters play in a media-saturated society.

Several scholars have written about Black satire, and my argument here owes a substantial debt to those works. In particular, Mel Watkins's encyclopedic history of African American humor identifies the forms and functions of African American satire. As Watkins demonstrates, African American comedy has historically skewered intolerance and hypocrisy in both out-group and in-group attitudes and institutions.[9]

Darryl Dickson-Carr explores African American satirical novels, making an important call for examining satire within specific media and genres, as well across them. "The novel," he writes, "allows . . . for sustained investigations and/or critiques of a wide range of subjects," because of the genre's heteroglossia, or its integration of a range of discursive styles and worldviews.[10] Consequently, he argues, the social and political consequences of the African American satirical novel differ from novels written by whites, as well as satire that appears in other types of expressive media or literary genres.

Perhaps more than the novel, broadcast television, especially sitcoms, integrate discourses from a wide range of perspectives to maximize their appeal and, thereby, their ratings. Dickson-Carr distinguishes between satirical novels, which "qualify as satires in toto," and texts with satirical moments or "passages . . . that a reader might find satirical only at remote points."[11] Situation comedies rarely function as satires as a whole. Instead, sitcoms typically use satirical characters within otherwise realist or parodic aesthetics. The distinction between satire and parody here is important to parse: satire is a comedic form of ridicule aimed at social types, institutions, or practices, while parody ridicules other modes of cultural expression, including other texts, genres, or media. Hence, *The Simpsons* is a parody of the domestic sitcom that also satirizes society at points.[12]

Most television comedies continue to deploy satirical humor "only at remote points," particularly those media texts that have popularized the Blerd.[13] Moreover, for scholars of humor and television, as well as for scholars of race and media, a more elaborated theory of satirical moments in otherwise conventional genres like the three-camera domestic sitcom can illuminate the political potential even in seemingly banal and politically regressive shows like *Family Matters*. While Black-cast satires do exist, including *The Boondocks* (Cartoon Network, 2005–2014), *The Nightly Show with Larry Wilmore* (Comedy Central, 2014–2015), and, to some extent, *The Bernie Mac Show* (FOX, 2001–2006), Black-cast series instead most predominantly fall into the conventional domestic sitcom genre, even as they utilize satirical humor liberally.

John Fiske argues that popular characters like Urkel should be understood as "figures" that gain their cultural force not by short-circuiting our cognitive processes but rather by gathering within themselves a broad range of extant discourses and affects, some of them consistent with one another, others wildly contradictory.[14] In other words, figures are the fundamental hyper-real objects that media-saturated societies employ to stage and work through deep-seated tensions. As a character, Urkel tapped into the long-standing figure of the witless Black buffoon and the more recent figure of the white nerd. But in combining those figures at a specific moment in history, for certain audiences, Urkel emerged as a cultural figure in his own right.

Urkel figured at least three charged cultural conflicts that continue to animate the Blerd figure today. The first conflict concerns proper performances of Black male racial identity. The disagreement between Poussaint and O'Connor is indicative of a class-based conflict surrounding Urkel and appropriate/inappropriate performances of Black masculinity at the time. In the late 1980s and early 1990s, as before and since, this class conflict centered assimilation, as evidenced in educational achievements, standardized speech, and conventional white dress versus Black difference and pride in one's dress, speech, and personal style.[15]

The second conflict, which was also a class conflict, was more televisual, stemming from the use of buffoonish or satirical Black characters in comedy. As Watkins points out, these concerns arose at a moment in history when African Americans began integrating into the American middle and upper-classes and became concerned about how the portrayal of Black buffoons might be influencing their new white neighbors and coworkers.[16] By contrast, working-class African Americans rightly considered such portrayals to be a long-standing element of traditional African American humor. Characters like J. J. Evans in *Good Times* (CBS, 1974–1979) and many of Eddie Murphy's films and TV characters are good examples of satirical characters that were popular with working-class Black viewers but troubling for their middle-class counterparts.

The final conflict concerned liberal white attitudes toward young Black men. In the post–civil rights white imagination, most Black men were still "gangbangers"—a term coined in 1969 and popularized throughout the 1980s to refer specially to Black male members of street gangs. A character like Urkel could become an object lesson for the kind of Black male behavior that white Americans found acceptable, allowing them to place the burden of continued poverty and violence back on young African American men rather than racist social practices and structures. In other words, Urkel staged the debate among whites over where responsibility for continuing Black poverty and skyrocketing Black male death rates lay. These powerful social conflicts—about what constitutes Black male identity, about satirical Black humor, and about the sources of social inequities for African Americans—continue to make the Blerd a relevant cultural figure in American society.

Navigating Urkel's Nerdiness

Family Matters debuted in the fall of 1989. Featuring as Carl Winslow Reginald VelJohsnon, who had recently starred opposite Bruce Willis in *Die Hard* (1988, dir. John McTiernan) as a Chicago police officer, and Mary Jo Payton as Harriet Winslow, *Family Matters* focused on a middle-class African American family with two school-aged children. When it ended its run in the spring of 1998, *Family Matters* had become the longest-running Black-cast sitcom in American history.

During the mid- to late 1980s, every network was looking to replicate *The Cosby Show*'s success by developing sitcoms focused on middle-class African American families, and *Family Matters* was ABC's contender. An inaugural member of ABC's TGIF programming block on Friday Nights, *Family Matters* was spun off from the popular *Perfect Strangers* (ABC, 1986–1993) and was the only predominantly Black-cast sitcom in the block. In its initial episodes, the series lacked anything unique to draw viewers. It did not have the star power of *Charlie & Company* (CBS, 1985–1986) with Flip Wilson and Gladys Knight; the aesthetic ornamentation of *Frank's Place* (CBS, 1987–1988); or the gritty realism of *Roc* (FOX, 1991–1994).

Industry lore suggests that Urkel was intended as a one-time character, but he was so popular with audiences that he became the center of the series.[17] Of course, as with all forms of industry lore, care must be taken to avoid giving this account too much credence; undoubtedly, the producers were looking for a hook to make the show stand out. Their initial efforts centered on extended family members, including Carl's wise-cracking mother, who moved in with the family in the pilot episode, and Harriet's sister Rachel, a widow with a baby, who had also moved in with the Winslows prior to the beginning of the series. Despite popular accounts of Urkel's sudden, meteoric rise, he had only cameo appearances for most of season one, showing up in only five episodes, typically as a comic relief in the show's cold open. As the series progressed, much like J. J. Evans on *Good Times* (CBS, 1974–1979), Urkel became the center of both the comedy and the narrative.

Urkel drew on a lineage of oddball characters in Black-cast sitcoms whose performance of Black masculinity were portrayed as suspect due to their pursuit of forms of success that were coded as white, typically business or educational pursuits.[18] Some of these forerunners include Roger Thomas in *What's Happening?* (1976–1979), Dwayne Wayne in *A Different World* (1987–1993), and Leonard Taylor in *That's My Mama* (1974–1975). Still, while characters such as these were ridiculed for overemphasizing their studies or careers, they were largely portrayed as realistic, unlike Steve Urkel, who remained largely a satirical caricature for the full run of *Family Matters*.

Urkel became best known for his nerdy character traits: his large glasses, "high-water" jeans with suspenders pulled up near his chest; his nasally voice and snorting laughter; his awkward, stoop-shouldered gait; and his love of science and school. His tendency for destructive, slapstick comedy, captured in his signature tag line, "Did I do that?" was also central to his comedy. In his initial appearances, Urkel is less definitively identified with slapstick and nerdiness. Instead, his humor arises primarily from costuming and performance. His costuming, while odd, can be read as a failed attempt at 1980s Black hipster style, à la Dwayne Wayne on *A Different World*. Likewise, his large glasses and signature voice and laugh tend initially to mark him more generally as an oddball rather than a Blerd. In this way, Urkel integrates two long-standing types in Black-cast sitcoms, the oddball character

In his first appearance in "Rachel's First Date," Urkel, wearing rainbow-colored suspenders, a blue cardigan, and a plaid shirt, walks into the Winslows' kitchen, where Carl is about to eat a large ice cream sundae. "You're not going to eat that, are you, Carl?" he intones in his nasally voice, reeling off a list of harmful ingredients that disgust Carl, making him storm out of the room, after which Urkel hops on the counter and begins to eat the sundae. Here, as in a couple of these early scenes, Urkel serves as a kind of trickster character who uses flattery and cunning to "get over" on more powerful characters and get what he wants—a characteristic that all but disappears as the series progresses.[19]

Urkel has a greater narrative purpose in episode 12, "Laura's First Date," where he asks Laura, the Winslows' daughter, to the school dance and gets rejected, only to have Carl ask him to take her, because Carl believes that she is having trouble getting a date. Of course, Laura ends up with several dates to the dance and ultimately goes with the boy she asked out herself. In a break from what had become typical for the series, Urkel does not appear in the cold open but in the first scene after the opening credits. Wearing a large shower cap, a bathrobe, and oversized flip-flops and carrying a live duck, he explains that Carl's mother allowed him to shower there because the hot water at the Urkel home isn't working. Later in the episode, he appears in several scenes, and the fact that Carl has set him up on a date with Laura becomes the core of the episode's storyline. Urkel's first substantial appearance in the series, then, reveals an inconsistent approach to his character, which can best be described as strange and awkward. Certainly, his nerdiness is one component of this portrayal, but it is not the only component or even the most prominent one.

These early episodes make clear the recognition of Urkel's comic potential but show uncertainty about how best to exploit that potential. As the season progresses, Urkel's portrayal as a nerd begins to predominate, as his association with school- and science-related scenes and storylines take center stage, though the character never loses his penchant for odd costuming and behavior. Clearly, the nerd was a common teenage character across film and media, and *Family Matters'* focus on teenaged children, as well as its positioning in a network programming block targeting teenaged viewers, made the nerd an obvious choice as the central satirical character in the series. The fact that it took *Family Matters'* producers much of the first season to settle on Urkel's primary characterization reflects the difficulty of imagining and integrating a teenaged African American nerd in popular culture.

URKEL, BLACK-CAST SITCOMS, AND THE SATIRIZING OF WHITENESS

As a satirical character whose humor often arises from slapstick comedy, Urkel joins a long list of African American television buffoons. While white sitcoms also employ buffoons, given the checkered history of racist Black buffoonery in Western popular culture, characters like Urkel are much more likely to arouse controversy among viewers and activists than their white counterparts. Consequently, US television series that employ satirical or buffoonish Black characters must be particularly careful about whom they ridicule and how. The complexity of integrating satirical characters into what Alfred L. Martin Jr. calls "the Black-cast sitcom" in a manner that doesn't offend some segments of the audience is one of the defining features of the subgenre.[20]

As mentioned previously, *Family Matters* managed to solve the riddle of how to integrate satirical characters into the Black-cast sitcom by using Urkel to ridicule white culture. A closer look at Urkel's alter ego, Stefan Urquelle, illustrates the centrality of white cultural allusions in the original Urkel character for the series' humor and Urkel's popularity. In the 1993 episode "Dr. Urkel and Mr. Cool," Urkel manages to isolate his "cool" gene, copy it billions of times, and drink a solution that turns him into a different person who introduces himself as "Stefan Urquelle." The differences between the two characters are telling. Stefan removes his suspenders, hikes down his jeans, loses

Fig. 6.1 Nerdy Steve Urkel meets his cool alter ego, Stefan Urquelle, on *Family Matters*.

his glasses, unhunches his shoulders, and stops moving around in a frenzied, halting manner. When he speaks to Laura, his voice is low and self-confident. He has become suave, charming, and sexy—the antithesis of Urkel. Later, when he appears at a party at the Winslow home, Stefan wears sunglasses, a long, white sportscoat with matching pants, a black turtleneck, and a black-and-white spotted vest. As he strides in, Laura and the other young women take notice. "Look at all the honeys in here," he says. "This party is the bomb." Stefan manages to charm the men as well, calling the Winslows' son, Eddie, "Eduardo" and asking Carl if he's lost weight. Later, when he dances with Laura, she loses control of herself and begins kissing him passionately.

Stefan thoroughly transforms the premise and appeal of the series, demonstrating Urkel's centrality to the show and its humor. Stefan is Ukel's Black alter ego: he is stylish, while Urkel is not; he is cool, while Urkel is nerdy; he moves and swaggers confidently, while Urkel is a disaster waiting to happen. Stefan clearly harkens back to a different Black male figure than does Urkel, one more associated with Billy Dee Williams's character in *Star Wars: The Empire Strikes Back* (1980, dir. Irvin Kershner), Lando Calrissian. This figure is a ladies' man, who is decidedly Black in his speech, movements, and sartorial choices. Stefan's appearance throws the white racial aspects of Urkel's character into stark relief: it is not simply Steve's penchant for polka music that marks him as white but also his speech patterns, his personal style, his physical and social awkwardness, and, by inference, his love of school and science.

With Urkel out of the picture, the episode finds its comedic targets in the other main characters: Eddie is no longer cool because he doesn't know the intricacies of Stefan's handshake; Carl is mocked for his vanity and weight; Laura is ridiculous because she is boy crazy. By moving the locus of ridicule from Urkel's performance of masculinity and refocusing it on other characters and their performances of Blackness, the show risks trafficking in stereotypes and racist ridicule. Moreover, the narrative focus itself shifts from the social and familial challenges of high school to the relationship between Stefan and Laura, from a teenaged sitcom to a romantic comedy. In other words, retaining Stefan would have required a significant reorientation of the series' narrative structure and ideological problematic.[21] Rather than a story in which the weird neighbor and his questionable performance of Black masculinity continually threaten the nuclear family, *Family Matters* would have had to become a romantic comedy where outsiders threaten the harmony of Laura and Stefan's relationship.

Urkel's performance of Black masculinity was also in dialogue with other Black male popular types at the time, particularly the "gangsta." Popularized in music, film, and television the Black male gangsta of the 1980s was portrayed as interested only in bodily pleasure, immediate gratification, violence, and hard masculinity. For many middle-class and aspiring viewers, Urkel offered a popular counterweight to gangsta—he was bookish, respectful, hardworking, and clearly upwardly mobile. His eponymous dance craze, "The Urkel Dance," was a series of awkward, largely asexual moves that drew more on country line dancing than popular Black dance styles of the day. The opposition between Urkel and gangsta rap was on full display in a television commercial from the time for Ralston's breakfast cereal Urkel-Os. Launched in 1992, the ad featured Urkel in his signature red cardigan, suspenders, and glasses, along with an oversized chef's hat, as he rapped about inventing a tasty cereal to make Laura fall in love with him. As he roamed around the kitchen/laboratory, he sang, "Hike up your pants and do the Urkel rap." Clearly, the humor of the ad arises from the disconnect between gangsta rap as a genre and Urkel's voice, lyrics, and movements.

Urkel not only prefigured the surge in Blerd characters and culture but also paved the way for several other satirical characters in Black-cast sitcoms whose connections with whiteness and white popular culture made them the prime targets of their series' ridicule. Most prominent among these was Carlton Banks (Alfonso Ribeiro) from *The Fresh Prince of Bel-Air* (NBC, 1990–1996), whose love of Welsh singer Tom Jones, goofy uncool dance moves, and idolization of Macauley Culkin, Bryant Gumbel, and William Shatner all identify him with white cultural tastes. In one famous scene, Carlton is denied admission to a Black college fraternity because the brothers consider him to be a "sellout." While *The Fresh Prince of Bel-Air* deployed Carlton to complicate definitions of Black masculinity, the show's main comic trope also ridiculed Carlton for performing white masculinity. Indeed, in defending himself to the fraternity brothers, Carlton complains, "You think I'm a sellout because . . . I like Barry Manilow?" after which Will explains to his fellow partygoers that "he meant Barry White."

The use of supposedly white traits to ridicule characters remains a central way Black-cast sitcoms contain widespread criticism of ridiculous Black characters; it is not the character's racial identity as Black that gets ridiculed but, rather, a suspect performance of Blackness that is too closely aligned with white culture. Much of the ridicule of Dre in *Black-ish* (ABC, 2014–2022) is in this vein, though his racial identity becomes the butt of jokes because of his wealth, not his nerdiness. Indeed, the portrayal of comedic characters in Black-cast sitcoms who exhibit supposedly white character traits goes back before *Family Matters* as well, to *The Jeffersons* and even *Sanford and Son*.

<h2 style="text-align:center">Understanding Urkel</h2>

As a recurring, satirical character, Urkel forced heated social conflicts into the mainstream of American culture. Contrary to what proponents of positive images insist, satirical characters are perhaps better at staging these kinds of fraught and urgent debates about culture and identity, of ensuring they remain in the popular consciousness, precisely because they are social types and cannot easily be read as individuated human beings.

Paul Attallah, writing about *The Beverly Hillbillies* (CBS, 1962–1971), makes the point that, in their absence of change or growth, their very lack of psychological depth as characters, the hillbilly members of the Clampett family never let viewers forget that they were social types, persistently staging the conflict between wealthy urbanites and the rural poor.[22] The struggles with classism, racism, sexism, homophobia, and transphobia that well-rounded characters encounter can be easily written off as having individualized causes and solutions. However, social types encountering systemic inequities are much more likely to be read as systemic critiques. This likelihood is even greater in the sitcom genre, which insistently returns to a state of ideological equilibrium at the beginning and end of each episode; when this state of equilibrium is one of social conflict rather than familial harmony, as in the case of *The Beverly Hillbillies* or *Family Matters*, that conflict also remains active in society and in viewers week after.

Popular satirical characters, then, have the capacity to offer more incisive political critiques than deep characters. Likewise, satirical characters in serialized narratives offer the opportunity to stage those critiques consistently for years. In this way, I argue, satirical television characters have greater potential to facilitate social change than similar characters in one-off cultural texts such as films or novels. The true legacy of Urkel is his continuing relevance over several years of the series run to social debates about Black masculinity, intellectual acumen, social change, and personal liberty.

Even today, Urkel appears in nearly every online list of Blerd characters, and references to Urkel continue to appear intermittently on television and other media. In 2021, Jaleel White began promoting a marijuana brand for 710 Labs called "Purple Urkel."[23] The fact that Urkel continues to be a cultural touchstone of Black nerdiness today is testament to the character's centrality in opening and sustaining a space for these debates.

The continued presence of Blerd culture and discussions about it in legacy and social media outlets reflect the ongoing social process of reconciling performances of intellect with Black male identity, particularly with values of cultural authenticity. Urkel enabled the discursive space within which these dialogues could begin to take place. Indeed, the case of Urkel shows the unique ways serialized television comedies can enable such discursive spaces through their persistent popularity over time and their tendency to appear intertextually across media genres and forms.

Timothy Havens is Professor of Communication Studies, African American Studies, and International Studies at the University of Iowa. He is author of *Global Television Marketplace*; *Black Television Travels: African American Media around the Globe*; and (with Amanda D. Lotz) *Understanding Media Industries*.

NOTES

1. Toby Mekeisha Madden, "The Rise of the Black Nerd in Popular Culture," CNN, March 31, 2012, https://edition.cnn.com/2012/03/31/showbiz/rise-of-black-nerds/index.html.

2. Alfred L. Martin Jr., "Doing Double Duty: Toward a Theory of 'Compound Otherness' on Television," *Flow*, August 18, 2011, https://www.flowjournal.org/2011/08/doing-double-duty/.

3. Mary Bucholtz, "The Whiteness of Nerds: Superstandard English and Racial Markedness," *Journal of Linguistic Anthropology* 11, no. 1 (2001): 84–100.

4. Patricia Hill Collins, *Black Sexual Politics: African Americans, Gender, and the New Racism* (London: Routledge, 2004).

5. Kristen J. Warner, "In the Time of Plastic Representation," *Film Quarterly* 71, no. 2 (2017): 32–37.

6. Joy Horowitz, "Snookums! Steve Urkel Is a Hit," *New York Times*, April 17, 1991, 11.

7. John J. O'Connor, "Blacks on TV: Scrambled Signals," *New York Times*, October 27, 1991, Arts & Leisure, 2.

8. John Fiske, *Media Matters, Race and Gender in US Politics* (Minneapolis: University of Minnesota Press, 1996), 70.

9. Mel Watkins, *On the Real Side: A History of African American Comedy from Slavery to Chris Rock* (Chicago: Chicago Review Press, 1999), 25.

10. Darryl Dickson-Carr, *African American Satire: The Sacredly Profane Novel* (Columbia: University of Missouri Press, 2001), 6.

11. Ibid., 10–11.

12. Jonathan Gray, *Watching with 'The Simpsons': Television, Parody, and Intertextuality* (New York and London: Routledge, 2012).

13. Dickson-Carr, *African American Satire*, 10.

14. Fiske, *Media Matters*, 70; Oscar H. Gandy, *Communication and Race: A Structural Perspective* (London: Arnold, 1998).

15. Todd Boyd, *Am I Black Enough for You? Popular Culture from the 'Hood and Beyond* (Bloomington: Indiana University Press, 1997).

16. Watkins, *On the Real Side: A History*, 21.

17. Joy Horowitz, "Snookums! Steve Urkel Is a Hit," *New York Times*, April 17, 1991, 11.

18. The idea that some African Americans "act white" because of their pursuit of educational or professional achievements is, of course, controversial, pejorative, and even destructive. Nevertheless, I do find compelling arguments that racial identities are social constituted through performance (see E. Patrick Johnson, *Appropriating Blackness: Performance and the Politics of Authenticity* [Durham, NC: Duke University Press, 2003]). Here, when I refer to the coding of certain character traits as "white," I mainly mean how a television series identifies particular characteristics as aberrant for Black characters by associating them with white culture.

19. Watkins, *On the Real Side: A History*, 73.

20. Alfred L. Martin Jr., *The Generic Closet: Black Gayness and the Black-Cast Sitcom* (Bloomington: Indiana University Press, 2021).

21. Mimi White, "Ideological Analysis and Television," in *Channels of Discourse: Television and Contemporary Culture*, 2nd ed., ed. Robert C. Allen, 161–202 (Chapel Hill: University of North Carolina Press, 1992).

22. Paul Attallah, "The Unworthy Discourse: Situation Comedy in Television," in *Interpreting Television: Current Research Perspectives*, ed. Willard D. Rowland Jr. and Bruce Watkins, 222–49 (London: Sage, 1984).

23. Pierre-Antoine Louis, "Jaleel White Wants to Sell You 'Purple Urkle [*sic*],'" *New York Times*, May 8, 2021, https://www.nytimes.com/2021/05/08/us/jaleel-white-purple-urkle.html.

7

GIVING (FUNNY) FACE

Prince and His Humors

Scott Poulson-Bryant

HEARING PRINCE

The first time I met Prince, at his Minnesota production facility Paisley
Park in 1991, he stepped up to me, offered his hand, and said, "Hi, I'm
Prince." Despite a rare star-struck-ness—by that time, I'd been interviewing music artists for a few years and had, I thought, trained myself out of
such responses—I was, in a way, speechless. Partly because this was *Prince*,
an artist who'd been for me, musically and emotionally, an emblem of "difference" in my boring, homogeneous town. But it was also because I was
thinking hard in that moment, trying to read the expression on his face as
he introduced himself. It was mysterious or, at least, a mystery to me. Was it
disdain for yet another journalist inserting himself into his space to ask more
questions? Was it smugness, a kind of performative acknowledgment of his
own greatness being mirrored in my star-struck eyes? Ultimately, I landed on
irony. In that moment, there was something in his affect that reminded me of
expressions I'd seen him exhibit in many of the visual products he'd released
to the public as part of his performance career, from various moments in the
film *Purple Rain* (1984, dir. Albert Magnoli) to the video for his 1986 single
"Kiss" and in various performances after that—a mix of humorous interest
in a moment and a cockeyed ironic distance *from* the moment, as if he was
watching himself and those around him, commenting on the moment while
participating in it.

100

The second time I was in his presence, at a Grammy party in New York in 1996, I saw him across the room just before he summoned me over from a table where I sat drinking with friends. He said, "I thought that was you over there." This time, that facial expression I'd experienced in Minnesota now manifested itself in his voice, in the tone of it, which I noticed even more when he said, "I heard what you said about me on VH1." I watched him watch me, as I wracked my brain, trying to recall everything I'd said about him on the TV talk show I regularly appeared on, on VH1 at the time, trying to remember if I'd said anything negative about him. After watching me think, he smiled and said, "I'm messin' with you, man. You only said good stuff about me." Relieved that he hadn't remembered my saying something I couldn't remember saying, I breathed a sigh of relief, and I smiled myself. Partly because of relief, but also because I realized he was doing some version of "playing the Dozens" with me (a humorous game of insults also called "signifyin'" or "sounding"). Perhaps he was enacting the power of his celebrity with a journalist. Perhaps he was so fully aware of the differences in our status but also conscious that I possessed my own "status"—as someone who'd moved from magazine writer to TV commentator with my own image to maintain—that he could play around with that hierarchy. The act of recognition—"I thought that was you over there"—followed by the summoning and then the opening question as the joking setup of a punchline: he was performing, for an audience of one but also slightly removed from the interaction, watching for my reaction to the joke. He was, indeed, signifying.[1]

I open this essay with these reminiscences of Prince to introduce two of the ways humor appeared throughout his sonic and visual oeuvres over the course of his long and storied career. At various times, from his recording debut in 1979 to his film debut in 1984, from his early videos on MTV to talk show appearances and award show performances, Prince (both as Prince and as the "Artist Formerly Known as Prince") utilized humor—sometimes bawdily, often sarcastically, almost always ironically—as a mode of expression which seemed to place him deeply within a Black tradition of blue humor while also simultaneously outside of more normative and expected performances of pop stardom, particularly in the overly sincere 1980s pop music era during which he experienced his greatest artistic and commercial achievements. In the process of being both part of but also removed from these cultural traditions, Prince enacted a long-running commentary on musical stardom, often walking thin, but embattled, lines between the meanings of "Blackness" and "whiteness," between the heteronormative and the queer, between culture industry expectations and artistic vision. Prince performed a kind of double consciousness throughout his career, deeply aware of his performative (public, artistic) self while also always deeply conscious of the myriad ways that performance of (public, artistic) self was always regarded through audience and industry questions about race, gender, and sexuality as well as how they all contributed to an artist's aesthetic and approach. He courted it while also commenting on it, often through humor, through his lyrical work and his embodied performance of those lyrics, using humor to provide audiences with a critique of Blackness, masculinity, and the expectations placed on him as a Black male artist. Through a close reading of lyrics from 1980s-era Prince songs, both hit singles and "album tracks," as well as a consideration of his 2014 appearance on *New Girl* (FOX, 2011–2018), a primarily white-cast sitcom, this chapter examines Prince and the signifying, ironic humor that often framed his public, artistic selfhood.

When Prince's double album *Sign O' the Times* was released in March 1987, it immediately became a critic's favorite, hailed by some as his best work, topping several best-of charts at the end of the year, and nominated for Best Album at the following year's Grammys. Showcasing the breadth of Prince's celebrated ability to mine, master, and materialize a deep trove of various sonic styles, the album's four sides spanned silky uptempo dance tracks, studied social commentary, story songs, and slow jams, each track more distinct than the last, building on his reputation for stylistic leaps and bold, unexpected arrangements, interspersed among the radio-ready, hook-laden singles that kept the album on the *Billboard* charts for fifty-nine weeks. Though four singles were released from the album, "Adore," the six-and-a-half minute slow jam that closes the album, became a Prince fan favorite without ever being released as a single, instead gaining its reputation through its frequent spins on late-night "quiet storm" radio shows immediately upon the album's release. Like many closing tracks on Prince albums up to that point, "Adore" is epic in scope, driven by lush horns, gospel-ish organ lines, and Prince's signature falsetto vocals, recounting a love story, full of come-ons, sexy compliments, and descriptions of lovemaking (on, as Prince describes, sheets made of "hundred percent Italian silk imported Egyptian lace"). And though it is in many ways a typical "'til the end of time" ballad—"from the first moment I saw you," Prince sings to his beloved, "I knew you were the one"—the bridge of the song is conceptually interesting: in the midst of sweet-talking his love (there are, Prince reveals, "heavenly angels" singing as they make love), the song's narrator tells a joke. He is so infatuated with this woman—she is "his fix," he sings, the reason that he has a "condition" he describes as "crucial"—that he'd even invite her to express her passion in the most performatively sadistic of ways: "U could burn up my clothes/Smash up my ride." Yet while chronicling this surplus of passionate behavior, the narrator pauses as the melody continues, deepens his voice a bit, and reneges on that last suggestion, using spoken word rather than sung-through falsetto, "Well, maybe not the ride."

It is a sudden tonal shift, a funny moment spliced into the heady rhythms of a sexy one. It is not often that one hears a joke in the middle of a love song, a spoken aside in the middle of a seduction, an aside that happens just a few couplets after the narrator deploys the only curse word in the song—"I ain't fuckin' just for kicks," he sings a few beats before the joke. The casual lyric use of a curse word—famously one of the "Seven Dirty Words" comedian George Carlin listed in 1972 as unable to be spoken on television—is not surprising; it had been appearing in Prince lyrics for years by the time "Adore" hit record stores in 1987.[2] And based mostly on the lyrical content of select songs and his album cover and concert appearance costuming, Prince had already garnered a reputation for producing controversial content, most famously through the Parents Music Resource Center (PMRC) adding his song "Darling Nikki" to another famous list, the "Filthy 15" songs, in 1985.[3] It is, however, the combination of the curse and the joke that emblematizes the bridge of "Adore" as quintessentially Prince. In a retrospective review of *Sign O' the Times* in 2002, Bomani Jones calls the mash-up of sweet-talking lyrics that culminate in "well, maybe not the ride" as "hyperbolic exaggerations tempered with realistic limits," and in many ways, Prince's lyrical choice can be read as based in a kind of masculinist realism steeped in the culture of "prized possessions," to which women have historically, misogynistically, been aligned and compared.[4] But, as music critic Chris Lacy asks in his review of the song and album, "Who else can tell a joke in the middle of one of the greatest love songs ever and not break the mood?"[5] That not breaking of the mood speaks to a recurring thematic approach in Prince's songwriting, his ability to understand popular musical expression—in this case the deeply gendered "love ballad" that presumes and caters to an audience's affective relationship to the narratives that become soundtracks to living, to loving—as always, already, performance. There is an extensive body of literature that positions Prince's work as whittling away at the thin line between the sacred and the profane, but "Adore" shows, in the moment of what critic Ill Mami called "comic relief," that Prince's work seeks to confront with irony the gendered expectations of popular music production and consumption.[6] In "Adore," Prince performs a moment of masculinist romantic posturing, but he is also stepping outside of that moment, and with a joke, with humor, pointing a finger at the impulse to take too seriously, in the sincere "quiet storm" way, those exact postures. He does it by risking making a joke in that lyrical moment to signify on the posturing that has defined lush love songs throughout pop history.

Other songs in the Prince canon engage humor in similar ways. Often those songs are recordings considered most explicit in their sexual content. "Let's Pretend We're Married," from 1999, his first double album, recounts a newly brokenhearted narrator who's looking for a new love or, at the very least, a new sex partner to occupy his time and help him "forget the girl that just walked out [his] door." Constructed as a seven-plus minute come-on, the song is less a seduction-with-a-backbeat than it is a funked-up sonic personals ad, its title alone introducing listeners to its seemingly tongue-in-cheek hint at a forever-after narrative. By the time the song reaches its climax—full of choruses punctuated with playful "mwah" kissing sounds—the narrator foregoes any pretense to "marriage" (even a play one) and goes in for (and with) the sexual gusto: "I want to fuck you so bad it hurts," he intones, repeating the phrase "it hurts" as the instrumentation subsides to an emphasized pulsating keyboard line and drum track that simulates the sound of a horny heartbeat. Then, he reveals his conquest's name: She's "Marsha." And Prince tells her directly, "Look here, I'm not saying this just to be nasty, but I sincerely want to fuck the taste out of your mouth." In this moment, the narrator is not just coming on to Marsha but also actually narrating the sexual escapade, commenting on the desire that heretofore he's only described having—again, he is in the moment but also outside of it.

Two words frame this posture, "just" and "sincerely": He isn't saying this solely ("just") to be nasty; he means what he says. He is advertising for a sexual liaison, but he imagines it as a "sincere" encounter, whether it results in marriage or not. It's a moment of come-on as commentary, a performance of testosterone-fueled desire but also a slyly polite acknowledgment of it. In the way that it seems to play on the African American reference to a potential fighting opponent as aiming to "knock the taste out of yo' mouth"—rendering the opponent simultaneously conquered, silenced, and senseless—the lyric plays like a humorous nod to the age-old "battle of the sexes" that has contoured pop lyrics for years. But Prince being Prince, there is another level to this gendered joking: the coda to this abject request, however, reels in the joke through sonically inflected vocalized play: his voice transitioning from falsetto to the computerized tenor of his natural speaking voice, Prince asks, "Can you relate?" In that moment, he performs a multidirectional, polyvalent call-and-response of sorts. Can *who* relate, exactly? Marsha? The audience of listeners dancing to the song? Himself, consumed at this point in the irony of asking such a question after making such a request? It's all pretend anyway, the lyrics seem to say, as they mirror the title of the song itself. This performance of overt sexuality gets cut through with a moment of humor that signifies on the over-the-top, overdetermined performance of desire it enacts. The fact that Prince's humor "lands" in the context of the song itself is the sheer in-congruity of the lyrical postures themselves, the way in which the humor dis-obeys rules of logic while rewriting new ones through the dashing of lyrical expectations. The violation of emotional patterns and expectations through wordplay or rhetorical shifts has a long history in humor and comedy.

In this moment, as he does in "Adore," Prince uses humor to perform an act of genre revision. Whereas in "Adore" the humor in the aside about "his ride" arrives mid-bridge, at a peak moment of shared passion, in "Let's Pretend We're Married" he embeds his sense of humor within his own self-aware vulgarity, pushing the limits of the sexual come-on by releasing it at the very end of the song, at the climax, simulating the sexual act while also commenting on it. In "Adore" he takes on the classic soul-man role (inspired, he has said, by the "quiet storm" intonations of singers like Luther Vandross), inflecting it with sonic and vocal phrasings redolent of Black church intona-tions but revises it with the use of humor.[7] In "Let's Pretend We're Married," Prince invites listeners along on his search for sexual activity, then constructs the song to behave as a come-on, and subsequently lands the joke at the end of the song, as if he understands how humor can both propel the seduction and provide a distanced, observed view of it, as if he's revising the four-on-the-floor sexual freedoms of disco, on which the song is based.

SEEING PRINCE

As it was not one of the singles released from *Sign O' the Times*, Prince never filmed an official music video for "Adore." I've often wondered what an "Adore" video might have been like, particularly the joke moment in the song's bridge that I have written about in this chapter. In early clips of songs from his first five albums—mostly filmed performances of Prince lip-syncing and his band playing to studio recorded tracks—Prince worked hard to es-tablish a visual mystique akin to his burgeoning reputation as a studio "boy wonder," the wunderkind out of Minneapolis who wrote all of his own songs, played all the instruments on his albums, and self-produced his records. In her 1983 essay on Prince, journalist Carol Cooper describes how Prince and his early band mate and cowriter Andre Cymone "used to sit up all night in the early days discussing the whole shtick . . .: the suggestive visuals [and the] the cultivated mystique" that Prince used as a way to build an audience for himself beyond what Cooper calls "the cosy [sic] ghetto exclusivity of the black teen" market.[8] When he performed the vaguely gender-bending 1979 hit "I Wanna Be Your Lover" ("I wanna be your mother and your sister, too," he sings) on *American Bandstand*, Prince performed in a pair of skintight gold metallic pants, his slightly hairy chest exposed under an open peach-colored shirt jacket, his hair a feathery, Farrah Fawcett–like perm.[9] Stylistically, he was in line with the moment, vaguely new wave, while still glittering, from the waist down at least, like an R&B star. But that episode of *American Bandstand*, as important as Prince's introduction to a wide audience became, enshrined itself in popular culture (and Prince) history because of his postsong interview with host Dick Clark, during which Prince responded to some of the questions with hand gestures instead of verbal responses, took extremely long pauses before answering, or gave outright exaggerations in response to questions (when, for instance, Clark asked how many instruments he played, he responded, after a long, considering pause, "one thousand"). Many of his responses elicited laughter from the kids in the audience, a seeming mix of discomfort and cross-generational identification, as they watched the old guy ask the hip young guy to describe himself and his band. Most interesting, to me, as I watch now, are Prince's nonverbal responses, the moments during which he lays his gaze directly on Dick Clark, unspokenly questioning the host with his eyes while also seeming to watch Clark from afar despite being only a few inches away from him. "This is not the kind of music that comes from Minneapolis, Minnesota," Clark says to Prince, who has one hand on his hip and the other atop his head, as if he was a cartoon character attempting to keep it from blowing off. There are moments where—as Clark points out—Prince's famous shyness is on display. But I argue, this is also an early example of Prince's public engagement with and performance of ironic distance, a commenting on the experience while experiencing it, an acceptance of the necessary maneuvers of the star-making machinery of popular culture but also a distance from it made clear by the smirk that seems to denote a desire to do things differently than expected. The irony I read as emanating from Prince's body and affect during the interview segment, and the way it seems to register with the youthful audience and elicit laughter from them—a verbalization of his affect, it seems, in reaction to Clark—seems to be indicative of what theorist Alfred Martin calls a "two-faced humor" (building on Freud's notion of the "tendentious joke"). In Martin's formulation, there is the person telling the joke and the person, the butt of the joke, imagined as "outside the intended audience for the joke."[10] It is a kind of "covert form of humor" in which Prince's posture, affect, and (sometimes) lack of vocal expression includes the youthful audience into his commentary, making humorous spectacle of Clark's outsider, perhaps sincere and earnest questions, which come off as outside the hip circle (and point of view) that envelops Prince and the young fans who "get the joke," as it were.

By the time Prince released the music video for his 1986 hit single "Kiss," he had expertly polished the contradictions inherent in that ironic smirk into a distinct and usable mode of performance. I think here of the ways in which Prince's performance as the Kid in *Purple Rain*, his first film (before *Under the Cherry Moon*, the 1986 follow-up, whose soundtrack, *Parade*, featured the single "Kiss"), brings those contradictory poses to the big screen. Structured as a story about an artist's development in the wake of family trauma, *Purple Rain* uses pop music—as Hollywood movies had long done—to stand in as the articulations of the inchoate yearnings and desires of youth. In the film, Prince's music acts as a soundtrack to the Kid's life *and* about his life, often, if not always, inflected by tensions about authenticity that are often connected to gender. For all the music in the film, however, the character of the Kid often performs his frustrations—sometimes legitimate, often immature— not through words but through gazes, smirks, and glances. A subplot about tensions within his cross-racial, cross-gender band The Revolution caused by the Kid's tightfisted artistic and musical control of them is explored early in the film. During an argument about whether the band will ever perform songs written by guitarist Wendy and keyboardist Lisa, the two women in the group, the Kid stares into the dressing room mirror, toying with a harlequin puppet. When he finally responds to his bandmates' concerns, he uses sarcasm to blunt their arguments before using the puppet to mount a defense of sorts. "Why should he use your music?" the puppet asks, ventriloquizing the Kid's words. After the women leave the room, frustrated by what they describe as his "paranoia," the Kid, alone in the dressing room, continues to use the puppet to articulate his thoughts, fixing his face into a pose of ironic annoyance. "You don't need those girls or their stupid music," the puppet says. "All you need is me. . . . Man, I don't know. Life's a bitch" (29:40). This moment of ventriloquizing to create distance between his "real" feelings and his seeming inability to connect with others is marked by facial expressions that allow Prince/the Kid to articulate both anger and humor. The broad style of this interaction—and the tension it showcases between gendered power games—is mirrored in the video for "Kiss."

The "Kiss" video showcased a Prince who had already starred in *Purple Rain*, and its accompanying videos (only one of which, "When Doves Cry," utilized new staging and choreography as opposed to the clips edited together and produced from movie scenes) as well as "Raspberry Beret," the lone video from *Purple Rain*'s surprise follow-up album, *Around the World in a Day*, located Prince and his band in a psychedelic fantasyland overlaid with animated characters depicting the narrative of the song. "Kiss" featured Prince and two women, the Revolution guitarist Wendy Melvoin and dancer Monique Mannen, who spends most of the video shrouded in a black sheath. The "Kiss" video has, in the strictest sense, no structured

Fig. 7.1 In *Purple Rain*, Prince / the Kid uses a puppet to articulate both anger and humor.

narrative: Prince dances around a relatively bare film set, chasing (or being chased by) Mannen, while Wendy sits on a stool strumming a guitar and watching the shenanigans.[11]

"Kiss" is the text in which Prince most readily combines the lyrical and visual humor that frames his irony and its mobilization as a mode of commentary on racial and gender performance and presentation. Clothed in a cropped shirt (which might be called a combination of halter and midriff-baring top if worn by a woman), tight black jazz pants, and a leather jacket, Prince's visual presentation eschews the overtly Edwardian-style excesses of his *Purple Rain* period and the psychedelic fashionings aligned with *Around the World in Day*. In "Kiss," Prince presents as a mix of Elvis Presley–era rocker and mascara-eyed ingénue, his hair cropped from the high, styled elegance of his recent past into a sleek, slicked-back pompadour. He has replaced the bombastic, concert stage–bound star-twirls of *Purple Rain* with a louche, snaky, almost Fosse-esque choreographic style. Prince moves through the video portraying both showman and showgirl, combining a masculine arrogance with almost feminine affect, allowing himself to be, at various points, both the hunter and the hunted (at the beginning and end of the video, Prince and Mannen trade places in the act of possessively biting the neck of the other, as if they're rock star vampires). I want to center a discussion of Prince's facial expressions throughout the video. During the first thirty seconds or so, Prince uses his heavily mascaraed eyes to gaze right into the camera, as if daring the viewer to interrupt the blend of bopping swagger and coy striptease he performs, removing the jacket from each shoulder in time to the martial beat of the drums and the acoustic strumming

Fig. 7.2 Prince giving (humorous) face in the music video for "Kiss."

of the guitar. He is in "seducer" mode, a familiar location for Prince, leering at the camera in some shots, marking his cheek with a make-believe tear in the next. A minute and half into the video, as he sings, "You can't be too flirty mama/I know how to undress me," as he does, in fact, perform a kind of "undressing" as he lifts his already-midriff-baring top over his head and gyrates his hips to the beat of the song. The camera stays on Prince throughout that lyric, but then, on the improvised "yeah" that closes the couplet, the clip cuts to Mannen, wearing her dark sunglasses and smiling lasciviously, mouthing the word "yeah" as if to acknowledge not just the sentiment of his lyric but also her own desire for Prince. The gender reversal here—Prince as the coy stripteaser, Mannen's female face lip-syncing the male (Prince's) recorded vocal—is followed by a quick cut to a close-up of Prince, his face twisted into a smirky grimace, his lips raised to the left, one eye almost squinting in confusion. Is he responding to the way the video clip has allowed Mannen to take on the masculine role, sonically and visually? Is he responding to the way Mannen's gaze is privileged in the shot exchange and staging here? Perhaps. But the confusion does not last. Next, he sings, "I want to be your fantasy" as the film cuts from the confusion of his grimace to the declarative image of his own hands rubbing against his twisting, gyrating ass, as if he's a stripper a few feet away from the pole.

That facial expression Prince strikes serves as comic relief while also acknowledging the jumble of gendered signifiers floating through the landscape of the video and, very often, landing on the bodies that people it. As the funny lyric about his ride simultaneously stops the action of "Adore" without quite neutralizing the forward momentum of the song (instead, one might argue, enhancing it), so does Prince's funny look in this "Kiss" video. That look, I argue, is a response to the action in the video but also an invitation to viewers, looking on, either confused by the gender switches, entertained by them, amused by them, or turned on by them. Prince, who spends time outside his texts, observing the commentary while also making it, displays the smirk as a part of the video's "narrative" of him as an object of desire while also understanding that this choice, as presented, isn't the traditional choice but is, indeed, the funny, ironic one.

In *On Racial Icons*, Nicole Fleetwood posits a theory of what she calls "giving face," in which she discusses the various "economic, cultural, and psychic functions" of celebrity icons, and analyzes "giving face" as a "mode of performance of face as an iconic form of modern celebrity." Thinking through this mode of performance as a "self-conscious and deliberate practice of elevating one's facial features . . . with the intention of producing desire, envy, and idolization," Fleetwood identifies it primarily as the domain of women entertainers, due in part to the use of makeup as one of the characteristic tools needed to produce the marketable, marketed face, through magazine covers, album covers, and other visual texts.[12] However, Prince also gives face. And it is never *not* a self-conscious mode of embellished embodiment tinged with humor and irony, dating back to his debut on *American Bandstand*. In the video for "Kiss" Prince gives face in the sense that he positions himself (or allows Rebecca Blake, the video's director to position him) as an object of desire while also aligning that ability to "give face"—the mascaraed eyes and pompadour-meets-bouffant hairstyle—to a larger critique of the clichéd and normative, masculinist sexuality of pop, R&B, and rock stardom. The power of his critique arrives bolstered, in the case of "Kiss," by not just his attention to the gender norms he seeks to break but also how it intersects with his attention to the racial contours of his lyric's jokes. "Act your age, mama/Not your shoe size," he sings, then adds, "You don't have to watch *Dynasty* to have an attitude." There he is again, signifyin' with the Dozens but also reaching into popular culture to enhance his "dis"—as it were—by comically ranking on television's (or celebrities giving face) ability to act as a prompter of identity formation and performance. You can have an attitude, he seems to say, but you don't have to learn it from the likes of Dominique Devereux to enact it in and on the world. As in "Adore" and "Let's Pretend We're Married," he buries the comic within the contours of the romantic/sexual song, pushing gender boundaries with (and within) racial(ized) humor.

In 2014, Prince appeared on the Super Bowl Sunday episode of *New Girl*, playing himself. In press reports surrounding the publicity and marketing of the episode, it was revealed that Prince was, indeed, a fan of the show and had asked to appear on an earlier episode of the show, a single-camera sitcom depicting the dating and professional lives of a group of friends after Jess, a schoolteacher played by Zooey Deschanel, moves into an apartment with three men. In the episode in which Prince appeared—titled "Prince"—Jess and her friend Cece, in a setup typical of sitcoms, land invites to Prince's party. Their guy friends (one of whom is Jess's boyfriend Nick, a huge Prince fan) do not have invitations. As Jess and Cece's limo starts to drive away, Nick blurts out to Jess that he loves her. In another typical sitcom moment, the guys have to finagle their way into the party—to meet Prince but also to allow Nick to take back his declaration or find out how Jess feels—while Jess cannot enjoy the party because she's stressing that she didn't return the words to Nick before driving off.

Just as he introduced himself to me in 1991 (was this just his "thing"?), Prince introduces himself to Jess and Nick at the party with "Hi, I'm Prince" and then hesitates and says, "I'm sorry, I haven't given you enough time to freak out yet. . . . You may do so now." They both scream; Nick faints. Later, while Jess and Nick sit squeezed on a bench, with Prince between them, they playfully make gun signs at Prince with their fingers, an inside joke between them. Prince glares at them and calmly says, "Don't point those things at me. They might go off." "That," Nick says to him, "is very much your flavor of humor." The episode is not terribly funny, but it does provide a showcase for a late-career Prince to perform "his flavor of humor" as he jokes about his public image as a mysterious, romantic, sexually all-knowing Pygmalion whose music and advice can bring much-needed heat to any audience who hears and experiences it.

What I found quite fascinating about the episode—other than the fact that Prince introduced himself to the characters the same way he introduced himself to me in 1991—was how Prince played up his dry humor to achieve his ironic distance in the prefabricated world of the sitcom, to use his face and the pitch of his voice, as he'd done in so many of his own sonic and visual productions, to create a Black humor space for himself as a guest star in a very white TV show. It reminded me of the way he used his face to comic effect in *Purple Rain* (even as those moments were in scenes often fraught with a distinctly '80s multiplex misogyny), *Under the Cherry Moon*, and the videos for "Kiss," "Cream," and "Raspberry Beret," as if he was signifying on the long history of bringing Blackness to white spaces and antinormative masculinity to more traditional spaces as he had since his debut on *American Bandstand*. Prince may not have been a comic, in the most formal sense, but he could always, as the song goes, make us laugh.

Scott Poulson-Bryant is Assistant Professor of Afro-American and African Studies at the University of Michigan. He is author of *Hung: A Meditation on the Measure of Black Men in America* and *The VIPs: A Novel*. His work appears in the *Journal of Popular Music Studies* and *Palimpsest*.

NOTES

1. Black humor historian Mel Watkins defines *signifying* as "verbally putting down or berating another person with witty remarks" and links the act to "ranking, sounding, or dissin'" (*On the Real Side: Laughing, Lying, and Signifying—The Underground Tradition of African-American Humor That Transformed American Culture, from Slavery to Richard Pryor* [New York: Simon & Schuster, 1994]).

2. "Filthy Words by George Carlin," January 23, 2011, https://web.archive.org/web /20110123114427/, http://www.law.umkc.edu/faculty/projects/ftrials/conlaw/filthywords.html.

3. For more on Prince's relationship to the 1980s activist work of Tipper Gore and the PMRC battles against record labels to sticker album releases, see Tobias Salinger, "'Darling Nikki': How Prince's Lyrics Angered Tipper Gore and Led to the Parental Advisory Label," *New York Daily News*, April 21, 2016, https://www.nydailynews.com/entertainment/music /prince-lyrics-led-parental-advisory-label-article-1.2610382.

4. Bomani Jones, "Rock's Last Great Double Album," *Ottawa Citizen*, May 23, 2002, 62.

5. "ChrisLacy1990's Review of 'Adore' by Prince," *Album of The Year*, accessed May 18, 2021, https://www.albumoftheyear.org/user/chrislacy1990/album/284787-adore/.

6. Ill Mami, "#2: Prince 'Adore,'" *Soul Bounce*, August 28, 2008, https://www.soulbounce .com/2008/08/2_prince_adore/.

7. Mike Joseph, "Prince's 'Adore' Is the Love Song to End All Love Songs," *Diffuser*, February 23, 2018, https://diffuser.fm/prince-adore/.

8. Carol Cooper, "Someday Your Prince Will Come (1983)," *Beat Patrol* (blog), May 6, 2009, https://beatpatrol.wordpress.com/2009/05/06/carol-cooper-someday-your-prince-wil l-come-1983/.

9. Dudu Freitas, "Prince on American Bandstand 1980," YouTube, 2017, https://www .youtube.com/watch?v=krEXzOEsP9I.

10. Alfred L. Martin, Jr., "The Tweet Has Two Faces: Two-Faced Humor, Black Masculinity, and RompHim," *JCMS: Journal of Cinema and Media Studies* 58, no. 3 (2019): 160–65, https:// doi.org/10.1353/cj.2019.0031.

11. Prince, "Prince & The Revolution—Kiss (Official Music Video)," YouTube, 2017, https:// www.youtube.com/watch?v=H9tEvfIsDyo.

12. Nicole R. Fleetwood, *On Racial Icons: Blackness and the Public Imagination* (New Brunswick, NJ: Rutgers University Press, 2015).

PART III

THE LIBERATION AND LIMITS
OF BLACK COMEDY

8

"I NEED MISS RONA TO START TAP DANCING AROUND IN THEM LUNGS"

Black Twitter's Political Humor in COVID-19 Times

Anshare Antoine and Mel Stanfill

In 2020, as the threat of the COVID-19 virus became the new normal for people around the world, the pandemic turned into a battleground in the United States: between political parties; between federal and state governments; between citizens who felt public health restrictions infringed on their rights and those who supported taking action; and every combination thereof. The pandemic was also racialized in the United States. In a tweet, then-US president Donald Trump dubbed COVID-19—the first cases of which were identified in Wuhan, China—the "Chinese virus." A University of California, San Francisco, study linked this nomenclature to a significant increase in anti-Asian sentiment on social media.[1] Moreover, hate crimes against Asians and Asian Americans increased by nearly 150 percent in 2020.[2] At the same time, the negative impacts of the virus itself were unevenly distributed by race. Data from numerous states showed that African Americans and other minority groups were disproportionately contracting and dying from the coronavirus compared to white people. Absolutely none of this is funny—not the mass death, the economic impacts, the politicization, or the racism. And yet African Americans widely joked about COVID-19 online as part of what is often known as Black Twitter. In this chapter, we examine this Black political humor, specifically how, at the intersection of politicization and racialization in a pandemic, Black Twitter users leverage humor for political commentary.

For this analysis, we collected tweets for the phrase "Miss Rona" posted between October 6 and October 9, 2020, using the Twitter Archiving Google Sheet.[3] The search term was selected after a preliminary survey of Black Twitter conversations about COVID-19 as the most common nickname (more frequent than variants like "Ms. Rona"); we excluded other nicknames like "The Rona" that were also widely used outside of Black Twitter enclaves and would have resulted in tweets from other communities. We collected a total of 3,798 tweets and then removed retweets from the data set before calculating word frequency using data mining software Orange to gain a broad overview of the data.[4] This high-level analysis showed a high frequency of words referencing Trump, then-US vice president Mike Pence, and their respective Twitter accounts, suggesting that the politicization of the pandemic should be our focus in examining humor practices. We subsequently took a random sample of one hundred tweets for initial qualitative analysis. Though retweets were removed in order to not skew these first two methods, we used retweet data to create a second sample of the most popular posts to oversample for comments that gained traction. The two authors independently coded both samples for major themes and then discussed both the themes and the keywords representative of the themes to reach a consensus. Those keywords were then searched in the full body of tweets to create a corpus of tweets for each of these three themes: references to political figures, direct addresses to Miss Rona, and projections of the future. These three corpora were examined to discern patterns in how users humorously engaged with both the coronavirus and the political landscape.

We begin our analysis from an understanding that "Black folk use the internet as a space to extol the joys and pains of everyday life."[5] Through examining these tweets, which appear to make light of a pandemic that has disproportionately affected Black Americans, we consider how these conversations go beyond laughing to keep from crying to engage in an explicit political critique of public policy failures through humor. Suggesting that Trump administration officials infected with COVID-19 were reaping what they had sown and connecting the pandemic's disproportionate killing of Black people to broader political implications, Black Twitter users articulated a critique of how Miss Rona has been handled using Signifyin' as a Black cultural technology with affordances such as humor, misdirection, and double meaning.

"Y'ALL PRESIDENT WILD": AAVE AND PLAYFUL LANGUAGE WITH A BITE ON BLACK TWITTER

Our site for this examination is colloquially known as Black Twitter. As defined by André Brock: "Black Twitter is an online gathering (not quite a community) of Twitter users who identify as Black *and* employ Twitter features to perform Black discourse, share Black cultural commonplaces, and build social affinities. While there are a number of non-Black and people of color Twitter users who have been 'invited to the cookout,' so to speak, participating in Black Twitter requires a deep knowledge of Black culture, commonplaces, and digital practices."[6]

Black Twitter, then, is a loose network of culturally Black practices on the social media platform. It is, in particular, what Alfred L. Martin, Jr. calls an "insider" group, where participants opt-in and act under the assumption that they are joking among friends—even if, as periodic incidents show, it is a leaky network in Wendy Chun's sense and tweets do not always stay among friends.[7] Black Twitter is, therefore, a space known for what Brock calls the libidinal and the ratchet—for refusing respectability.[8] These characteristics contribute to the creation of what Catherine Squires calls a "satellite public sphere," where participants "do not feel compelled to hide or change cultural particularities" but exist with little or no regard for dominant publics.[9] Such spaces allow Black people to ignore respectability politics—which "has sought to modify embodied, sensual, and 'deviant' Black behaviors toward standards of middle-class whiteness"—as they engage with political and social issues within their communicative traditions and culture.[10] These are practices and spaces to which the white gaze is irrelevant.

The Blackness of Black Twitter happens in large part through the use of African American Vernacular English (AAVE), a common feature in our tweet corpus. Within many pandemic-related tweets by Black American Twitter users, AAVE demonstrates a skillful level of wordplay, synonymous with the Black American community, that delivers savvy political commentary imbued with humor, Black identity, and joy that only Black Americans can fully understand and engage with. While AAVE has often been perceived as "bad" or "broken" standard English, it is in fact a distinct dialect of English.[11] While scholars disagree about the exact origins and development of AAVE, it is generally understood to have combined aspects of the various western African languages spoken by enslaved people with American/European English into a distinct dialect.[12] AAVE is, in particular, a resistive language against Eurocentric expectations of civility in speech.

Rhetorically, AAVE embodies Black culture and identity in its practice of Signifyin' that subverts linguistic norms and centers the identities and experiences of Black Americans. As Henry Louis Gates describes, "The Afro-American rhetorical strategy of Signifyin(g) is a rhetorical practice that is not engaged in the game of information-giving" but rather "turns on the play and chain of signifiers"; this form of wordplay has distinctive "black rhetorical tropes" such as "marking, loud-talking, testifying, calling out (of one's name), sounding, rapping, playing the dozens, and so on."[13] While Signifyin(g) is a routine practice in Black communities, the character-limited, playful, and insider characteristics of Black Twitter make it particularly common. Importantly, as Jessica Lu and Catherine Knight Steele note, "While perhaps appearing coarse and even cruel to outsiders, both signifying and 'playing the dozens' are rhetorical strategies that are embedded in the pursuit of communal sharing and joy."[14] These practices are important for their role in "allowing Black Twitter users to perform their racial identities 140 characters at a time."[15] That is, Signifyin' involves clever verbal games that are distinctively Black.

Humor is a key part of these Signifyin(g) practices, and Black Twitter participates in broader histories of Black humor. On the one hand, as Daryl Cumber Dance notes, Black people often "laugh, as the old blues line declares, to keep from crying. We laugh to keep from dying. We laugh to keep from killing. We laugh to hide our pain, to walk gently around the wound too painful to actually touch."[16] That is, these practices are often cathartic releases in the face of violence and trauma. On the other hand, as Dance also argues, African Americans often "use our humor to speak the unspeakable, to mask the attack, to get a tricky subject on the table, to warn of lines not to be crossed, to strike out at enemies and the hateful acts of friends and family, to camouflage sensitivity, to tease, to compliment, to berate, to brag, to flirt, to speculate, to gossip, to educate, to correct the lies people tell on us, to bring about change."[17] Humor serves here as a mode of critique.

We see AAVE in calling the coronavirus "Miss Rona" in the first place. As Sarah Florini explains, "Miss" and "Auntie" are "honorifics used in many Black communities to refer to older women," particularly one "known for her sharp tongue and no-nonsense approach."[18] Giving the coronavirus a nickname in AAVE highlights the Black community's deference to and fear of a virus that inconspicuously appears with flu-like symptoms—much as an older woman might seem unthreatening—but is approximately ten times more deadly than the flu.[19] Black communities are painfully aware that the coronavirus is not to be trifled with (just like a Black elder whom you respect or fear), hence the honorific title of "Miss." Additionally, humor is found in Black Twitter's nickname for the virus, "Rona," which sometimes appeared with an image of the coronavirus with glossy, thick lips and a hand with long nails held up in a sassy pose, wearing large hoop earrings and fake eyelashes, as demonstrated in figure 8.1. In such ways, as Dance argues, we "observe that when African American women are joking around, they often slip into an idiom that is uniquely black."[20] While Black Americans rightly fear the virus

Happy birthday to this hot girl summer Miss Rona aint got nobody time for dat bicccc

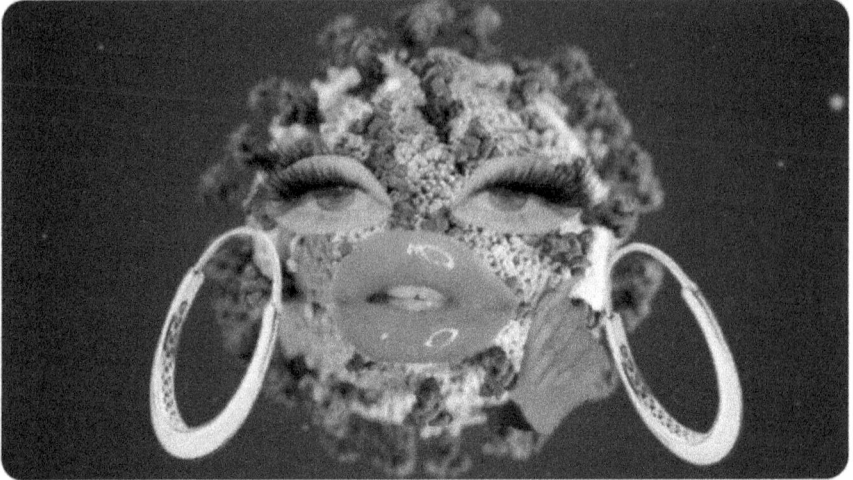

Fig. 8.1 Image of the coronavirus as if seen under a microscope, but photoshopped with human features and accessories, including eyes, large hoop earrings, fake eyelashes, glossy thick lips, and a hand with long nails held up in a sassy pose.

and the destruction it causes, they collectively share and cope with these facts by putting COVID-19 in this liminal position between absurd and dangerous. "Miss Rona" is thus in itself a form of Signifyin' that performs Black identity and participates in the African American tradition of finding joy in pain through humor.

Additionally, we observe practices of oblique but skillful insult in both Black culture in general and our tweet corpus in particular. One tweet addresses Ivanka Trump, daughter of Donald Trump, by asking several questions in a witty one-sided banter: "WHAT ABOUT @IvankaTrump? Girl, you doin alright? A little feverish? Mild cough? Daddy gave you everything . . . did he give you Miss Rona too?" The user playfully engages with several facets of the social and political climate: rising coronavirus infections in the Trump White House, where Ivanka worked as a senior adviser throughout her father's administration; the nepotism of Trump appointing his daughter to a senior position in his administration; and the ways Ivanka was privileged throughout her life due to her father's wealth (and whiteness). While on the surface the questions appear solicitous of Trump's health, the full meaning of the tweet is in understanding the intonation of the words and questions, steeped in AAVE, wherein the real humor lies. Far from caring about Ivanka

Trump, the tweet encompasses the tragedy of the COVID-19 pandemic, the privilege of the white and rich, and the general displeasure among African Americans with the then-ruling party's inequitable handling of the pandemic.

Another tweet that is both more direct and more embedded in AAVE says, "Y'all president wild. please come thru miss rona. do what you came to do." As Florini notes, "Nonstandard spellings are used by most Twitter users of all backgrounds as a strategy to cope with Twitter's 140-character limit. However, many Black users seem to use preexisting grammatical constructions derived from Black Vernacular English and phonetic spellings that convey specific pronunciations."[21] This tweet employs the common AAVE practice of copula deletion, removing *is* from "[your] president [is] wild." It also structurally declares that Trump is not the tweeter's president, instead referring to him with the second person plural possessive *y'all's*, truncated to *y'all*. The term *wild* originates from Black Twitter and expresses incredulity about how crazy or "out of pocket" a person, action, statement, or situation is; here it critiques how then-president Trump handled the COVID-19 pandemic; specifically, as we'll discuss later in the essay, the tweet likely responded to Trump ending negotiations on a stimulus package until after the election. Those most affected by Trump's policies in general, and coronavirus in particular, were minority groups. The user's call for the coronavirus to punish Trump as just recompense in a witty use of AAVE—"come thru . . ." is simultaneously playful and serious. Calling on Miss Rona to do something was a significant feature of the tweet corpus. This kind of projection of what should happen in the future demonstrates Brock's argument that "while Black culture is often in dire need of political and moral reassurance that the present is not the future, the linguistic features of AAVE indicate a comfort and willingness to live in an elastic now or . . . a postpresent that is not quite the future but a moment to be present within."[22] In such ways, while some of the meaning and humor of these tweets is broadly available, AAVE adds layers that are distinctively Black, positioning this as humor by and for Black people.

"Miss Rona Is Really Clapping the White Supremacists": Black Twitter Humor and Political Critique

The coronavirus pandemic in the United States was deeply politicized. Trump had asserted that the virus was a hoax, that it would not be a problem in America, that it was just another strain of the common flu, and that the American people had nothing to worry about. The more than 400,000 lives lost by the end of his presidential term showed the heavy cost of those falsehoods. In October 2020, when we collected our tweets, many members of the Trump administration had recently been diagnosed with COVID-19, and this was widely viewed in light of this downplaying of the pandemic. While schadenfreude over Trump having contracted coronavirus was widespread, the disproportionate toll of COVID-19 on Black Americans as a result of systemic racism made it particularly acute on Black Twitter. Moreover, Black Americans have historically been shunned and excluded from mainstream political conversations, resulting in their ingenious repurposing of spaces, such as barbershops or Black Twitter, as sites of political discussion and critique; in these nontraditional spaces, Black Americans feel safe, seen, and valued as they express and share their political commentary within their Black oral tradition, which oftentimes involves a significant amount of humor and wit.

Moreover, tweets using "Miss Rona" as a colloquial Black Twitter name for the coronavirus also participate in broader histories of political humor. Scholars have shown that political humor attempts to work through problems and contradictions in the political realm, often specifically "imagining a different moral order."[23] It is a vehicle for critique.[24] This critique can target either the government at large or specific politicians due to their incompetence or malfeasance.[25] In terms of form, political humor is characterized by "antagonism and contempt" as well as being "exaggerated, distorted, displaced, inverted, or stylized."[26] Moreover, humor is also central to politics on social media more specifically.[27] In particular, Jenny L. Davis, Tony P. Love, and Gemma Killen argue that social media humor "acts as a vehicle for meaningful political participation."[28] Humor is in fact a preferred way to engage with politics on Twitter; Kevin Driscoll and colleagues found that "tweets containing humor may reach greater visibility and longevity than breaking news messages."[29]

For both of these reasons, one of the key themes in the Miss Rona tweets connected the virus to the broader political moment. One user tweeted, "Miss rona is in Trumps lungs going IN! 😭😭," with an image from the popular cartoon *SpongeBob SquarePants* (Nickelodeon, 1999–present) showing a character with an aggressive expression clinging to a spinal column after apparently karate chopping a lung completely off from its twin (fig. 8.2). The image humorously demonstrates the violence coronavirus is imagined to be doing to Trump's lungs, while the caption signals cultural identity through AAVE in the phrases "Miss Rona" and "going in." The "crying from laughing" emoji makes clear that the user is participating in schadenfreude, taking pleasure in Trump's misfortune; against the background of the disproportionate harms of Trump's policies to Black communities, we can understand why lung problems might have been seen as just deserts.

A second tweet shows how Black Twitter users leveraged humor to comment on political reality. The user quote-tweets a news report about Trump

Miss rona is in Trumps lungs going IN! 😭 😭

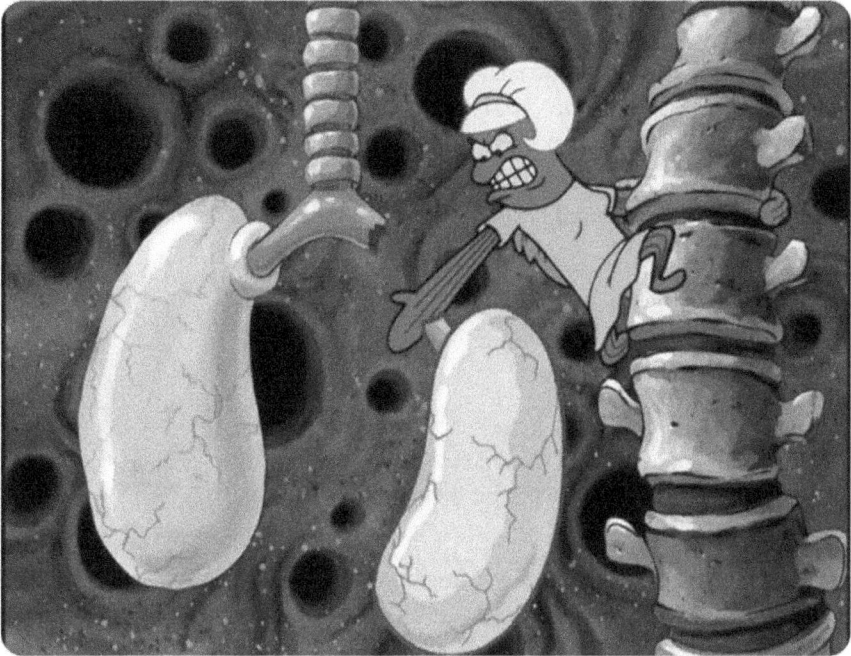

Fig. 8.2 This image from the popular cartoon *SpongeBob SquarePants* (Nickelodeon, 1999– present, Season 3, episode 5, "Mermaid Man and Barnacle Boy IV," aired January 20, 2002) shows a fish character with an aggressive expression clinging to a spinal column after apparently karate-chopping the right lung off the trachea.

administration adviser Stephen Miller being diagnosed with COVID-19 and says, "Miss Rona is really clapping the white supremacists, I can't be mad at her." This tweet uses the African American slang "clapping," which denotes a form of violence enacted against someone. The word can also be used to refer to a rough sexual act. In this context, either meaning is appropriate because the user is contending that this negative event for Miller is deserved because he is a white supremacist, which makes the tweet a clever form of Signifyin', employing multiple levels of meaning. With either meaning of "clapping," the implication is that white supremacists like Miller, the architect of the Trump administration's policy of deliberate cruelty to migrants at the US-Mexico border to discourage migration, are receiving what they deserve: retribution for the injustices they have created, supported, or encouraged.[30] "White supremacists" here refers broadly to all members of the Trump administration who had recently been diagnosed with the virus at the time of the tweet; this reflects the user's recognition that Donald Trump's platform was white nationalist from his campaign through the end of his term.[31]

In both tweets, humor is political commentary that resonates with Black communities because the tweets reference Black trauma during the pandemic. While it did not appear in our data set specifically, other Black Twitter participants linked COVID-19 to broader, ongoing issues of racial violence and white supremacist ideology. In late May 2020, when the murder of George Floyd prompted nationwide protest, one user tweeted:

> -George Floyd
> -Amy Cooper
> -Blackface
> -Ahmaud Arbery
> -Breonna Taylor
> -COVID-19 killing Black folks
> -Reopen protestors with confederate flags
> FYI: WE don't make everything about race.
> Systems do that for us.

While this particular tweet is not humorous, it shows how users explicitly connected heightened vulnerability to the virus to other risks and harms facing Black Americans. The pandemic happened alongside the murders of Ahmaud Arbery (pursued and fatally shot by two white men while he was out jogging), Breonna Taylor (fatally shot in her apartment by officers serving a warrant on someone else), and George Floyd (murdered by a police officer who kneeled on his neck for over nine minutes after responding to a call about an alleged counterfeit twenty-dollar bill). This state and vigilante violence, the white nationalism of those who refused to take the pandemic seriously, and the disproportionate deaths of Black Americans from the pandemic all coalesced to encourage people to see these disparate events as linked through systemic racism.

These tweets demonstrate the broader applicability of Dance's argument about Black women in particular that "if there is any one thing that has helped us to survive the broken promises, lies, betrayals, contempt, humiliations, and dehumanizations that have been our lot in this nation and often in our families, it is our humor."[32] COVID-19 and the political landscape it both reflected and amplified were not funny in any normal sense of the word, but humor was a beneficial strategy to critique these traumas, especially for Black people, without facing them head-on. In such ways, we liken Black Twitter users' approach to humor and the coronavirus to what Bambi Haggins describes as Black humor's usefulness as an "unabashed tool for social change, for the unfiltered venting of cultural and political anger, and for the annunciation of blackness."[33] Overall, Black Twitter users leverage humor not just to comment about general injustice, but often to specifically comment about the political and electoral landscape.

"Legit Holding the Whole Country Hostage": Black Twitter Responds to Ending Stimulus Negotiations

As noted previously, the "y'all president wild" tweet came in the context of then-recent reports that Trump had ended COVID-19 relief bill talks until after the 2020 election.[34] In this section, we focus specifically on Black Twitter's responses to this news, which were characterized by hoping for Miss Rona's retribution. One user tweeted, "This nigga is legit holding the whole country hostage in exchange for an election victory and nobody with the power to challenge him on it is doing anything about it." This user addresses Trump's shenanigans in his efforts to win another presidential term and calls out other political leaders who allegedly allow Trump to play these political games at the expense of the public. The first part of the tweet expresses anger and frustration in a serious tone and the user employs the "n word" to address Trump in a way that functions on two levels at the same time: on the one hand, it is a social leveler that removes the differentiation between the high status afforded to Trump as the president of the United States of America and the lower status afforded to a Black man living in the United States of America, placing both men on equal standing; on the other, it is a positive reinforcement of the user's Blackness, regardless of who is being addressed, through the use of AAVE. In this context, the word *nigga* has no racial connotation for the user or toward the receiver; rather, the user employs the word to call Trump out in a derogatory manner that is synonymous to saying "this bitch" or "this motherfucker." The humor comes into play when the user continues with "I really need Miss Rona to show her ass right about now and start tap dancing around in them lungs." The user code-switches from the use of a serious tone and standard English (after the first four words) in the first half of the tweet to a humorous political statement expressed in AAVE. Her tweet contends that those who fail to challenge Trump's (in)actions are complicit, and therefore, it is up to "Miss Rona" to secure justice for those who are powerless and oppressed. This tweet thus exemplifies "words that, with poignant playfulness, serve to concretize a response to social, political, and economic realities of oppression."[35]

In a similar style of Signifyin', another user quote-tweets the news about Trump halting the COVID-19 relief bill with the caption, "I fucking hate it here." This references a common meme in Black Twitter, often appearing as an animated .gif, taken from a scene in the 2010 film *The Karate Kid* in which Jaden Smith's character complains, "I hate it here. I wanna go home!" The statement is frequently used by Black Americans to reinforce how terrible, unbelievable, or funny a situation is, suggesting that a particular situation is a bad place to be. This user expresses her anger that Trump would halt work on a bill that would bring much-needed relief to Americans as part of his political strategy. The user follows up with another tweet that states, "Miss Rona gotta turn that shit up because we need a resolution." Just as with the previous user's mid-tweet change, this user switches from more standard English in her first tweet to AAVE in her second tweet, adding humor with the reference to Aaliyah's 2001 hit song, "We Need a Resolution."[36] The song is about a situation in which two people are in a bad relationship and something needs to be done about it. Applying this context to the tweet, the user is "asking" the virus to do its worst with Trump ("Miss Rona gotta turn that shit up") because "we need a resolution" to the problem that is Trump himself; the virus's threat to Trump's health is viewed as the resolution. Furthermore, the second tweet exemplifies Gates's assertion that signifyin' is "not engaged in the game of information-giving" in that without accurate knowledge of and personal participation in Black culture, one would not easily recognize the reference and connection to one of Aaliyah's hit songs.[37] In the previous tweets, the humor is intertextual because the user expertly intertwines popular Black cultural references with her anger at how COVID-19 was being handled by the Trump administration to create a level of meaning that speaks to the Black in-group interpretation of the tweets and appeals to Black humor.

The code-switching in these tweets invokes what it means to be an African American: a political body that is simultaneously and separately American and Black. The rhetorical strategy of code-switching in the aforementioned tweets also challenges the idea that Black Twitter is "'immature' and 'ineffective' because its creative and discursive practices, in their viscerality and sensuality, do not directly lead to Black political or economic empowerment," because these tweets do not need to give up play in the name of political critique.[38] In such ways, as Brock argues, "Blackness employs multiple, interlocking strategies to manage the matrix of American white supremacist ideology."[39] In their concurrent seriousness and humor, the tweets engage the political implications of the pandemic when viewed from the perspective and within the lived-in experiences of Black people, who laugh to keep from crying.

CONCLUSION

Historically, Black Americans have been excluded from governmental politics and mainstream media's political conversations because they were thought to have nothing of value to add. Therefore, they sought out or created alternative publics to discuss and participate in political issues that frequently had a negative impact on the well-being and human rights of Black communities. Within these alternative publics, Black communities used their communicative traditions to engage with political and social issues, which may have seemed ineffectual to outsiders, but were strategic, empowering, and liberating. Today, the convergence of Black communicative practices and alternative publics, such as Twitter, are shaping public conversations about social and political issues, including governmental politics.

However, it is essential to take seriously that these political counterpublic practices need not be serious. Humor is a core feature of both Black political culture and AAVE that then plays out in online spaces. In such ways, as Brandy Monk-Payton notes, "Social networking becomes a crucial platform for generating humor as a form of protest against systemic anti-Blackness in the United States."[40] It is both humor and protest, and we must recognize it as both. The Miss Rona tweets exemplify Lu and Steele's point that "joy as a mode of resistance [is] particularly applicable to Black users in digital spaces."[41] The COVID-19 pandemic and the governmental failures to manage it were (literally) deadly serious, but Black Twitter users nevertheless joked about it, bringing to bear a tradition of sharp political critique couched in humor.

Anshare Antoine earned her PhD in Texts and Technology from the University of Central Florida. She is a technical content writer contracted with Synergis .

Mel Stanfill is Associate Professor of English with a joint appointment in the Texts and Technology Program at the University of Central Florida. They are author of *Exploiting Fandom: How the Media Industry Seeks to Manipulate Fans.* Their work appears in *New Media and Society, Critical Studies in Media Communication,* and *Cinema Journal.*

NOTES

1. Yulin Hswen et al., "Association of '#covid19' Versus '#chinesevirus' With Anti-Asian Sentiments on Twitter: March 9–23, 2020," *American Journal of Public Health* 111, no. 5 (March 18, 2021): 956–64, https://doi.org/10.2105/AJPH.2021.306154.

2. Kimmy Yam, "Anti-Asian Hate Crimes Increased by Nearly 150% in 2020, Mostly in N.Y. and L.A., New Report Says," NBC News, March 9, 2021, https://www.nbcnews.com/news/asian-america/anti-asian-hate-crimes-increased-nearly-150-2020-mostly-n-n1260264.

3. Martin Hawksey, "Twitter Archiving Google Sheet," TAGS, accessed February 11, 2021, https://tags.hawksey.info/.

4. Janez Demšar et al., "Orange: Data Mining Toolbox in Python," *Journal of Machine Learning Research* 14 (2013): 2349–53.

5. André Brock Jr., *Distributed Blackness: African American Cybercultures* (New York: NYU Press, 2020), 6.

6. Ibid., 81.

7. Alfred L. Martin Jr., "The Tweet Has Two Faces: Two-Faced Humor, Black Masculinity, and RompHim," *JCMS: Journal of Cinema and Media Studies* 58, no. 3 (2019): 161, https://doi .org/10.1353/cj.2019.0031; Wendy Hui Kyong Chun, *Updating to Remain the Same: Habitual New Media* (Cambridge, MA: The MIT Press, 2016).

8. Brock defines the libidinal economy as "the value-laden tension underlying the beliefs within which we operate *where* we operate," which he connects to affect and the visceral; ratchetry is characterized by a "refusal to apologize for or assimilate to out-group and in-group notions of appropriate behavior and aesthetics" (Brock, *Distributed Blackness*, 10, 130).

9. Catherine R. Squires, "Rethinking the Black Public Sphere: An Alternative Vocabulary for Multiple Public Spheres," *Communication Theory* 12, no. 4 (2002): 464, https://doi .org/10.1111/j.1468-2885.2002.tb00278.x.

10. Brock, *Distributed Blackness*, 172.

11. John Baugh, "At Last: Plantation English in America: Nonstandard Varieties and the Quest for Educational Equity," *Research in the Teaching of English* 41, no. 4 (2007): 465–72.

12. John R. Rickford, "The Creole Origins of African American Vernacular English: Evidence from Copula Absence," in *African American English*, ed. Salikoko S. Mufwene, John R. Rickford, Guy Bailey, and John Baugh (London: Routledge, 1998); Donald Winford, "On the Origins of African American Vernacular English—A Creolist Perspective: Part I: The Sociohistorical Background," *Diachronica* 14, no. 2 (January 1, 1997): 305–44, https://doi.org/10.1075 /dia.14.2.05win.

13. Henry Louis Gates Jr., *The Signifying Monkey: A Theory of African-American Literary Criticism*, reprint ed. (New York: Oxford University Press, 1989), 52.

14. Jessica H. Lu and Catherine Knight Steele, "'Joy Is Resistance': Cross-Platform Resilience and (Re)Invention of Black Oral Culture Online," *Information, Communication & Society* 22, no. 6 (May 12, 2019): 825, https://doi.org/10.1080/1369118X.2019.1575449.

15. Sarah Florini, "Tweets, Tweeps, and Signifyin' Communication and Cultural Performance on 'Black Twitter,'" *Television & New Media* 15, no. 3 (March 1, 2014): 224, https://doi .org/10.1177/1527476413480247.

16. Daryl Cumber Dance, ed., *Honey, Hush! An Anthology of African American Women's Humor*, edition unstated (New York: W. W. Norton, 1998), xxii.

17. Ibid.

18. Sarah Florini, "Enclaving and Cultural Resonance in Black 'Game of Thrones' Fandom," *Transformative Works and Cultures* 29 (March 15, 2019), para. 5.7, 5.5, https://doi .org/10.3983/twc.2019.1498.

19. Lisa Lockerd Maragakis, "Coronavirus Disease 2019 vs. the Flu," April 29, 2021, https:// www.hopkinsmedicine.org/health/conditions-and-diseases/coronavirus/coronavirus -disease-2019-vs-the-flu.

20. Dance, *Honey, Hush!*, xxxiii.

21. Florini, "Tweets, Tweeps, and Signifyin' Communication and Cultural Performance on 'Black Twitter,'" 233.

22. Brock, *Distributed Blackness*, 240.

23. David L. Paletz, "Political Humor and Authority: From Support to Subversion," *International Political Science Review* 11, no. 4 (October 1, 1990): 483–93, https://doi .org/10.1177/019251219001100406; Tanja Petrović, "Political Parody and the Politics of Ambivalence," *Annual Review of Anthropology* 47, no. 1 (2018): 204, https://doi.org/10.1146 /annurev-anthro-102215-100148.

24. Arthur Power Dudden, "The Record of Political Humor," *American Quarterly* 37, no. 1 (1985): 50–70, https://doi.org/10.2307/2712762; Petrović, "Political Parody and the Politics of Ambivalence."

25. Dudden, "Record of Political Humor"; Don L. F. Nilsen, "The Social Functions of Political Humor," *Journal of Popular Culture* 24, no. 3 (Winter 1990): 35; Paletz, "Political Humor and Authority."

26. Dudden, "Record of Political Humor," 69; Petrović, "Political Parody and the Politics of Ambivalence," 208.

27. Jenny L. Davis, Tony P. Love, and Gemma Killen, "Seriously Funny: The Political Work of Humor on Social Media," *New Media & Society* 20, no. 10 (October 1, 2018): 3898–916, https://doi.org/10.1177/1461444818762602; Kevin Driscoll et al., "Beyond Big Bird, Binders, and Bayonets: Humor and Visibility Among Connected Viewers of the 2012 US Presidential Debates," *Social Media + Society* 4, no. 1 (January 1, 2018): 2056305118761201, https://doi .org/10.1177/2056305118761201.

28. Davis, Killen, and Love, "Seriously Funny," 3912.

29. Driscoll et al., "Beyond Big Bird, Binders, and Bayonets," 2.

30. Sahil Kapur, "Stephen Miller Reveals Trump's Immigration Agenda If He's Re-Elected," NBC News, October 30, 2020, https://www.nbcnews.com/politics/immigration/trump-adviser -stephen-miller-reveals-aggressive-second-term-immigration-agenda-n1245407.

31. White nationalism, as Stephanie Hartzell notes, is a "formation of white supremacy premised on racial separatism, the desire for a white ethnostate, and the preservation of white racial hegemony." Stephanie L. Hartzell, "Whiteness Feels Good Here: Interrogating White Nationalist Rhetoric on Stormfront," *Communication and Critical/Cultural Studies* 17, no. 2 (2020): 131, https://doi.org/10.1080/14791420.2020.1745858.

32. Dance, *Honey, Hush!*, xxi.

33. Bambi Haggins, *Laughing Mad: The Black Comic Persona in Post-Soul America* (New Brunswick, NJ: Rutgers University Press, 2007), 4.

34. Kelsey Snell, "Trump Halts Coronavirus Relief Talks Until after the Election," NPR, October 6, 2020, https://www.npr.org/sections/latest-updates-trump-covid-19-results /2020/10/06/920828075/trump-pausing-coronavirus-stimulus-talks-until-after-the-election.

35. Haggins, *Laughing Mad*, 13.

36. Aaliyah Dana Haughton, mostly known as just Aaliyah, was a beloved Black American R&B singer during the 1990s. She has been credited with redefining contemporary R&B, hip-hop, and pop and has been dubbed the Princess of R&B. In 2001, she died in a tragic airplane accident in the Bahamas.

37. Gates, *Signifying Monkey*, 52.

38. Brock, *Distributed Blackness*, 87.

39. Ibid., 170.

40. Brandy Monk-Payton, "#LaughingWhileBlack: Gender and the Comedy of Social Media Blackness," *Feminist Media Histories* 3, no. 2 (April 1, 2017): 29, https://doi.org/10.1525 /fmh.2017.3.2.15.

41. Lu and Steele, "'Joy Is Resistance,'" 824.

9

"CAN YOU SAY P-FAILURE?"

The Secret Diary of Desmond Pfeiffer and UPN

Kelly Cole

In the mid-1990s, demographers noted that the weekly list of top-ten TV shows were different for Black and white households.[1] The revelation that African Americans didn't like *Seinfeld* was offered up as evidence of the deep fragmentation of American society. However, this rift spelled opportunity for some. When Viacom launched the United Paramount Network in 1995, in a heated horse race with Time Warner's The WB to become the fifth network, its strategy was to follow the model set by FOX: seek out underserved audiences to compete with the Big Three. And like FOX in the early 1990s, UPN soon found a foothold in the TV market by targeting African American viewers with Black sitcoms. Despite some criticism that it had begun to "ghettoize" these programs, the network's focus made it a viable player.

But in the fall of 1998, UPN made a spectacular misstep by unveiling *The Secret Diary of Desmond Pfeiffer* (*Pfeiffer*). The sitcom was set in the Civil War era and revolved around a Black British butler and confidant to Abraham Lincoln. Ostensibly a satire of the Clinton White House—complete with jokes about telegraph sex—it immediately sparked controversy for its historical setting and references to slavery. Before the first episode aired, the network was slammed with a wave of criticism and protests. UPN canceled the show shortly after it debuted, citing poor ratings as the sole reason. Though it lives on mostly as a footnote to TV history, making numerous "worst TV shows ever" lists, there is much to be learned by revisiting *Pfeiffer*. The gulf

Fig. 9.1 Promotional image from UPN's failed *The Secret Diary of Desmond Pfeiffer.*

between what the creators thought would happen (audiences will embrace a comedy about the Civil War) and what did happen (the NAACP and numerous community groups condemned the show) can teach us a great deal about American culture and the TV industry in the late 1990s.

In the pantheon of failed TV shows, *Pfeiffer* was by any metric a bad idea. The premise was problematic: a Black British nobleman beset with gambling debts flees England on a slave ship with his white manservant and ends up a trusted advisor in the Lincoln White House at the beginning of the Civil War. The execution was worse, with plots revolving around an infantilized, sex-starved Lincoln, a perpetually drunk General Grant, and a sex-crazed, binge-eating Mary Todd Lincoln who is regarded as offensively unattractive. Ironically enough, given the outrage over a "slave-com," the four aired episodes contain no direct references to slavery. Rather, the show is full of misogynistic, homophobic, and antisouthern jokes. Still, much of the show's humor hinges on the presence of the lone Black main character and, regarded in the context of late '90s television, speaks volumes about racial representation at the time.

While there is a tendency to look back on bad ideas, particularly bad TV shows, with a bemused eye roll, the rhetorical question "What were they thinking" is a useful one to answer—starting with who are *they*? Television programs can make for difficult academic subjects as there is no single

"author" of a television text. Rather, there is a collaboration of writers, direc-
tors, and network and studio executives who work within a larger economic
system made of production companies, parent corporations, advertising
agencies, sponsors, and ratings systems. All are united in one common goal
of identifying and targeting audiences. As scholars like Amanda Lotz and Fe-
lica Henderson have demonstrated, an accounting of creative and industrial
practices in television is crucial to understanding the programs themselves.[2]

To understand why UPN thought this show would be a good way to reach
audiences, an examination of the industrial conditions in which it emerged,
the social conditions in which it failed, and the legacy it left for the relationship of network television to the audience it needs is necessary.

The Creation of UPN and the Race to Fifth

In the early 1990s, amid seismic waves of corporate mergers, media conglomerates like Time Warner and Viacom felt pressure to own an in-house
television network to maintain a competitive edge for their TV production
companies. Thanks to the significant scaling back of ownership regulations
(like the financial interest and syndication, or Fin-Syn rules), they were finally
allowed to do so. Unfortunately, the major networks, NBC, CBS, and ABC,
had already been subsumed into larger conglomerates.[3] The next best option
was to create a new one, as Newscorp did in the 1980s, and follow the lead of
FOX. Each "netlet," as they became known, tapped a former FOX president
to lead their team, and each followed FOX's strategy for building a schedule.

UPN debuted in January 1995 with five programs spread over two nights
of the week, Monday and Tuesday, and no coherent identity. (The WB
claimed Wednesday nights.) Building around its one recognizable property,
Star Trek: Voyager, the netlet selected four new sitcoms, all in pursuit of the
same eighteen- to thirty-four-year-old (white) male demographic. By June, it
had scrapped these shows in favor of hour-long dramas, still seeking young,
white, educated men. UPN's second (first full) season began with three
science-fiction dramas, but by the middle of 1995–1996, the netlet had shifted
course again, this time bringing on two sitcoms featuring Black casts. One,
appropriately titled *Minor Adjustments*, did not last the season. The other was
Moesha, which became central to the UPN's growth over the next five years
and set the course for its new demographic: Black audiences.

This demographic had recently made headlines with the 1996 release of
ad agency BBDO's annual *Report on Black Television Viewing*, which found
virtually no overlap among the list of top-twenty shows in white and Black
household viewership (only *ER*, *Monday Night Football*, and *NBC'S Monday Night Movie* made both lists).[4] Further, amid audience erosion due to

cable and VCRs, the "underserved" Black audience was proving quite loyal to broadcast TV: according to Nielsen data, the average Black household watched seventy-five hours of television a week as opposed to the average white household's fifty hours.[5]

In the 1996–1997 season—the height of NBC's "must-see-TV" era—critics began to call attention to the lack of diversity on major network lineups, with one saying it "looks like a group photo snapped at a suburban Rotary Club dinner, circa 1953."[6] By this time, FOX had also gravitated toward white audiences, with shows like *Beverly Hills 90210*, *Melrose Place*, *Party of Five*, and *X Files*, and traveled afield of its "urban" audience—a journey that is thoughtfully well-documented in Kristal Brent Zook's definitive *Color by Fox*. Still, it straddled the racial divide, holding on to *Martin*, *Living Single*, and—the number 1 show with Black audiences—*New York Undercover* (which ranked 122th with white audiences).

The WB, having weathered a rocky debut, had expanded to two nights for its second season, keeping its Black-cast sitcoms, *The Wayans Bros* and *The Parent 'Hood*, and picking up two more, *Sister Sister* and the short-lived *Cleghorn!* A smattering of other shows, *Kirk*, *Pinky and the Brain*, and *Savannah*, rounded out the lineup; these programs, like the quirky frog mascot, made for a random network identity but kept the door open for The WB to be oriented toward "a family audience." As the netlet struggled to find its footing, the strategy was clear: "We are basically targeting the same old Fox demos," stated heads of marketing Bob Bibb and Louis Goldstein (imported from FOX), "We want to convey the same attitude of hip."[7] And for its 1996–1997 season, The WB brought on the *Jamie Foxx Show* and the *Steve Harvey Show*, making the lineup predominantly reliant on Black sitcoms—with the exception of Monday nights, which was reserved for one-hour dramas *Savannah* and *7th Heaven*. All the while, executives downplayed the idea that they were targeting Black audiences, telegraphing a new pivot with a midseason replacement called *Buffy the Vampire Slayer*, according to head of programming, Garth Ancier (also a FOX alum), "We want to do more shows with empowered female leads."[8]

For its part, UPN capitalized on this moment by putting a string of Black-cast sitcoms on the air, picking up *Sparks*, *Malcolm & Eddie*, *Homeboys in Outer Space*, and *Goode Behavior*. Looking back on the season, Herman Gray observes, "Of the six commercial television networks, WB, UPN, and Fox had a combined total of *sixteen shows* that could be identified as black or black-oriented"; in fact, UPN had the most.[9] These shows were predominantly comedies, and some of them came under fire for the quality and depth of the representations.[10] In writing about stages of programming with Black casts, Robin Means Coleman and Charlton D. McIlwain characterize the 1990s as the "neo-minstrelsy" era on television (identifying *Pfeiffer*'s premiere as the moment "Black Sitcoms hit an all-time low.")[11] UPN was soon facing criticism for "ghettoizing their schedule." [12]

By the start of the next television season, the divergence in Black and white viewership went from an observed phenomenon to a cause for alarm. The blame for what the *New York Times* called "the widening racial divide" was laid squarely at the feet of the new networks: FOX, The WB, and UPN.[13] As one reporter remarked, "The racial chasm in television viewing is relatively new. That's because until the last several years there weren't enough shows with black casts to fragment the audience."[14] Ironically, this argument both celebrates the emergence of "new black media images" and blames them, for they "polarized America's viewing habits, underscoring the depth of the nation's ambivalence about race and identity."[15]

This racial polarization was troubling—not just as an indication of social division, but for its impact on ad revenue for networks, whose executives worried whether shows that only attract Black audiences would be profitable (conventional wisdom said they would not). Analyzing the 1998 season, Herman Gray observes, "Since they remain the idealized subjects of television advertisers, studios, and networks, the culturally pressing question is still whether white viewers will watch shows about the lives of people different from them, and whether networks and studios will take the financial risk of programming these shows."[16] At the time, The WB's Ancier put it more bluntly: "Our advertisers are totally conscious that we be [sic] very crossover. . . . The message is, if you don't make shows that appeal to white audiences, you fail."[17]

The 1997–1998 television season saw an overhaul of programming in response to the prior year's criticism. The major networks' fall lineups were hailed for their racial diversity; much fanfare made of the fact that new and returning shows featured Black or Latinx characters in lead roles. NBC, which had come under particular fire the previous season for not having a single Black lead, had created minority roles in each of its eight new sitcoms and dramas. Meanwhile, the smaller networks seemed to be overcorrecting in the other direction.

Building on the modest success of *Buffy* to appeal to a teen girl audience, The WB added the angsty (white) teen drama *Dawson's Creek*. While FOX jettisoned the two most popular series in Black households, *Living Single* and *New York Undercover*, because the shows, "have not attracted significant numbers of white viewers."[18] UPN also modified its schedule, dropping

Homeboys and *Goode Behavior*, two underperforming Black shows, to pick up programs with multiethnic casts (the equally underperforming *Head Over Heels* and *Hitz*).

Midway through the season UPN revamped its leadership as well, dropping network president Lucie Salhany and replacing her with Dean Valentine, a veteran of Disney Television, who took the helm with a clear strategy to become an "inclusive" network.

Put into practice, the theory of inclusivity came to be known as "reverse integration," which meant either adding white characters to Black shows or placing Black characters in multiethnic settings—in the words of one headline, "TV's Black 'Ghetto' Opens Its Doors to White Characters."[19] All of broadcast television seemed to be moving toward this "inclusivity," as one reporter observed, "Not one new comedy this season features an all-black cast."[20] Established comedies were not immune either. On UPN the producers of *Moesha* decided to send the main character to a white school, and on The WB, as Steve Harvey recounted, "We have had to place white faces on our show this year. We didn't ask for it. It came down on us."[21] In this context, a show like *Pfeiffer* begins to make sense.

By the time it rolled out its fall 1998 lineup, The WB had found its audience with the success of *Buffy the Vampire Slayer* and *Dawson's Creek* and added *Charmed* and *Felicity*. These programs coincided with the recent cultural discovery of a new juggernaut teen girl market and gave the netlet an enviable niche.[22] But even as it created its own version of "must-see-TV," the netlet maintained a space for its Black sitcoms—just as FOX had. As Bibb and Goldstein's now-classic image campaigns conspicuously celebrated the fresh young faces of WB's "New Tuesday," Thursday nights quietly belonged to Jamie Foxx, Steve Harvey, and the Wayans brothers.

UPN, however, was still struggling. For the 1998 season it dropped *Sparks*, *Good News*, and *In the House*, dismantling its Monday night "black-block" lineup and taking three more of the top shows in Black households off the air.[23] Given the precarious nature of their situation, one couldn't fault UPN executives for taking a risk. Nor could one entirely blame them for thinking *The Secret Diary of Desmond Pfeiffer* might be a good bet. It featured Chi McBride, a Black actor who would go on to star in Fox's *Boston Public*, as the lead in an otherwise white ensemble (thus checking the "inclusive" box). Further, *Pfeiffer*'s writers came with strong television pedigrees. The two white creators, Barry Farano and Mort Nathan, had won an Emmy award for their writing on *The Golden Girls*, while Bill Boulware, a Black writer/director, hired as a consulting producer, had credits including *227*, *Fresh Prince of Bel-Air*, and *The Parkers*. Interestingly, the three men had previously worked together on the beloved '80s show *Benson*, about a Black butler / trusted adviser in the governor's mansion.

But unlike the '80s feel-good classic that spoke to its contemporary setting, the premise of *Pfeiffer* was more fraught. And this is where the benefit of the doubt becomes more difficult. For while a bawdy comedy about a Black man in the White House during the Civil War might seem overly provocative in any era, in 1998, it was particularly inflammatory.

Slavery was at the forefront of national discourse, as a heated congressional debate raged over the issue of reparations and whether the US government should apologize. President Clinton struggled with this throughout 1997 as his special Race Advisory Board conducted a yearlong "national conversation about improving race relations in America." Ultimately, he stopped short of an apology when, on a visit to Uganda in 1998, he denounced slavery, calling it "wrong." That year also witnessed the steady dismantling of affirmative action policies in states across the country. Meanwhile, in the television industry, the FCC was forced to abandon its twenty-year-old Equal Employment Opportunity (EEO) regulations. Tensions over "race relations" were felt more directly as examples of police brutality, especially in Mayor Rudy Giuliani's New York, made national headlines. The $8.75 million settlement to Abner Louima for the violent assault by police officers in the bathroom of a precinct stationhouse had indicted not just individual officers but also the system itself. And the tragic murder of James Byrd Jr. in the summer of 1998 by three white supremacists who beat him and dragged him to his death behind a pickup truck in Jasper, Texas, served as a violent reminder that the racism of the past was not in the past. It was certainly not a fertile source for humor in the present.

PFEIFFER COURTS CONTROVERSY

Before its debut, *Pfeiffer*'s pilot episode was prescreened to "industry insiders and television critics, many of whom labeled the series the worst show of the season."[24] Though two particularly objectionable references to slavery were cut from an early version on the pilot, others remained. For example, in one scene, Pfeiffer says to a "brandy-swilling" incompetent Ulysses S. Grant, "With you at the helm, I better get my cotton-picking skills ready."[25]

In September 1998, a grassroots movement led by the Beverly Hills/Hollywood chapter of the NAACP, the Brotherhood Crusade, and other leaders in the Black community launched a protest to get the show canceled before it was aired, citing the historical era as off-limits for a comedy. Protesters were reportedly "particularly dismayed at UPN, which has targeted much of its programming toward a black audience and has a loyal African American viewership."[26] In the week leading up to the show's premiere, three hundred people marched outside Paramount Studios, "brandishing signs with such comments as 'Slavery is not funny.'"[27] In response, UPN announced it would postpone the pilot episode, out of "respect [for] our African American viewers";[28] however, it would continue with the premiere, beginning with the second episode instead. As the protests continued, UPN entertainment president Tom Nunan remained confident in his decision, "It was clear to us that any kind of misunderstanding about this show would be forever silenced once people saw the second episode."[29]

In the second episode, *Pfeiffer*'s opening credit sequence references documentary filmmaking à la Ken Burns; a Shelby Foote quotation scrolls across sepia-toned historical war photographs as a male voice reads: "The Civil War defined America. Both the good and the bad. It was the crossroads of our being, and it was a hell of a crossroads. Who would have thought there was a comedy in all that? Well, we did!"

Civil War images dissolve into photos of the cast striking farcical poses. Though slavery is unmentioned, framing the credits as a documentary only emphasizes its implicit (and unacknowledged) presence. That the show premiered directly opposite the PBS special *Africans in America: America's Journey through Slavery* would have made the connection that much more immediate.[30]

This episode, entitled "AOL: Abe Online," establishes Desmond as the lone competent man (and person of color) in a sea of white characters who are either bumbling or belittled. In classic sitcom style, the interior sets are filmed with a multicamera setup, facilitating the rapid dialogue and reaction shots of the ensemble; the comedic plots are peppered with punch lines and sight gags. Most notably, in the tradition of Black-cast sitcoms of the late '90s, "the action and emotional cues were pumped up and pushed along with laughter provided by enthusiastic studio audiences and laugh tracks."[31] Focusing on the laugh track as performing "a hegemonic function," Alfred Martin observes that its "presence within Black-cast sitcoms attempts to control where humor can be found and where it is not supposed to be found."[32] This helps explain the relentless, often hysterical laughter that permeates *Pfeiffer*'s episodes. Indeed, the participation of the audience represents a sixth member of the ensemble.

The plot centers on Lincoln's addiction to "telegraph sex" with an anonymous woman; the president's obsession becomes an impediment to the South's attempt to surrender the war via telegraph. The episode culminates with a sexual/homoerotic miscommunication that unintentionally escalates the war. A message intended for Lincoln's paramour mistakenly reaches

Grant at the Southern headquarters, who reads, "You're gonna get the lickin'
of your life," and indignantly responds, "We'll see who licks who!" He fires
back his reply, "Prepare to be brought to your knees!" Lincoln responds lust-
ily from his desk at the White House, "Keep tappin' lady!" Standing beside
him, Desmond becomes disgusted, exclaiming, "This is the Oval Office,
you're the leader of this country, and if I may be so bold sir, you're acting no
better than a . . . horny hillbilly from Arkansas!" The laugh track roars with
the contemporary reference to President Bill Clinton.

The show's writing attempted to capitalize on the bawdy, risqué sexual
humor that was circulating around the Clinton sex scandals. A generous review would interpret this as drawing from a carnivalesque tradition, as *Entertainment Weekly* (in a characteristically high-theory reference) observes,
"There is something almost Rabelaisian about the vulgarity of *Desmond Pfeiffer*."[33] However, despite displaying some of the more superficial elements
of the Mikhail Bakhtin's Carnivalesque—the irreverent treatment of the
"sacred" history of Lincoln or the reliance on bodily humor—it is distinctly
not Rabelaisian laughter in which the hyperactive studio audience engages.
Pfeiffer did not display the "utopian freedom" and bottom-up revolutionary
spirit that "marked the suspension of all hierarchical rank."[34] Rather, every
element in the show works to reinforce the hegemonic order.

Pfeiffer premiered to low ratings and dismal reviews.[35] The protests continued outside of Paramount Studios as the activists redoubled their efforts,
turning to economic and political tactics to pressure UPN to cancel the show,
and the controversy made headlines widely.[36] This drama was more compelling than the show itself, tapping into larger societal debates about race
and representation. The protesters fought to ground the show in its historical context, "We want our children to understand what happened, and that
it will never happen again."[37] They were met with equally strong attempts
from UPN, the writing team, and the actors to disarticulate it from any social
context; UPN's president insisted that the "the sitcom was not about slavery
except for being set during Lincoln's Presidency."[38] Further, he invoked colorblindness to defend his position, "Instead of Chi, what if we had cast a Cau-
casian in that role? Would it still be wrong to do a comedy set in the Lincoln
White House? I'm totally baffled by that."[39]

Days after the show's premiere, LA city councilman Mark Ridley-
Thomas, an African American representing South Los Angeles, called it
"irresponsible" and "embarrassing" and led the council in unanimously
passing a motion condemning the sitcom as "a bad idea, destined to fan
the flames of racial discord."[40] Valentine rebutted the criticism as "political correctness . . . gone haywire" and "a scary harbinger for freedom of

expression."[41] Bill Boulware echoed Valentine saying, "It's extreme censorship to say you can't do a comedy about a particular period in time."[42] Even McBride, the show's star, spoke out, calling it "political correctness—a fancy word for censorship."[43] UPN's response exemplified, as Kristen Warner points out, how the complementary discourses of colorblindness and political correctness work together: "Because we have been socialized into 'not seeing race,' when issues arise that are consciously or unconsciously informed by racism, color-blindness renders claims of discrimination and prejudice moot. More specifically, assuming 'we are all the same' makes claims of racism appear as 'oversensitivity' and the result of political correctness."[44]

Valentine implied that the *councilman* was irresponsible: "I've got to believe that the guy who sponsored this resolution—who represents a constituency that is not affluent and that is constituted of people who are struggling to make a day-to-day living and get potholes filled in their neighborhood—you have to wonder if he doesn't have anything better to worry about than what UPN is putting on Mondays at 9."[45]

Nothing could be farther from the day-to-day concerns of South Los Angeles than the second episode, "Up, Up, and Away." This plot finds Lincoln, Desmond, and his white manservant Niblet in a downed hot-air balloon stuck behind enemy lines and surrounded by Southern soldiers, who are immediately identified by exaggerated accents and homosexual proclivities. Desmond wonders, "What kind of disguise could possibly conceal the identity of a large black man, a British inbred imbecile, and the president of the Union?" Cut to Lincoln in drag, Niblet in a young boys' sailor suit, and Desmond still in his original clothes. "What are *you*, Desmond?" Lincoln asks. At that moment, Confederate soldiers emerge from the bushes and say, "Freeze, y'all." Desmond, rifles pointed at his face, puts up his hands and says, "I'm a dead man." The audience laughs.

Thinking quickly, Desmond adopts a Foghorn Leghorn accent and identifies himself as a "lily-white son of the South" traveling with a mother-son team to "infiltrate the Northern infrastructure." One soldier is confused by Desmond's large vocabulary, so another translates, "He's sayin' he's a phony colored guy." The three are invited to Confederate headquarters, where Lincoln embarks on a scheme to retrieve secret battle plans while "Colonel Beauregard Desmond" charms the officers. They raise a toast to Desmond's "sacrifice," elaborating, "it must be awfully hard on you to even temporarily go through life as a Neeegro" (modest laugh track laugh). "Oh, it hasn't been that bad," he replies, lounging on the couch, "I have been able to get a lot more white women" (uproarious laugh track laugh).

One officer compliments his disguise, "You look like a genuine, simple-minded Negro" but claims that as a "true Southerner," he could never be fooled. Desmond responds in his exaggerated accent, "Not even if I was to call you an ign'ant, butt-scratchin', banjo-pickin', cousin-lovin' cracker?" The audience howls as the officer ignores the insult, "I remain unimpressed." Desmond then escalates to a physical assault, "Well what if I was to . . . bang yo' head against the wall," as the officer allows himself to be shoved, beaten, and finally kneed in the groin. The audience laughs and the other officers look on genially as Desmond smiles and waves. Meanwhile, the Southern general, who has fallen in love with Lincoln in drag, will not stop chasing him around a table until Lincoln is forced to reveal himself and the protagonists are exposed as spies.

The three are marched into the woods at gunpoint by a Confederate officer who—in a twist—fires his gun in the air, pulls off his face, and reveals himself to be the actor Sherman Hemsley playing a Union spy in whiteface.[46] He takes his leave of the president with his signature George Jefferson line, "You better get to movin' on up sir," and the stolen battle plans are returned to General Grant.

Given the preoccupation with colorblindness, the writers' focus on Desmond's physicality in this episode is striking, as it is remarked on multiple times in dialogue and is central to the plot. Desmond's character is called on to literally perform Blackness, bringing his "authenticity" to scenes for comic effect. There is an element of reveal each time Desmond drops his genteel accent and uses a Black vernacular, but his otherness is also completely contained and deployed in the service of white (heterosexual) masculinity. As a butler, he is in their service; as an agent of the Northern government, he serves his country. Meanwhile, the Southern soldiers are clearly coded as "other": unintelligent, emasculated, and racist. Their racism is benign (despite the rifles) and laughable, as we know they lost the war. This configuration uses the superiority theory of humor to allow the audience to both mock and deny the existence of structural racism: These people were wrong and we triumphed over them, so clearly we are right.

Lurking on the periphery of *Pfeiffer*'s fictional world is the knowledge that systemic racism, policy brutality, rape, eating disorders, sexual harassment, and hate crimes exist. Every so often, this knowledge peeks through in a chilling way. The *only* way to find the show funny is to take on the subject position of a straight white man. This is arguably true of most television texts; as Herman Gray reminds us, white viewers "remain the idealized subjects of television advertisers, studios, and networks."[47] But it becomes painfully obvious in *Pfeiffer*, as the relentless laugh track defies the viewer to disagree, be a killjoy, or take it too seriously. For example, in the third episode, Desmond prevents his "lesbian bitch" archnemesis from assassinating Lincoln. The fact that *this* was the program UPN chose to target "white audiences" underscores how truly restrictive the working definition of *white* is in a network context and how much racism, sexism, and homophobia it takes for granted.

The task of unpacking exactly where the humor in Pfeiffer lies (or, for that matter, finding humor at all) depends a great deal on the intended audience. One can imagine how Mary Todd Lincoln being the prize in a bowling competition where the challengers "don't want to keep her, we just want to pass her around!" might be less funny when approached from a female perspective. To watch *Pfeifer* is to witness how much labor goes into establishing and reaffirming a hegemonic subject position. The show ultimately collapses under that labor, as it is offensive on so many fronts at once. In his defense against allegations of racial insensitivity, Valentine said, "I can see where people might find it morally or sexually offensive, but not on the issue of race."[48] And indeed, it's as if the effort to avoid racist humor forced the writers to compensate with more socially acceptable sexist and homophobic humor. Viewing *Pfeiffer* today makes one reconsider the other wildly misogynistic texts that thrived in the late '90s (but were not canceled due to a racially inflammatory premise).

"Desmond Pfeiffer Became the Symbol of UPN's Disastrous Season"

When UPN canceled *Pfeiffer* one month into its run, network executives "downplayed the furor over the show as a factor . . . citing instead its chilly reception from viewers," a plausible explanation as it ranked 133 out of 135 prime time shows on the six networks.[49] Meanwhile, the show's opponents, a coalition that had grown to include several high-profile national figures, claimed their victory, due in no small part to having persuaded nineteen out of twenty sponsors to pull their ads from the program.[50] In a fitting tribute to the market considerations that had inspired UPN to pursue Black audiences, the coalition had wielded that economic power to punish UPN.

The failure of *Pfeiffer* was not the only dismal news for UPN; the netlet was down 39 percent in the ratings during fall sweeps—the most precipitous slide of all the networks that year.[51] The industry consensus was that "Valentine's effort to broaden UPN's programming beyond predominantly black-targeted sitcoms" was to blame.[52] Entertainment president Tom Nunan agreed, "We've been brutally aware of how important the African-American audience . . . is to UPN's health and success. . . . And I think we were pretty naïve and unconscious about how deep the impact would be should that core constituency depart."[53]

To correct course, UPN picked up *Between Brothers*, a comedy about four young African American professionals as a midseason replacement. The show had been on FOX for only a season but was the number-one rated program in African American households for 1997–1998.[54] UPN paired the show with *Malcolm & Eddie* in a block on Tuesday nights. It also added four other new series with Black leads or an all-Black cast: *The Parkers*, *Grown-Ups*, *Shasta McNasty*, and *Secret Agent Man*. Though UPN began the next season with a formal announcement that it would also be targeting young men—it picked up the rights to air *WWF Smackdown* from 8:00 to 10:00 p.m. on Thursdays—it would continue to reserve plenty of room on its schedule for African American sitcoms. Dean Valentine finally appeared to appreciate the audience he had tried to leave behind. "We have a deep commitment to reflecting on the air the way the country looks," he said in July 1999. "I think it's short-sighted to alienate an entire community."[55] That summer, when the NAACP launched a national campaign admonishing the networks for "whitewashing" their lineups and threatening boycotts and litigation, UPN was notably exempt from criticism.

When UPN and The WB were announced six days apart in a crowded television marketplace, each team knew that the odds were stacked against it. Jamie Kellner proclaimed, "There's only room for one more network. There's no way there's room for two."[56] While Salhany declared, "We'll survive. Warner Brothers has been left behind."[57] By 2006, when the netlets shuttered operations and merged to become The CW, both their statements would prove prophetic. But in 1995, they were the starting gun for a decade of competition, and this competition opened a space for some of the most diverse programming the airwaves had seen before—or, arguably, since. As a glaring misstep, *Pfeiffer* highlights the phenomenon of successful Black programming on UPN (*Moesha*, *Girlfriends*, *The Hughleys*) and The WB (*The Steve Harvey Show*, *Wayans Bros*, *Sister Sister*, *Jamie Foxx Show*). The cultural legacies of these programs are discussed by Zook and alluded to by Gray, "While not particularly remarkable aesthetically, the fact is that these shows helped to sustain a black presence, albeit separate, in the mediascape of American network television."[58]

Along the way as networks searched for identities and market share, the need to gather an audience led executives to take risks and provided opportunities for writers, producers, showrunners, and actors. The successes of this period of television launched careers, yet an examination of its failures demonstrates how many lessons remained unlearned because the engrained assumptions of the industry toward audiences proved so immovable and entrenched.

Kelly Cole is Lecturer in the English Department and Core Faculty in the Film and Media Studies Program and the American Studies Program at Georgetown University.

NOTES

1. "The Season at a Glance," *TV Guide*, September 12, 1998, 33.

2. Amanda D. Lotz, "Segregated Sitcoms: Institutional Causes of Disparity among Black and White Comedy Images and Audiences," in *The Sitcom Reader: America Viewed and Skewed*, ed. Mary M. Dalton and Laura R. Linder (New York: SUNY Press, 2005), 139–50, https://www.sunypress.edu/p-4180-the-sitcom-reader.aspx; Felicia Henderson, "The Culture Behind Closed Doors: Issues of Gender and Race in the Writers' Room," *Cinema Journal* 50, no.2 (2011): 145–52.

3. See Ken Auletta's *Three Blind Mice: How the Networks Lost their Way* (New York: Knopf Doubleday Publishing Group, 1992); Ben Bagdikian's *The Media Monopoly* (Boston: Beacon Press, 1997).

4. David Zurawik, "Races Diverging in Viewing Habits," *Baltimore Sun*, May 2, 1996.

5. Bill Carter, "Two Upstart Networks Courting Black Viewers," *New York Times*, October 7 1996, C11.

6. Steve Johnson, "Is Television Reverting to Black & White?," *Chicago Tribune*, August 27, 1996, 1.

7. David Tobenkin, "Plotting WB-ification," *Broadcasting and Cable*, July 25, 1994, 15.

8. T. L. Stanley, "'Buffy' to Slay Small Screen; New Action Thriller for the WB Television Network," *Mediaweek*, February 17, 1997, 9.

9. Herman Gray, *Cultural Moves: African Americans and the Politics of Representation* (Berkeley, CA: University of California Press, 2005), 81.

10. Greg Braxton, "Groups Call for Changes in Portrayal of Blacks on TV," *Los Angeles Times*, February 8, 1997, 1.

11. Robin R. Means Coleman and Charlton D. McIlwain, "The Hidden Truths in Black Sitcoms," in *The Sitcom Reader: America Viewed and Skewed*, ed. Mary M. Dalton and Laura R. Linder (Albany: State University of New York Press, 2005), 125–38.

12. Carter, "Two Upstart Networks."

13. James Sterngold, "A Racial Divide Widens on Network TV," *New York Times*, December 29, 1998, A1.

14. Nancy Haas, "A TV Generation Is Seeing Beyond Color," *New York Times*, February 22, 1998. 1.

15. Ibid.

16. Gray, *Cultural Moves*, 79.

17. Hass, "TV Generation Is Seeing Beyond Color."

18. John Carman, "Fox's Fall Leaves Out Black Hits," *San Francisco Chronicle*, May 21, 1997, D1.

19. Allan Johnson, "Integration? TV's Black 'Ghetto' Opens its Doors to White Characters," *Chicago Tribune*, September 30, 1998, 1.

20. Ibid.

21. Sterngold, "Racial Divide Widens on Network TV," A1.

22. Linda Lee, "Attack of the 90-Foot Teen-Agers," *New York Times*, November 9, 1997, sec. 9, 1.

23. Leon E. Wynter, "TV Programmers Drop 'Black-Block' Lineups," *Wall Street Journal*, September 2, 1998, B1.

24. Greg Braxton, "A Controversial 'Diary,'" *Los Angeles Times*, September 19, 1998, 1.

25. Ibid. They were oblique references: two masked bodies hanging from a tree and mention of "a ship headed to the southernmost part of America."

26. Ibid.

27. Greg Braxton, "300 Protest at Studio against TV Comedy Set in Slavery Era," *Los Angeles Times*, October 1, 1998, 3G.

28. Greg Braxton, "UPN Postpones, Reviews Its 'Desmond Pfeiffer' Pilot," *Los Angeles Times*, September 30, 1998, 2.

29. Jefferson Graham, "Protest Greets UPN's New Season," *USA Today*, October 5, 1998, 3D.

30. Eric Deggans, "TV Takes Two Angles on Slavery," *Emerge*, November 1998, 64.

31. Gray, *Cultural Moves*, 82.

32. Alfred L. Martin Jr., *The Generic Closet: Black Gayness and the Black-Cast Sitcom* (Bloomington: Indiana University Press, 2021), 104.

33. Ken Tucker, "The Secret Diary of Desmond Pfeiffer," *Entertainment Weekly*, October 9, 1998.

34. Mikhail Bakhtin, *Rabelais and His World* (Bloomington: Indiana University Press, 2009), 10.

35. Jack White, "Dumb and Dumber," *Time*, October 12, 1998, 106.

36. Don Aucoin, "An Uncivil War Over 'Desmond,'" *Boston Globe*, October 3, 1998, C1.

37. Braxton, "Controversial 'Diary.'"

38. Laurie Mifflin, "Black Protest Delays Sitcom Episode," *New York Times*, October 3, 1998, B12.

39. Braxton, "Controversial 'Diary.'"

40. Julian Borger, "Black Rage at White House Slavery and Sex Satire," *Guardian*, October 6, 1998, Foreign Page, 15.

41. Braxton, "300 Protest at Studio."

42. Braxton, "Controversial 'Diary.'"

43. Lisa de Moraes. "'Pfeiffer' Star Lambastes Show's Protesters," *Washington Post*, October 12, 1998, B5.

44. Kristen Warner, "A Black Cast Doesn't Make a Black Show: *City of Angels* and the Plausible Deniability of Color-blindness," in *Watching While Black: Centering the Television of Black Audiences*, ed. Beretta Smith-Shomade (New Brunswick, NJ: Rutgers University Press, 2012), 50.

45. Lisa de Moraes, "L.A. Council Pans 'Desmond Pfeiffer,'" *Washington Post*, October 1, 1998.

46. Best known for *The Jeffersons*, Hemsley also starred in UPN's short-lived *Goode Behavior*.

47. Gray, *Cultural Moves*, 79.

48. Braxton, "Controversial 'Diary.'"

49. David Bauder, "UPN's Downturn Makes It a Struggle to Survive," Associated Press, November 20, 1998; Greg Braxton. "'Desmond Pfeiffer' Is Deep-Sixed," *Los Angeles Times*, November 7, 1998, 1.

50. Ron Dungee, "Unity Works: Black Community Celebrates UPN's Cancellation of 'Desmond Pfeiffer,'" *Los Angeles Sentinel*, December 3, 1998, A1.

51. "UPN pulls 'Desmond Pfeiffer' from Monday Lineup," *Jet*, November 9, 1998, 14.

52. John M. Higgins, "Viacom Stands behind Valentine," *Broadcasting & Cable*, November 9, 1998, 14.

53. Allan Johnson, "With 'Brothers,' UPN Aims to Rebuild Black Audience," *Chicago Tribune*, January 19, 1999, 1.

54. Ibid.

55. Phil Kloer, "Struggling UPN Gives Black Actors a Home," *Atlanta Journal-Constitution*, July 20, 1999, 4C.

56. "Time Warner Plans Its Own TV Network, Battling Paramount," *Austin American Statesman*, November 3, 1993, D3.

57. Larry Bonko, "Fifth Network UPN to Take Off Beginning in January," *Virginian-Pilot*, November 3, 1994, E1.

58. Gray, *Cultural Moves*, 83.

PART IV

PRODUCING COMEDY

10

GERALDINE AND ME

Flip Wilson's Legacy and This Black Female Sketch Comedy Artist

Ellen Cleghorne

THE INTRODUCTION

This chapter is about the power of sketch comedy in the transmission of the Black narrative, our struggle for equality and personhood. It specifically concerns Flip Wilson's work. Born Clerow Wilson in Jersey City, New Jersey, Flip Wilson became television's first Black superstar.[1] His eponymous NBC-TV comedy variety show topped the ratings from 1970 to 1974, second only to *All in the Family*. *The Flip Wilson Show* (NBC, 1970–1974), a prime-time, half-hour comedy variety show, won Wilson a Golden Globe and two Emmy Awards and racked up eleven Emmy nominations before the show's finale on June 27, 1974. His iconic drag character, Geraldine Jones, a fearless high-fashion (many of her clothes were designer labeled) registered nurse by profession, was a fan favorite. The Reverend Leroy, pastor of the Church of What's Happening Now, was another of Wilson's characters that helped usher in a new era of Black performance on television. Reverend Leroy transformed the American cultural lexicon by satirizing all televangels and Black American evangelicals. Geraldine's catchphrases "what you see is what you get" and "the devil made me do it" inspired top music billboard hits and were used by Madison Avenue advertising agencies to sell, among other things, Diet 7UP. In his time, Wilson opened the doors for the likes of Richard Pryor and George Carlin, as well as others, and changed the perception of Black people in the quotidian.

146

Fig. 10.1 Flip Wilson and his alter ego, Geraldine, on the December 1970 cover of *Ebony* magazine.

This chapter gives a detailed narrative of who Wilson was and argues that Wilson's work on NBC during the post–civil rights era shifted hegemony even if ever so slightly by using humor to humanize Black bodies in the aftermath of the violent civil rights era. His work challenged the Jim Crow laws and ideology that delineated white-only spaces. His work is often overlooked and forgotten. This essay is, therefore, also an argument for his contribution to today's Black stand-up and sketch comedy. My claim is that his work has inspired every sketch comic and stand-up in the post–civil rights era and beyond. Never before through the medium of television had Black people been welcomed into so many non-Black homes and neighborhoods. Even more groundbreaking than writing and starring in his own Emmy Award–winning sketch comedy show was the fact that Wilson used his own production company, Clerow Productions, to produce *The Flip Wilson Show*.

Furthermore, this chapter investigates, through a close reading of the "Night Nurse" sketch, just how Wilson was able to cross racial boundaries using Black sketch and stand-up comedy that was not self-deprecating and attracted fifty million viewers weekly, the second-largest diverse viewership of any type of programming, behind only *All in the Family* (CBS, 1971–1979), which drew sixty million viewers weekly. How did Wilson attract almost sixty million viewers weekly to watch his show only two years after the assassination of Dr. Martin Luther King Jr.?

And finally, this chapter draws a connection from Wilson's iconic work to my work as a stand-up comedian and Emmy Award–winning sketch artist on *Saturday Night Live* (NBC, 1975–). His work inspired me as a child to want to become a comedian. Years later, I would stand on the same stages he stood on, and I am forever grateful.

THE FLIP WILSON SHOW: GERALDINE'S SCENE WITH BILL COSBY—A DEEP READ

This sketch is an example of how Wilson ignored Jim Crow laws using sketch comedy. The following is a close read of the sketch "Night Nurse" starring Gina Lolabrigida and Bill Cosby.

It is a little after 8:00 p.m. on a Saturday night in the early 1970s. *The Flip Wilson Comedy Show* returns from commercials. Network television runs on corporate sponsorship in the form of advertising. According to Meghan Sutherland, *The Flip Wilson Show* "proved to the industry . . . the Black comedy-variety genre" was "profitable prospects for corporate liberalism's brand of multiculturalism; it was integration for capitalists."[2]

The audience erupts in prompted applause. I have been to enough television tapings to know that when you return from a commercial break, neon "clap" signs flashing like traffic lights, as well as the stage manager, are in the audience, out of camera view, prompting the audience to applaud.

On set, Bill Cosby lies in a hospital bed attended by a curvaceous white nurse played by '70s international actress/sex bomb Gina Lollobrigida. In the sketch, Cosby plays himself, the individual successful Black man; he represents the idea (of 1970s postrace America) that racial equality has arrived. Not only is racial equality real, but also Cosby has experienced so much racial equality that he is exhausted to the extent that he needs to be hospitalized. The subtext: Too much racial equality will make the Negros sick. Lollobrigida's shift has come to an end, and she is waiting for the night nurse to relieve her and admonishes Cosby to rest.

At the mention of the night nurse, the audience squirms with anticipation. The literary irony is palpable. Everyone knows Flip Wilson as Geraldine Jones will make an entrance eminently as the night nurse, and Wilson in full and fabulous drag (pre-RuPaul) will deliver the funny! Cosby and Lollobrigida's exchange is packed with standard comedic techniques. Taboo is the predominant comedy force that drives the first half of this sketch. The taboo of a Black man and a white woman in a consensual intimate exchange paints a patina over the performance. The banter is quick witted, and the dialogue is rife with misunderstandings and puns and physical irony that push the boundaries of the acceptable amount of sexual tension between a

Black man and an almost white woman (she is Italian) in a nonsegregated America.

Italians were not always considered white in America. Most famously was the mass lynching of eleven Italian immigrants in New Orleans, Louisiana, followed by the apology from then-president Benjamin Harrison and financial reparations to the families of the lynched victims.[3] An exemplar of the banter between Cosby and Lollobrigida follows:

DAY NURSE [*to Cosby*]: You must try to avoid excitement. [*Nurse Lollobrigida crosses, preparing the room for the shift change.*]
COSBY [*to Lollobrigida as he watches her walk away*]: Then you should try not to walk that way.[4]

The (multiracial) audience laughs, blushing at the deployment of the double entendre embedded in the word *excitement* and Cosby's overt heterosexual arousal by the shapely temptress. Cosby and Lollobrigida represented the banality of cross-racial sexual contact, a trope as old as Shakespeare's Antony and Cleopatra and Othello and Desdemona and the biblical Solomon and Sheba ("she was Black but comely"). The script allows the actors to dance around with the language and walk the tightrope of prime-time propriety; the audience enjoys the athleticism and noncontact word play. For example, the word *excitement* is rife. The sexual charge in the deployment of *excitement* is multidimensional, grounded by the medical definition of the word, which carries equal weight. *Excitement* as a pun has an obvious implication of a potential sexual tête-à-tête, but the flirt falls flat when Lollobrigida doesn't respond in kind; she doesn't even acknowledge that she has been objectified as the possible source of "excitement." The rejected advance and Lollobrigida's seeming obliviousness to racial taboo elicits laughter. Her insensitivity or lack of hypersensitivity belies the national narrative relative to the potential danger in cross-racial intimate exchanges. Emmitt Till was murdered fifteen years earlier because he was thought to have simply whistled at a white woman. Blackness has its own dialogue, one that carries equal potential for a tragic turn; however, in Geraldine's world, in which a Black man being attended by an almost white nurse can engage in casual flirting, the audience that looks on is not happily anticipating a lynching, like those iconically captured in postcards at the beginning of the century but eagerly awaiting the funny turn of the script—Geraldine's own entrance.

In the post–civil rights era, a cross-dressing Black man is a talisman that wards off evil spirits. Comedy as pretense, therefore, has the power to move an entire society out of racial tragedy. Pretense as comedy, or the "comedy of pretense," can only exist when both the pretense and the "real" correspond to the shared ideologies of the masses—which is to say, we are not laughing at Cosby, a Black man, pretending to be an articulate intelligent human being, nor are we laughing at the impossibility of cross-racial attraction; rather, we are laughing at a circumstance where racial inequality does not exist.[5] Laughter is a release of repressed ideologies qua realities; we, therefore, are collectively laughing at the power of the ubiquitous repression of sexual desire. Freud links sexual desire to excitement and argues that sexual excitement is caused by two opposing forces happening simultaneously.[6] The audience and the actors are trying to reconcile a pleasurable feeling of desire with an unpleasant feeling. Simply put, Cosby as a patient expresses the repressed desires of the masses: the desire for the absence of racial tension. This is a revolutionary moment not only in post–civil rights television history but also in American history writ large.

Black people, by law, were prohibited from drinking water from the same fountains as whites in most parts of the country. Ironically, that separate was equal highlighted Blackness as synonym for all things inferior and contradicted everything Wilson presented. While most of the country masqueraded under the pretense of a shared ideology Black as abjection, the quantifiable evidence of Black and white social/sexual cohabitation as equals was undeniable. This Black performance continued the legacy of creating a space for social harmony. Black performers and performance spaces have a rich history as a mechanism working in opposition to racial inequality. According to W. T. Lhamon's work on Blackface minstrelsy,[7] cross-racial desire and class have always backgrounded popular culture in America, while white supremacy after the abolition of slavery used Black performance as the main weapon for dehumanizing Black people and Black performance.

Considering the beginning of the scene is a discourse in interracial equality, comedy is the vehicle for racial harmony. The desire for public displays of interracial affection is registered in the bursts of laughter; the laughter confirms the scenario as a hidden secret embedded in American culture and dying to get out.

On *The Flip Wilson Show* stage, in that comedic moment the taboo of public displays of cross-racial flirtation, which had been the so-called crime that "justified" Till's murder, was laid bare as unjustified and buried as a rationale for killing Black men and boys. This sketch makes it clear that cross-racial exchanges are harmless. It is as if the sketch replays what may have happened between Till and Carolyn Bryant in that store in Money, Mississippi, in 1955. In 1970, audiences were asked if this human exchange should be punishable by death. Even as the nation reached its two hundredth anniversary, the racial divide was clearly entrenched in national ideology. The generally expressed moral taboo regarding cross-racial love surely wasn't passé; even today, biracial relationships carry a negative charge or at least something akin to it, but on that day, in that space, the taboo was forced into the background by the collective social flow of libidinal fluids evidenced in the group burst of laughter.

Geraldine, Wilson in drag, finally enters. The integrated live audience erupts into shrieks of happiness and conspiratorial satisfaction at the first glimpse of Geraldine Jones. In Wilson's 1998 obituary published in the *New York Times*, Geraldine is described as a "sassy but proud black woman whose flamboyance . . . was recognized by millions." Her catch phrases—"When you're hot you're hot, when you're not you're not"; "The devil made me do it"; and "What you see is what you get"—were in everyone's vocabulary in the 1970s. Wilson's drag character is the perfect Black woman; in this sketch, she is the night nurse. Geraldine is not the Black night nurse, just the night nurse who is Black, a spectral image. She is obviously Black, not light-skinned mixed race or "exotic," just Black. But the jokes are not about the absence of whiteness or putting down whiteness. The jokes are not tendentious jokes aimed at Blackness. The jokes are based on Geraldine's absolute belief and knowledge that she has the power to be in control of her image within the confines of the historical culture of Blackness by summoning the gestures of Blackness, the way we think, talk and respond to our environment. More accurately, Wilson explicates to his forty million viewers how he understood and translates the Black woman.

She is perfect. She is wearing a light blue nurse's uniform and light blue classic stiff cap. The uniform is tailored to create and accentuate her curvaceous frame yet the neckline keeps her appropriate and dignified. In the unspoken, her uniform defines her station, rights, responsibilities, levels of experience and education, and demand for respect. She is flawed and perfect, which shows us that to be perfect is to be flawed. This uniform is in stark contrast to her usual attire: in many of her appearances, Geraldine is wearing designer Emilio Pucci dresses valued at $500 and $50 designer shoes.[8]

Geraldine enters dancing, which is not the "perfect" way to enter a hospital room. But it shows that the Black woman has life and music in her body. Wilson's character Geraldine is also flawed in her speech. It is by no means standard English. She uses African American Vernacular English, which at the time was called street talk by white people. That "flaw" is perfect for communicating to her community. It links her to a temporality and history beyond the present. When Black folks hear Geraldine, they know immediately that she speaks for us or shows us that we can speak for Black folks or shows

Black folks that Black folks can speak without shame or insecurities. This encouragement comes from the audience's response. What I mean is that in my home, my family and I were the audience. I am a Black person, and I was encouraged and emboldened by her unapologetic imperfections. I saw my parents laugh. The next day, I heard my friends repeat Geraldine's catch phrases while laughing. It felt good.

The applause in the studio was full and heavy and extended; not only was Geraldine the perfect 1970s Black woman, but she is also the white woman's '70s liberated woman. The post-Vietnam women's liberation zeitgeist was more of a white woman's liberation that destigmatized white women's "choice" to enter the workforce; Geraldine showed that Black women were also employable and employed historically. Slavery didn't discriminate based on gender or sexuality. That Geraldine was a Black man disguised as a beautiful, employed, childless, self-sufficient Black woman shows that drag is a diachronic/synchronic articulation of Black womanhood/manhood/personhood. Wilson made Black humanity visible through sketch comedy.

I argue that Black sketch comedy is an analogy for the tireless ontological transitioning by African American women. By that I mean, we (Black women) are constantly tasked with the mandate to change, and change again, and quickly change and then return to the character that feeds us and keeps us alive, the one-off and the recurring character. This was the essence of my work on *SNL* from 1991 to 1996. This work mandated ontological transitioning. Constant transitioning was also the work of the master sketch artists Flip Wilson and Eddie Murphy, both of whom also appeared on *SNL*.

As far as I am concerned, sketch comedy is an analogy of the tireless ontological transitioning African American woman. By that I mean, we, Black women, are constantly tasked with the mandate to change, and change again, and quick change and then, return to the character that feeds us and keeps us alive; the one off and the recurring character. This was the essence of my work on *Saturday Night Live* from 1991–1996. I became an Emmy Award–winning comedian and the first Black female cast member on the iconic sketch comedy show, *Saturday Night Live*. I always clarify that claim by acknowledging the great and talented Denetra Vance, who was the first *credited* Black woman to last a full season as a *featured player* on SNL. She left after one season. I was given an eight-year contract as a cast member many, many years later. It was a monumental watershed moment for me and for the network, in its nineteenth season. This mandated ontological transitioning, is in the work of master sketch artists like Flip Wilson.

What You See Is What You Get: Social Mobility in Black Cross-Dresser Sketch Comedy

Wilson's drag character Geraldine Jones was a woman of the '70s. She was the Black Mary Tyler Moore. She was mod, hip, and an embodiment of the '70s woman who could have it all—economic independence and love—and look good while she was at it. Geraldine's tagline "What you see is what you get" so infected the 1970s soundscape that it inspired The Dramatics' hit R&B song "What You See Is What You Get" in 1971. Geraldine had an extra element—she had "Blackness," among other *extras*. However, it was this Blackness that allowed her to bring Black and white audiences together in a convivial national play space. Cross-dressing allowed for an exchange across the color line and across socioeconomic stratifications. What was it about a Black man dressed like a Black woman that united a nation in the aftermath of the turbulent '60s? Who was this Flip Wilson and how could I be him/her?

Wilson bringing the nation together for an hour a week was a monumental feat. America—both Black and white—was (and continues to be) racist and chauvinistic. The Memphis sanitation workers' protest was still fresh, having taken place only two years prior to the premiere of Wilson's show. It was Wilson's training as a Black comic and acute business acumen that changed the comedy landscape in America forever.

Wilson, according to Meghan Sutherland, was a solid comedian before he hit the national stage.[9] He was also a "trailblazing businessman," according to newspaper writer Bill Britt, who penned a heartfelt tribute to Wilson in the *Washington Post* after Wilson died in 1998. Rising from the depths of poverty, Flip Wilson was the founder and president of Clerow Productions, which took its appellation from Wilson's given name.[10] Clerow Productions was the company that oversaw *The Flip Wilson Comedy Show* and shared production credit with NBC; a business move that enabled the comic to retire comfortably after only four years on the air. Britt wrote in 1998 after Wilson's death, "Even today, it's unusual for a star to actually produce his own series, yet" Wilson had the "foresight and self-sufficiency" to do so.[11]

Born on December 8, 1933, Clerow Wilson was one of twenty-four children (eighteen surviving). When his mother left the family, Wilson was seven years old. His father struggled with alcohol dependency and Flip—then Clerow—was surrendered to the custody of the state. Young Wilson, as the story goes, ran away from foster care "thirteen times," finally finagling his way into the US Air Force at sixteen. He said, "I wasn't patriotic"; he joined the air force because he was "just tired of being ashamed of [his] clothes."[12] While in the air force, Wilson practiced the Eastman theory of comedy and tried out his jokes on his fellow soldiers in Guam.[13] It was in the air force that Clerow became "Flip," because he often "related stories in a multitude of dialects."[14] Wilson left the air force in 1954 and headed for San Francisco, where he worked at the Manor Plaza Hotel as a bellhop and performed stand-up comedy in local San Francisco comedy clubs before hitting the road on the Chitlin' Circuit.[15] He spent four years performing for mostly Black audiences and building a reputation alongside comics like Dick Gregory, Godfrey Cambridge, Richard Pryor, and Redd Foxx.

Wilson ended his show after four years because, as Christine Acham has recorded, he said at the end of *The Flip Wilson Show* in 1974, "[I wanted to] give my kids their chance. I went through *five foster* homes when I was a kid and I knew my kids needed me. . . . Television made me a hero to other people's kids, but I knew I needed to be a hero to my own kids. I had to do that. And I did."[16]

Although he ended his show, he did not end performing. His relevancy is found in his profound tenacity, belief in the American dream, and passion for performing, which he testifies he found at an early age. Prophetically enough he got his "big break" at age eight playing a nurse in a school play. "That was my first gig—playing a girl. The play became a comedy, and it was a smash."[17]

Wilson's narrative was an inspirational saga reconfiguring the American promise of equality and the myth of the "hard work makes dreams come true" ethic. Hard work alone did not make the Black subject's dreams come true in the historical narrative of America. America is not a meritocracy. Wilson's ability to find and focus on humanity and human exchanges and desires enabled him to transcend racial barriers. This is the case for all groundbreaking comedians, including Pryor and Chappelle, who both opened the door to the truth about racial inequity.

After appearing on and guest hosting *The Tonight Show* (NBC, 1962–1992), performing often on *The Ed Sullivan Show* (CBS, 1948–1971), and spending years on Chitlin' Circuit stages, Wilson was ready—or, rather, allowed—to host his eponymous variety show. It had been on the air for two years when *Time* magazine dubbed him "TV's First Black Superstar" in 1972. Geraldine Jones was the centerpiece of the show. By centerpiece, I mean Geraldine was undeniably the show's franchise player. Kevin Cook wrote that Wilson grew "tired of Geraldine but what was he supposed to do? *She's* his meal ticket."[18] Geraldine Jones was an amalgamation of southern Black femininity and urban Black womanhood; it didn't matter that she was a man. Wilson was selling a brand of middle-class Black femininity, and the nation was buying it. She was perfect: always employed, on vacation, or interviewing for jobs for which she was well qualified. She had a boyfriend, Killer. Her reddish-brown hair was always coiffed, her nails polished, and her stockings runless. She

Fig. 10.2 Wilson's sketch comedy, particularly his Geraldine, centered women as invaluable to the community, whereas the 1968 Memphis Sanitation Strikes seemed to exclude Black women and Black womanhood.

was irresistible to any man she played opposite from the "man's man" John Wayne to football star Joe Namath. She exuded confidence without being pretentious or acting "white." She was unapologetically a Black woman, and she liked it. However, she was not a real person. She was a man in drag.

The irony and bravery of the character is magnified in the anti-Black feminism movement of the late '60s and '70s. These were turbulent times in both Black and white communities.

Whites were resisting integration. Dr. Martin Luther King Jr. was assassinated. Malcolm X and Medgar Evers were gunned down. There was no racial equality or gender parity. It is important to remember that most Black women always had to work outside the home to maintain the family. So, while white women were just finding feminism, Black women wanted intersectional equality. Often Black women's daughters earned as much if not more than their male counterparts, which became a source of contention. In an iconic photograph from the era, two years before the show's premiere, Black men are captured during a protest event wearing double-faced placards and carrying picket signs that read, "I AM A MAN," the slogan for the 1968 Memphis, Tennessee, garbage workers strike supported by Dr. Martin Luther King Jr.

Black men employed by the Memphis refuse collection service earned less than seventy dollars per week. According to the historian Michael K.

Honey, the workers went on strike to protest low wages and dangerous working conditions. Earlier that year, two sanitation workers were killed when a sanitation truck malfunctioned. The sanitation workers' protest brought attention to the fact that Black women and girls were working outside the home for the survival of the Black family. Black men felt emasculated because Black women were earning wages equal to or sometimes greater than their male counterparts. This protest was, therefore, also a protest against Black women and Black women's contribution to the maintenance of the culture was devalued. Wilson's sketch comedy centered women as invaluable to the community.

Currently, I play Michael Che's mother on *That Damn Michael Che* on HBO, now in its second season. I hope I continue the legacy of Flip Wilson and *The Flip Wilson Show* and find ways to move racial and gender boundaries. Wilson's work was groundbreaking. I know I would not be a doctor of philosophy, Emmy Award winner, or mother of an oral and maxillofacial surgery doctor of dentistry if it wasn't for the Black family who raised me to know my history and Wilson's ability to make me laugh.

I learned from Geraldine that my gift for humor was a secret weapon that could neutralize hypermasculinity and racism. Using sketch comedy, I could be fearless and speak truth to power both within the Black community and outside of it.

Ellen Cleghorne is a former cast member of *Saturday Night Live* and the series' first African American woman to win an Emmy as a writer and performer. She can be seen on HBO's *That Damn Michael Che.* Cleghorne earned her doctorate in Performance Studies from New York University and teaches Black humor studies at The New School.

NOTES

1. Mel Watkins, "Flip Wilson, Outrageous Comic and TV Host, Dies at 64," *New York Times*, November 27, 1998, https://www.nytimes.com/1998/11/27/arts/flip-wilson-outrageous -comic-and-tv-host-dies-at-64.html.

2. Meghan Sutherland, *The Flip Wilson Show*, TV Milestones Series (Detroit, MI: Wayne State University Press, 2008), 51.

3. Fred Gardaphé, "We Weren't Always White: Race and Ethnicity in Italian American Literature," *Lit: Literature Interpretation Theory* 13, no. 3 (2010): 185–99, https://doi.org/10 .1080/10436920213855. This essay outlines the transition from Italian immigrant to white American. Italians are currently considered a protected class in New York and protected under antidiscrimination laws.

4. *The Flip Wilson Show*, 1970, season 1, episode 7, directed by Tim Kiley, aired October 29, 1970 on NBC.

5. Stefano Luconi, "The Impact of Italy's Twentieth-Century Wars on Italian Americans' Ethnic Identity," *Nationalism and Ethnic Politics* 13, no. 3 (August 16, 2007): 465–91, https://doi .org/10.1080/13537110701451637.

6. Sigmund Freud, "Three Essays on the Theory of Sexuality (1905)," in *The Standard Edition of the Complete Psychological Works of Sigmund Freud, volume VII (1901–1905): A Case of Hysteria, Three Essays on Sexuality and Other Works*, ed. James Strachey and Anna Freud (London: Hogarth Press, 1953), 125–245.

7. W. Lhamon Jr., *Raising Cain: Blackface Performance from Jim Crow to Hip Hop* (Cambridge, MA: Harvard University Press, 1998).

8. Louie Robinson, "The Evolution of Geraldine—Flip Wilson's TV Creation Is a Classic Comic Character," *Ebony* 26, no. 2 (December 1970): 176–78, 180, 182.

9. Sutherland, *Flip Wilson Show*, 55–57.

10. Bruce Britt, "Leaping Barriers with Laughter; Flip Wilson, a Comic for the Times," *Washington Post*, November 28, 1998, F01, *ProQuest*.

11. Ibid.

12. Sutherland, *Flip Wilson Show*, 55–56.

13. Max Eastman, *The Sense of Humor* (New York: Charles Scribner & Sons, 1921); Eastman, *Enjoyment of Laughter* (New York: Routlege, 2009).

14. Sutherland, *Flip Wilson Show*, 58.

15. Kevin Cook, *The Inside Story of TV's First Black Superstar: Flip Wilson* (New York: Viking, 2013).

16. Christine Acham, *Revolution Televised: Prime Time and the Struggle for Black Power* (Minneapolis: University of Minnesota Press, 2004), 83.

17. Cook, *Inside Story*, "Rags" chapter.

18. Cook, prologue to *Inside Story*. Emphasis added.

11

FROM NETWORK COMEDY TO STREAMING DRAMEDY

How *The Game*'s Creator Challenged the Boundaries Placed on Black-Themed Sitcoms

Felicia D. Henderson

I have been a working television writer-producer-director for twenty-five years. Nearly a decade into my writing career, while obtaining an MFA at UCLA, I became interested in studying the industry in which I was employed. I was sitting in one of two required critical studies courses when a classmate presented an oral critical analysis of Showtime's *Soul Food* (2000–2004), a one-hour drama series I created. He did not know that his classmate was the show's creator. He surmised that although the show's credits identified several executive producers, Kenneth "Babyface" Edmonds, the most powerful on the list, was clearly running the show. The male gaze on the lives of the three sisters at the center of the show was demonstratively insensitive to the women characters in a manner that someone who wrote pop songs for a living would believe to be appropriate. Several examples of "proof" followed.

I raised my hand and explained that Babyface was able to negotiate an executive producer title on the series simply because he was the executive music producer of the feature film on which the series was based and agreed to write the theme song for the series. The student eyed me suspiciously and then replied, "That doesn't change my conclusions. Men are clearly in charge." The student was wrong. In fact, Edmonds had only visited the set for three days when he guest starred on the show. I, in fact, was "in charge"—a true hood feminist. However, I became quite curious. How could my work and my message have been decoded in this way? Thus began my interest in television studies, specifically production studies. I wanted to take advantage of my privileged position as a content creator to turn a critical and self-reflexive eye on the medium that employed me. The following year, I applied to the PhD program in critical studies (now the Cinema and Media Studies Program) at the UCLA School of Film, Television and Theater. I was interested in studying my workspace in a research method that anthropologist Deborah Reed-Danahay describes as "autoethnography"—an approach that acknowledges the connections between the personal and the cultural.[1] The autobiographical and self-reflexive nature of my research allows me to, as William M. Sughrua describes, use my experiences "as representative of a larger community."

It is as the executive producer and showrunner of the Netflix drama *First Kill* (2022) who began her career as a sitcom writer on the seventh season of *Family Matters* (1989–1998) that I approach this study of *The Game*'s journey from a traditional half-hour sitcom with a laugh track on The CW to its reboot as a "dramedy" on Paramount+. I watched *The Game* (CW, 2006–2009; BET, 2011–2015; Paramount+, 2021–2023) during its BET run and have known its creator, Mara Brock Akil, for over twenty years. With this chapter, I investigate Brock Akil's attempts to resist the traditional constraints of Black-themed sitcoms in pursuit of creative authenticity[2]—the ability to create stories based on the showrunner/head writer's vision of a world or environment, inhabited by characters with specific conflict, traits, and behavioral motivations—as opposed to writing a show overly determined by the sensibilities of the studio and outlet executives who oversee it. I argue that Brock Akil's journey was motivated by an attempt to redefine the boundaries of the Black-themed comedy subgenre. She desired to ground the experience of Black characters in a range of emotions that were not contained by artificially added laughter, whose use signaled to the audience that Black characters' challenges could be dismissed with humor. I also argue that, ultimately, Brock Akil's efforts were thwarted by The CW's position in a hegemonic system that used Black-themed sitcoms to build networks in the 1990s, only to abandon that audience for the more advertiser-coveted eighteen- to thirty-four-year-old White female viewer. As explicated by Amanda Lotz:

> In the 1990s, upstart networks added a new chapter to the already complicated history of Black sitcoms as their need to attract audiences led them to seek out groups underserved by ABC, CBS, and NBC. Targeting a Black niche audience yielded success for FOX with sitcoms and variety-comedies that offered a diversity of series dominated by Black actors and performers. . . . The representations of African Americans in these series have been the source of extensive academic debate (Bogle; Gray; Means Coleman; Zook), yet from an

institutional standpoint, FOX's mid-1990s strategy of intentionally counter-programming ethnically diverse representations against a successful slate of programming that neglected non-White audiences was quite successful. As the network gained in its competitive position, however, its programming shifted to target White audiences.[3]

Lotz's was an analysis of Fox Broadcasting Company; however, it is relevant here in that it describes a strategy that was also employed by The CW, and UPN and The WB before it. As a brief history, in 1995, Viacom and Chris-Craft Industries' United Television launched United Paramount Network (UPN) with *Star Trek: Voyager* as its flagship series. By 2000, the upstart network, as stated earlier, followed FOX's lead and began to heavily program Black-themed sitcoms as a means of growing its overall viewership. In 2006, it merged with The WB network, the Time Warner–Tribune partnership netlet—also launched in 1995 and employing a similar programming strategy—to become The CW.

Brock Akil's attempts to creatively question sitcom format norms by pushing the boundaries of acceptable story themes created a tension between The CW's previous identity and the new identity it desired and was actively shifting toward—a tension that ended with the network's cancellation of *The Game*. Eventually, the show would make its record-breaking cable debut on BET Networks. While Brock Akil found more creative freedom at the show's new home, its cancellation on network television was proof that Black-themed comedies had little value beyond their ability to build the networks that would go on to abandon them.

The Game was the first series I observed in an autoethnographic production study that is the foundation of my dissertation research, an exploration of the creative culture in the comedy series writers' room. During *The Game's* third season on The CW, Brock Akil granted me permission to observe the writers' room. My goal was a critical analysis of a writing staff's creative workspace on a series on which I had never been employed, from the vantage point of someone who is intimately familiar with how stories are broken in this space.

With no hesitation or conditions, Brock Akil agreed to my request. "Why not? It'll be interesting to see what you uncover," she said matter-of-factly. Brock Akil and I had been friends since meeting as writers on *Moesha* (UPN, 1996–2001). Brock Akil is self-assured, easily discusses difficult subjects, and enjoys a healthy debate in her writers' rooms. When I commented on how comfortable the writers were with challenging each other's ideas, she replied, "How else are you going to get to the good stuff?" One might argue that she was forthcoming with me because we have a long-standing relationship.

However, I had witnessed her exhibit the same traits before we were friends, when the *Moesha* writing staff gathered for the first time over two decades earlier. She is naturally gregarious and thoughtful. She trusted me and did not appear to have much concern for what I might learn. The Hawthorne effect—a change in behavior due to an awareness of being observed—appeared to be minimal.[4]

I observed the writers for two weeks. My access included eight- to twelve-hour workdays, while the writing staff was breaking stories for the season's episodes. I was allowed to remain in the conference room during nonworking and working lunch hours. I also accompanied the writing staff to the production stage three times per week for producers, studio, and network rehearsals (also called "run-thrus") and on production days when the show was shot. Not including Brock Akil, the writing staff was composed of eight racially and ethnically diverse men and women who ranged in age from late twenties to late forties. In 2009, when I initially investigated *The Game*, it was in its third, and what would be its final, season on The CW. Both *Girlfriends* (UPN, 2000–2008) and *The Game* were produced by Brock Akil's Happy Camper Productions and Kelsey Grammer's Grammnet Productions under television production deals with Paramount Studios.

Several months after my study, *The Game* was canceled on The CW. According to Brock Akil, at the end of the season, she met Dawn Ostroff, The CW's president of entertainment, to discuss Brock Akil's ideas for turning the half-hour show into a one-hour drama. The network had recently shuttered its comedy development department and was focusing on one-hour dramas, as was every other network by the end of the 2000s. Brock Akil saw the writing on the wall and was formulating a plan to keep *The Game* on the air. She believed she had done an excellent job of sharing her vision for the one-hour version of the series. The show had slowly abandoned the traditional multicamera sitcom format for one that was more of a hybrid. It was no longer shot in front of a studio audience, as most broad sitcoms are. While it still incorporated broad comedic moments it also tackled dramatic stories.

In her seminal study of Fox Broadcasting's early programming strategies, Kristal Brent Zook outlines four key elements of Black-produced television. The fourth of these is "The struggle for drama," a marked desire for complex characterizations and emotionally challenging subject matter. Whereas traditional sitcom formats demanded a "joke a page," many Black productions of the 1980s and '90s resisted such norms by consciously and unconsciously, "Drafting dramatic episodes, with less explicit storylines, unresolved endings, and increasingly complex characters, those 'dramedies' allowed for exploration of painful in-group memories and experiences"[5]—dramedies such as *Moesha, Roc* (FOX, 1991–1994), and *South Central* (FOX, 1994).

This "struggle for drama" was evident with *The Game's* writing staff. Brock Akil encouraged the show's writers not to feel obligated to end every scene with a "button" (a joke at the end of the scene). Further, the show attempted to go beyond struggling at the boundaries. Brock Akil wanted to break new ground. Rather than being a half-hour comedy that sometimes tackled dramatic stories, she wanted her show to be a half-hour drama with occasional comedy when it suited the story. However, after programming multiple Black-themed comedies to draw Black viewers and a footing in the broadcast television space, The CW no longer needed the audience whose households historically watch more television. In a programming strategy Alfred Martin calls "Fox Formula 2.0," The CW (and FOX before it), created "programming targeted at 'urban' (which is always code for black) viewers by featuring shows with black stars, almost all of them comedies. . . . Once they [The CW and its predecessors UPN and The WB] became a force to be reckoned with . . . black viewers, and hence 'black shows' were no lo longer needed and were unceremoniously dumped from the network."[6] Three years after its debut, The CW shuttered the programming that had been instrumental in the network's launch and discontinued its comedy programming all together.

In the Beginning: The CW Seasons

In the fall of 2006, *The Game*, a multicamera, half-hour comedy, premiered as the anchor on The CW's Sunday night schedule of prime-time Black-themed comedies. It was the only new comedy to be added to the network's fall schedule that year and one of only two series that were not inherited from either UPN or The WB.[7] The Sunday lineup included Chris Rock's *Everybody Hates Chris* (The CW, 2005–2009), the Will Smith–produced *All of Us* (UPN, 2003–2007), and the first series Brock Akil created, *Girlfriends*, the Traci Ellis Ross starrer from which *The Game* had been a spin-off. As originally conceived, *The Game* starred Tia Mowry as a first-year medical student who forgoes acceptance into Johns Hopkins University School of Medicine to follow her boyfriend, a rookie professional football player (Pooch Hall), to San Diego, California. Other cast members included Brittany Daniel, Coby Bell, Hosea Chanchez, and Wendy Raquel Robinson.

In the 2006–2007 broadcast season, *The Game's* first on The CW, it averaged 4.35 million viewers. In its second season, both *The Game* and *Gossip Girl* (2007–2012), in its inaugural season, averaged 2.35 million viewers. Considering the difference in the network's promotion of the two shows, their

Fig. 11.1 Members of the original cast of *The Game* on The CW (*left to right*: Pooch Hall, Tamera Mowry, Hosea Sanchez, Wendy Raquel Robinson, Brittany Daniel, and Colby Bell).

identical average viewership is significant. In an interview about her show's move to BET, Brock Akil said BET was presenting her show with an opportunity that it never had at The CW. "What we never had before was the marketing component to support the show."[8]

A disgruntled Brock Akil publicly shared her complaints about The CW's lack of marketing support for her show. Although *The Game* often outperformed *Gossip Girl*, the latter series was heavily promoted by the network. It immediately became the show that defined what the network desired to be—young, rich, indulgent, and white. The press coverage of *Gossip Girl* was overwhelmingly positive. The City of New York supported and promoted the show and its setting, Manhattan's Upper East Side. By its second season, *New York* magazine had declared *Gossip Girl* the greatest teen drama of all time, suggesting, "The best, and most addictive, aspect of *Gossip Girl* is that the delectable tangle of jealousy, loyalty, confusion, and general teen angst coils and recoils at such a frenetic pace. . . . The show has resurrected the potential for scripted dramas to be effective social satire—to present a world more accurately than a 'reality' program can."[9] "Summer's been good to this girl," claimed *Entertainment Weekly*, which awarded the series its highest grade of A.[10]

According to Ostroff, with shows like *Gossip Girl* and the remake of *Beverly Hills 90210*, "we knew going in there were hurdles to climb. . . . But when we discovered that our sweet spot was young women, we focused on building that demographic."[11] In January 2012, during *Gossip Girl*'s fifth season, after the show had produced its one hundredth episode, New York City's Mayor Michael Bloomberg declared January 26, 2012, "Gossip Girl Day." He visited the set of the show and proclaimed, "While *Gossip Girl* is drawing fans in with its plot twists, the show also attracts many of them to visit New York, contributing to our incredible 50.5 million visitors last year. In fact, the economic impact of *Gossip Girl* and other television shows and films that are made in New York really can be felt directly in all five boroughs. The 100th episode of Gossip Girl is a real landmark, and I want to congratulate the show's cast and crew."[12]

With the success of shows like *Gossip Girl*, The CW was ready to redefine itself. No matter how compelling Brock Akil believed her retooling presentation to be, "no amount of tweaking could have turned the show's cast members into moody, misbehaving teenagers. . . . Or make them white."[13] As Lotz points out, "As a result of increasing segregation of sitcom cast composition, as well as the dichotomization of networks airing series with Black and White casts, viewership of series also became segregated."[14] As she also states, scheduling and promoting to segregated audiences becomes an institutional challenge, "Amidst a schedule designed to appeal to White teen girls and boys, respectively."[15]

After being bandied about on the schedule from Monday to Sunday to Friday nights, *The Game* finally dropped to a 1.75 million viewer average in its third season. One of the show's uber fans, Stacey Mattocks, created a Facebook fan page in the early days of the show. She became more active when she heard rumblings about the show's possible cancellation. However, neither the fan page nor the cast's online campaign persuaded The CW, and the series was canceled in 2009. Ms. Mattocks believed The CW had neglected the show, partly by moving it into less favorable time slots.[16] Ms. Mattocks's Facebook page "continued to gain fans, and when BET ordered new episodes of the show last May, it embraced her page—with three million fans—instead of creating one. The channel [was paying] her to run the fan page parttime, in addition to her job at an insurance company in Florida."[17]

THE MIDDLE: THE BET YEARS

Nearly a year after the show was canceled by The CW, *The Game*'s first three seasons on The CW were licensed to BET, which did not immediately categorize the show as a comedy or drama. BET's website simply described it as a series that follows "the lives of professional football players and their significant others as they navigate fame, family and friends."[18] As a network

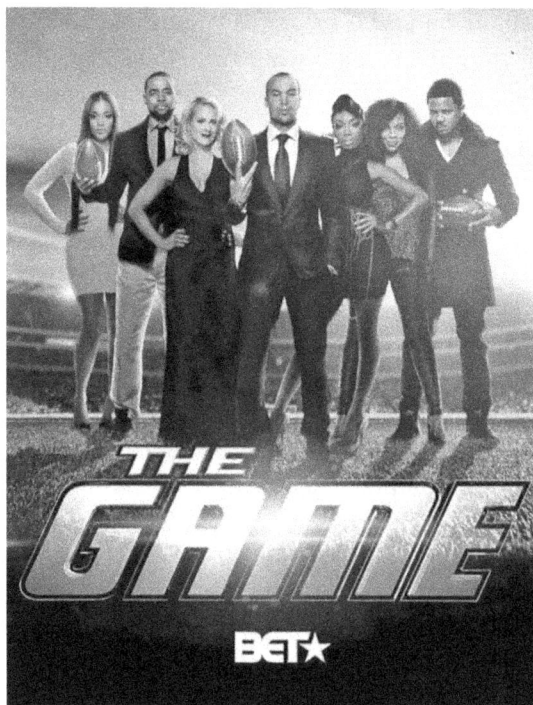

Fig. 11.2 Promotional image of the cast of *The Game* on BET reflected its more hybrid tone, mixing comedy and drama (*left to right*: Lauren London, Pooch Hall, Brittany Daniel, Colby Bell, Brandy Norwood, Wendy Raquel Robinson, and Hosea Sanchez).

committed to programming for Black viewers, the boundaries of what a half-hour Black-themed show was were more fluid because those boundaries were not being defined through a mainstream (white) outlet.

The Game is not the first series to be canceled by one network and picked up by another. However, it is one of the first to find itself more popular in syndicated repeats after being canceled by its original network. Much like *The Family Guy* (FOX, 1999–), whose viewers made it a hit in reruns on cable's Comedy Central channel and the second-highest-selling television series DVD in history, *The Game* had fans who did not merely give a struggling show another chance.[19] In 2009, fans gave the show its first ratings hope when BET began airing repeats of the episodes that had initially aired on The CW. BET viewership of the old episodes was consistent and became instrumental in the record-breaking viewership of the show's first new episode on the channel, nearly three years after it was canceled by The CW. Although The CW averaged 60 percent more viewers in prime time than BET, *The Game* immediately garnered higher Nielsen ratings on its new network.[20]

Approximately six months before the show's debut, BET began its traditional marketing campaign. On-air promotions announcing *The Game*'s return to television began appearing on BET, including a promotion filmed on a college football field depicting the cast strutting through the opening of the stadium's tunnel, flanked by enthusiastic viewers wildly applauding the show's return. However, it is likely that the dedication of one fan, who had been rooting for the show since its debut on The CW, made the biggest impact on *The Game*'s newfound success.

After the first three seasons of the show (The CW years) did so well on BET, the network negotiated with *The Game*'s parent company, CBS, to develop new episodes of the series. The show's physical production moved from Los Angeles to Atlanta, and its BET premiere was announced at the April 2010 Upfronts.[21] On January 11, 2011, in its fourth season, its first on BET, *The Game* returned to television and garnered a cable viewership record-breaking 7.7 million viewers.[22] The series was immediately renewed for a fifth season (twenty-two episodes), which premiered on January 10, 2012. At the 2012 BET Upfronts in April 2012, the network revealed that *The Game* had been renewed for a sixth season.[23]

How did *The Game* manage to garner cable viewership record-breaking ratings? In acknowledging the competitive role reality television plays in programming in an interview with the *New York Times*, Salim Akil, the series' in-house director and Brock Akil's husband, acknowledged that he and his wife were mindful of how times had changed. "The digital age, YouTube, reality TV—everything is now, in the moment, in the second," said S. Akil.[24] This realization on the part determined the press campaign. In addition to traditional marketing placement, BET bet heavily on advertising the show on the home pages of AOL, YouTube, and social media sites. Research showed that much like television viewership, Blacks overindexed as early adopters of most forms of social media. The gamble paid off, leading to the cable channel viewing record.

While moving to BET may have afforded Brock Akil more creative freedom, the most significant challenge she faced as *The Game*'s executive producer–showrunner was a budgetary one. When *The Game* moved to BET, due to budget constraints, the individual episodes would no longer be produced over a five-day week. Instead, each episode was shot in three days, alleviating two full production days from the process. This new system included a table reading (cast members reading the script, for the first time, around a conference table) of the show on day one, rehearsals in the afternoon of that same day, and shooting the show on days two and three. In a traditional network setting, the table read happens on day one. There are light rehearsals for the rest of that day. Additional rehearsals occur on days two and three. Day four is used to block and light the show for cameras and the show is performed and recorded in front of a studio audience on the evening of the fifth day. Sometimes, elaborate or lengthy scenes are preshot before the performance in front of an audience. A series that has aired for several seasons and becomes a well-oiled machine will often condense the production schedule to a four-day week. On the fifth day, the actors are on a one-day hiatus (day off), and the writers can work uninterrupted by the needs of production. However, in a system where an episode is produced every three days, the production process is strained significantly. Writers are on a tighter schedule to produce scripts, the department heads have less time to prep episodes, and the actors have less rehearsal time.

"We are all blessed to be working. This time last year, our show was canceled, and we were all sad to leave the people with whom we'd become a family, and worse, we were all looking for work. No, the schedule is not easy. It's hard. But at least we're working," said Wendy Raquel Robinson, one of the stars of the series when I asked her for her thoughts on shifting from The CW to BET.[25] However, the writers continued to work in Los Angeles, although the series was being produced in Atlanta, which was also done as a financial consideration. As many states have done to compete with foreign countries that offer tax breaks to incentivize US film and television production, Georgia now offers a 30 percent tax incentive to film and television projects. "I know it will get better as we go forward, but right now, being in LA, with the show shooting in Atlanta, we feel disconnected from it," said Kenya Barris, writer–consulting producer, about the new workflow. Lengthy rehearsals and the luxury of rewriting until it was right had no place in the new paradigm.

According to Brock Akil, the initial budget at BET was approximately 20 percent less than the episodic budget the show enjoyed at The CW. However, after the show premiered to record-breaking basic cable numbers and continued to do well, the budget slowly "crept up a little," according to Brock Akil, but still compared unfavorably to its past budget. "And then there are the realities of moving the show [from Los Angeles] with the added costs that come with travel and getting a new labor force up to speed. Initially, this process costs the show a lot of money in overtime," said Brock Akil.[26]

The realities of the creative freedom/financial constraints paradigm the show was forced to navigate also included a smaller writing staff. Fewer writers meant that all writers, regardless of seniority—trainees to coexecutive producers—have more responsibilities. For example, on a major network hit comedy with a dozen writers, a trainee or staff writer (entry-level writing staff positions) might be expected to pitch jokes but not to break a cohesive story; on a show with a smaller budget, trainees and staff writers are expected to contribute more ideas of every kind, not only jokes. Midlevel writers (coproducers and producers) might be expected to take on more supervisory responsibilities (approving wardrobe, meeting with the music composer to discuss the score). Upper-level writers (supervising producers, coexecutive producers) might be expected to competently run *the room* when called on because the showrunner has been called into meetings with the studio or network, as opposed to simply taking a break until the showrunner returns to the writers' room.

Brock Akil had given up the traditional multicamera shooting structure partway through the show's tenure on The CW. There was no studio audience. In the producers' efforts to utilize a hybrid visual style—a cross between a multicamera and single-camera production—the show was shot on a "block and shoot" schedule.[27] This allows the writers more creative freedom and the opportunity to reinvent the show's format. Consequently, the show's storytelling became more dramatic and ambitious. While its visual aesthetic often mimicked a brightly lit sitcom, the content was more dramatic. This led to a disconnect for some fans, who complained that the show had changed since its final season on CW. The producers heard the criticism but remained proud of the work. "The fans have taken a ride with us. . . . Our team, cast, crew, and writers left it all on the field. People will say what they want to say, but we did it," said Brock Akil.[28]

During its first season on BET (its fourth season on television) *The Game* eventually settled into an average of about 3 million viewers per episode, a far cry from 7.7 million BET debut, but a great number in the land of fractured cable audiences. The show was the number-one scripted cable sitcom among adults eighteen to forty-nine (the coveted advertiser demographic) for the five years it aired on the channel outlet.[29]

The End: Back to The CW

In December 2019, thirteen years after the show helped launch The CW, *The Game* was on its way back to the network that had originally broadcast the series. Brock Akil's agents and lawyers had initiated discussions with The CW regarding the show's return to the broadcast network while it was in its sixth and final season at BET (the show's ninth season, overall). The CW's president, Mark Pedowitz, was slow to come around to the idea until the network's longtime current (as of this writing) programs executive, Traci Blackwell, aggressively championed the show's return. Blackwell and Brock Akil had started their careers together—Blackwell as a junior executive assistant, Brock Akil as an entry-level production assistant. Blackwell had always believed her network had unceremoniously dumped *The Game* without a proper opportunity for a finale and convinced Pedowitz that bringing the show back to The CW was the right way to correct this wrong. Eventually, Pedowitz decided that the show deserved a second chance. However, this had taken a while; Brock Akil had gone on to executive produce The CW's *Black Lightning* (2018–2021) and create her next series, *Love Is* (2018–2019), for OWN. Given her schedule, she decided to engage a writing partner to assist with the development of *The Game's* hour-long reboot. Together, Brock Akil and Devon Greggory, who was on Brock Akil's writing staff on *Being Mary Jane* (2013–2019), would write the reboot of *The Game*. The new one-hour drama would see the series setting move from San Diego, California, to Baltimore, Maryland, to give it an East Coast flavor. Several of the original cast members would either star or guest star as the show's out-of-touch old-timers determined to help a bunch of pompous tyros navigate the complex world of professional football on and off the field.

By late January 2020, several media outlets were reporting that after the delivery of the pilot script, The CW had made the decision not to go forward with the reenvisioned CBS Studios–produced show. According to Deadline. com, The CW was not enamored of the creative direction of the new show and offered to redevelop the series again.[30] However, Brock Akil said "I felt comfortable, strongly so, about what I delivered. That was my vision. Asking me to redevelop it meant that [The CW] didn't share my vision, so we parted ways."[31] The creator-showrunner's unreserved stance points to the tension between Brock Akil's desire for tonal and narrative authenticity and the limitations of Black-themed broadcast network shows. Her creative need for situational authorship, negotiated or not, had been evident since the show's solid yet embattled three-year run on The CW.[32] The opportunity to revisit the series as a one-hour drama appealed to Brock Akil because it provided her an opportunity to go beyond the limitations of the rules and rituals associated with the sitcom format, particularly for Black-themed half-hour comedies. From *Amos 'n Andy* (1951–1953) to *Julia* (1968–1971), from *Good Times* (1974–1979) to *The Cosby Show* (1984–1992), Black-themed sitcoms have had the sociopolitical burden of socially, economically, and politically representing the "Black experience" for a Black audience while, conversely, depicting and reinforcing the meaning of "Blackness" for mainstream America. Historically, whether the images were too Black, too stereotypical, or not Black ("authentic") enough, the constraints of the format have served as boundaries and borders, or what Alfred Martin calls "representational practices for Black-cast sitcoms," to contain the meaning of Blackness for mainstream audiences.[33]

In twenty years as an executive producer or coexecutive producer, with the exception of three series on BET and *Soul Food* on Showtime, the shows

I have produced have been supervised by white executives. Who Black characters should be are often determined by non-Black decision-makers with little or no knowledge of what Black audiences might respond to. As Martin points out, "This lack of diversity suggests (other than a real problem with Hollywood's employment practices and pipelines) that Black viewers are imagined in a way that may be out of step with how they exist in fact. These viewers are likely wholly different than the cardboard cutouts that industry executives imagine. As Larry Gross suggests, 'when groups or perspectives attain visibility, the manner of that representation will itself reflect the biases and interests of those elites who define the public agenda.'"[34]

Since the show's first placement on a television schedule, Brock Akil has been searching for the right to determine *The Game*'s artistic, political, and social relevance. When The CW rejected Brock Akil's and Greggory's one-hour pilot, it was a rejection of the writers' attempt to move beyond the limitations of the Black-cast sitcom format, in general, and the roles, rituals, and boundaries of the Black-themed comedy. Brock Akil's refusal to redevelop the one-hour drama script she delivered was a rejection of being in that box.

Epilogue: A Paramount+ Dramedy

One year after The CW rejected Brock Akil and Greggory's hour-long script format for a reboot of *The Game*, David Stapf, the president of CBS Studios, contacted Brock Akil to express interest in *The Game* for the newly relaunched Paramount+. Brock Akil said Paramount+ "wanted it to be more comedic than dramatic. That meant it was going to be a half-hour. And because it's streaming and you can have a full thirty-minutes versus the 19–21 minutes on broadcast, we felt it could work."[35]

The third incarnation of the series was executive produced by the Akils, Grammer, and showrunner Greggory. Although Brock Akil suggests that as a half-hour show, by definition it will be more comedic, the May 2021 press release announcing the show claimed the reboot "offers a modern-day examination of Black culture through the prism of pro football. The team will tackle racism, sexism, classism, and more as they fight for fame, fortune, respect, and love—all while trying to maintain their souls as they each play *The Game*."[36] At the time, Greggory confirmed that the series would not be comedydependent at Paramount+'s presentation at The Critics Association (TCA) event in August 2021. He explained that the new show would be a modern-day examination of racism, sexism, classism, and more. "We're going to come deep with some deep issues because 2021 is different than 2008," he said.[37] The disparity between Greggory's and Brock Akil's descriptions proves that Greggory believes himself to have successfully negotiated the

Fig. 11.3 Promotional image from *The Game*'s debut on Paramount+, this time as an hourlong dramedy, not a "straight" sitcom or comedy.

representational boundaries traditionally placed on Black-themed half-hour shows through branding the show a "dramedy" and publicly announcing that he would pursue subject matter usually reserved for serious dramas.

Brock Akil's comments demonstrate her skepticism about whether barriers can be broken in the subgenre's half-hour format, no matter what it is called. However, she also left room for Greggory's ability to redefine the space. "The entire experience is new for me. I support Devon's vision. It's not my vision and that has been the biggest transition for me. Letting go, allowing and making room for a new voice to emerge. It's part of my evolution as a 'super producer.'"[38]

By agreeing to allow Greggory to helm the creative management of the show alone, Brock Akil agreed to put its creative direction in someone else's hand—hands that are not the show's original creator's. For the first time since *The Game* originally aired on The CW, Brock Akil would not be struggling to break through boundaries to define the Black experience, and Greggory would be responsible for the reboot's creative vision. The series revival premiered on Paramount+ in November 2021. The second season premiered in December 2022 and was described on the Paramount+ website thusly: "The second season doubles the laughs and heightens the drama as the beloved characters and their relationships fight to survive the storms of change they face."[39] Despite Brock Akil's subversive attempts to battle network expectations of Black-themed shows, *The Game*'s journey was a circuitous onback to the studio that originally produced it, back to the format that launched it.

Felicia D. Henderson is creator of Emmy Award–nominated and three-time NAACP Image Award Best Drama winner *Soul Food*. She has written and produced many high-profile shows, including *Empire, Gossip Girl, Fringe, Everybody Hates Chris*, and *Moesha*. She is a PhD candidate in Media Studies at the University of California–Los Angeles.

NOTES

1. Deborah E. Reed-Danahay, *Auto/Ethnography: Rewriting the Self and the Social* (Oxford: Berg, 1997).

2. I purposely differentiate "Black sitcoms" and "Black-themed sitcoms." Black sitcoms are shows that simply have a Black lead actor but whose content is culturally, purposely, nonspecific to attract a mainstream, predominantly white audience. Black-themed sitcoms are ones in which the characters and content, for the most part, are purposely culturally and racially specific.

3. Amanda D. Lotz, "Segregated Sitcoms: Institutional Causes of Disparity among Black and White Comedy Images and Audiences," in *The Sitcom Reader: America Viewed and Skewed*, ed. M. Dalton and L. Linder, 136–50 (Albany: SUNY Press, 2005).

4. E. A. Spencer and K. Mahtani, "Hawthorne effect," Catalogue of Bias 2017, Sackett Catalogue of Bias Collaboration, accessed August 22, 2021, https://catalogofbias.org/biases /hawthorne-effect/. The original experiment to determine the proper amount of light in the Western Electric plant in Hawthorne, Illinois, in the 1920s was further studied in the 1950s. In reevaluating the study, researchers found that employees' productivity had increased simply because they were being watched.

5. Kristal Brent Zook, *Color by Fox: The Fox Network and the Revolution in Black Television* (New York: Oxford University Press, 1999), 5–9.

6. Alfred L. Martin, Jr., "FOX Formula 3.0? TBS, Cougar Town, and the Disappearing Televisual Black Body," *Antenna*, June 18, 2012, http://blog.commarts.wisc.edu/2012/06/18 /fox-formula-3-0-tbs-cougar-town-and-the-disappearing-televisual-black-body/.

7. The United Paramount Network (UPN) and the WB (Warner Bros. network) were the fifth and sixth broadcast networks to begin broadcasting schedules (ABC, CBS, NBC, and FOX are the four that came before them). In 2006, the two merged and became the CW, a joint venture between Paramount Studios (now CBS Corp.) and Warner Bros. Studios.

8. Trevor Kimball, "*The Game*: Season Four Starts on BET in January 2011," Canceled & Renewed TV Shows, *TV Series Finale*, October 12, 2010, https://tvseriesfinale.com/tv-show /the-game-season-four-bet-18759/.

9. Jessica Pressler and Chris Rovzar, "The Genius of Gossip Girl," *New York Magazine*, April 18, 2008, http://nymag.com/arts/tv/features/46225/index1.html.

10. "Gossip Girl Reviews at Metacritic," *Metacritic*, September 1, 2008, http://www .metacritic.com/tv/shows/gossipgirlseason2?q=gossip%20girl.

11. Marc Berman, "The CW Has Some Bright Spots, but Lingering Issues," *Adweek*, November 3, 2008, https://www.adweek.com/convergent-tv/cw-has-some-bright-spots -lingering-issues-110207/.

12. Sam Levin, "Mike Bloomberg Hangs with 'Gossip Girl' Cast," *Village Voice*, August 27, 2018, https://www.villagevoice.com/2012/01/26/mike-bloomberg-hangs-with-gossip-girl-cast/.

13. Jon Caramanica, "'Game' On: More Real Than Reality TV (Published 2011)," *New York Times*, February 4, 2013, http://www.nytimes.com/2011/01/09/arts/television/09game.html?_r=1&ref=television.

14. Lotz, "Segregated Sitcoms."

15. Ibid.

16. Brian Stelter, "'The Game' Is a Winner, Helped by BET Loyalists," *New York Times*, January 17, 2011, https://www.nytimes.com/2011/01/17/business/media/17bet.html.

17. Ibid.

18. BET homepage, show descriptions, accessed December 15, 2010, http://www.bet.com/shows.html.

19. Gloria Goodale, "Cult Fans Bring 'The Family Guy' Back to TV," *Christian Science Monitor*, April 22, 2005, http://www.csmonitor.com/2005/0422/p12s01-altv.html.

20. Stelter, "'The Game' Is a Winner, Helped by Bet Loyalists."

21. Jawn Murry, "The Game Sitcom's Return on BET," *AOL Black Voices*, accessed April 22, 2009, http://www.bvbuzz.com/2010/03/15/the-game-sitcoms-return-on-bet-nearly-finalized.

22. Kimball, "The Game: Season Four Starts on BET in January 2011."

23. Caramanica, "'Game' On: More Real than Reality TV (Published 2011)."

24. Ibid.

25. Wendy Raquel Robinson, interview with the author, May 27, 2012.

26. Mara Brock Akil, interview with the author, June 5, 2012.

27. *Block and shoot* refers to a shooting schedule whereby each scene is rehearsed and shot out of narrative order, much like the shooting schedule in feature films, one-hour dramas, and single-camera half-hour comedies. In general, multicamera half-hour comedies are taped before a studio audience. The show is rehearsed all week, and the entire episode is shot in narrative order. It is unusual to block-and-shoot a multicamera show, but it is done when the producers are attempting to facilitate a single-camera or "filmic" look on a multicamera show budget.

28. Emily Yahr, "'The Game' Is over and Everybody Won: How BET's Comedy Helped Make TV History," *Washington Post*, July 28, 2015, https://www.washingtonpost.com/lifestyle/style/changing-the-game-how-the-bet-comedy-helped-make-tv-history/2015/07/28/6245ed08-3546-11e5-94ce-834ad8f5c50e_story.html.

29. Ibid.

30. Nellie Andreeva, "'The Game' Reboot Not Going Forward at the CW," *Deadline*, January 31, 2020, https://deadline.com/2020/01/the-game-reboot-dead-not-going-forward-the-cw-1202847460/.

31. Mara Brock Akil, interview with the author, April 18, 2021.

32. *Situational authorship* is a term I coined to describe a system of authorship that considers the convergence of television format rules and rituals and how they influence the symbiotic relationship between content creators and buyers but neither falls back on ideas of individual authorship nor concedes that it is a product of the system.

33. Alfred Martin Jr., *The Generic Closet: Black Gayness and the Black-Cast Sitcom* (Bloomington: Indiana University Press, 2021), 183.

34. Ibid.

35. Mara Brock Akil, interview with the author, June 1, 2021.

36. Andrea Towers, "'The Game' Returns to TV after 6 Years with New and Old Cast Members," *EW*, May 13, 2021, https://ew.com/tv/the-game-returns-to-television-revival/.

37. Alexandra Del Rosario, "'The Game' Showrunner Devon Greggory Says Dramedy Needed 'an Opportunity to Reboot Itself': Paramount+ Sets Premiere Date—TCA," *Deadline*, August 31, 2021, https://deadline.com/2021/08/the-game-showrunner-devon-greggory

-says-dramedy-needed-an-opportunity-to-reboot-itself-paramount-sets-premiere-date
-tca-1234824603/.

38. Mara Brock Akil, interview with the author, June 1, 2021.

39. Paramount+, "The Game Season Two Kicks of Dec 15 on Paramount+," posted October 21, 2022, https://www.paramountplus.com/shows/the-game-2021/news/1010495/the-game
-season-2-kicks-off-dec-15-on-paramount-plus/.

12

"LOOK AT ME!"

Jackie's Back, Lifetime, and the Production of Black Camp

Alfred L. Martin Jr. and Ken Feil

Lifetime, from its 1984 launch, successfully used its original films to tar-get what was considered a "niche" audience: upscale white women, and white women in general.[1] However, by July 1999, Lifetime's then–executive vice president Dawn Tarnofsky-Ostroff informed *Cable World* that the net-work was engaging with material understood as "too controversial for the broadcast networks."[2] Slightly veering from its upscale white women core audience, Tarnofsky-Ostroff pointed to original films like *Jackie's Back* (Lifetime, 1999) to exemplify the kinds of "risks" the network was taking in its attempt to reach Black female viewers as networks like FOX, UPN, and The WB had done throughout the late 1980s and 1990s.[3] As scholars like Jen-nifer Fuller have argued, in the 1990s and 2000s cable channels often used programming with Black protagonists and costars to mark the quality of programing through "edgy" and "risky" content, like *Any Day Now* (Life-time, 1998–2002), which centered racial tensions—a marked departure from Lifetime's damsel-in-distress fare.[4] As if responding to Tarnofsky-Ostroff's comments to *Cable World* two decades later, *Jackie's Back* star Jenifer Lewis declared, "Here's the thing, [Lifetime audiences] weren't ready. It was before its time, darling. They weren't ready for that. They weren't ready for me nor were they ready for the drag queen coming out. . . . It was before its time."[5] Lewis's statement gestures toward how risk, quality, camp, and Blackness converged in the production and reception of Lifetime's *Jackie's Back*.

Jackie's Back premiered on June 14, 1999. Cowriters Mark Alton Brown and Dee La Duke, a white gay man and white woman who have been friends with Lewis since their college days, created a mockumentary chronicling the career and most recent comeback of Jackie Washington, a fictional pop/soul diva from Kinloch, Missouri—Lewis's hometown. *Jackie's Back* immediately and deliberately blurs many lines: between star and character, quality and camp, and Black popular culture and white mainstream as well as gay culture. *Jackie's Back* was risky, something Lewis, Brown, and La Duke relished.

From the first frame, *Jackie's Back* innovates camp, which Steven Cohan defines as "a queer recognition of the incongruities arising from the cultural regulation of gender and sexuality,"[6] by committing to a Black camp parody of the quality television Lifetime courted and the whiteness underpinning quality television discourses. *Jackie's Back* opens overflowing with parody of the cultural codes of whiteness and quality. The introductory classical horn strains mimic Masterpiece Theater's (PBS, 1971–) theme and signify the alleged seriousness of the proceedings, and so does the mise-en-scène, a palatial hall with polished wood walls and embroidered furniture. A title appears: "Jackie's Back: Portrait of a Diva." Edward Whatsett St. John (Tim Curry) introduces himself in an obnoxiously Anglicized accent and then says, "When I was first approached to make a documentary about Jackie Washington, I thought they meant the legendary baseball player who famously broke the color barrier. Once I was set straight, I was compelled to ask, who is Jackie Washington?"

Following a brief montage of clips tracing Jackie's career from "former child star" to adult "pop diva" and then "down-and-out boozing, has-been," the film segues from the repressive, constipated, PBS tone to a jubilant, soulful "Yeah!" that announces the theme song, which blends gospel musical stylings alongside diva worship. A cavalcade of stars, including divas Liza Minnelli, Diahann Carroll, and Dolly Parton, situate Jackie Washington in a fictional pantheon of pop culture goddesses while real-world music experts like *Soul Train* (syndicated, 1971–2006) host Don Cornelius and singers, including Taylor Dayne and Melissa Etheridge, help *Jackie's Back* blur the line between fact and fiction. In fact, Cornelius suggests that there were three great child singing stars—Michael Jackson, Stevie Wonder, and Jackie Washington—before going on to say, "I might get grief for saying this, but Jackie had the most raw talent." Thus, *Jackie's Back* quickly identifies the target of its pastiche and parody: "stuffy" documentaries, the institution of celebrity, and Jackie Washington and her less-than-stellar stardom.

As a Black camp celebrity diva, Jackie also materializes as a "morally questionable" antihero. Similar to the "great white men" of quality television

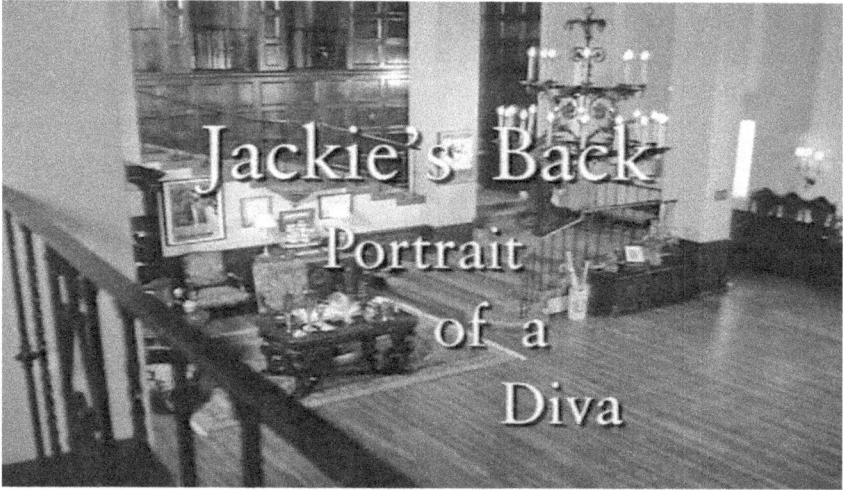

Fig. 12.1 *Jackie's Back* overflows with parody of the cultural codes of whiteness and quality, such as the opening travesty of PBS's *Masterpiece Theater*.

series like *The Sopranos* (HBO, 1999–2007), the diegesis positions Jackie as a generally unlikable, unsympathetic character. Thus, while scholars have rightly argued that antiheroes are infrequently women, when the female antihero emerges, she does not often "receive the same critical accolades and attention" as her male counterparts in quality TV.[7] Although some critics, like *Variety*'s David Kronke, commended *Jackie's Back* as "one of the more adventurous efforts" from Lifetime and praised Lewis's performance as "terrif," the film was not a ratings success for the network.[8] However, gesturing toward its resonance with Blackness and not necessarily "mainstream" notions of quality, *Jackie's Back* was nominated for an NAACP Image Award for Outstanding Television Movie/Mini-Series/Dramatic Special. That it lost to HBO's *Introducing Dorothy Dandridge* (HBO, 1999) starring Halle Berry, a lavish $9.2 million biopic about a real Black celebrity, hinted at how far Lewis and company diverged from perceptions of mainstream taste and quality television.

This chapter explores *Jackie's Back*'s engagement with and production of Black camp at the end of the twentieth century. Although camp is often understood as a white gay practice, an assumption perpetuated by Susan Sontag's colorblind dissection of "modern sensibility," Marlon B. Ross has more recently posited camp as among "the formal and material practices that mark sexual identity as a resource for racial identification and racial identity as a resource for sexual identification within and across historical moments within and across cultural traditions."[9] Using primary interviews with Lewis, Brown, and La Duke, we argue that Lewis incorporates camp as a "resource" to encode Blackness in *Jackie's Back*, a project with multiple consequences: opposing network television's presumptions about "quality," representations of Blackness, and constructions of audiences as well as materializing an open address to Black queer audiences. Inasmuch as camp typically concentrates on outdated culture, the Black camp of *Jackie's Back* and Jenifer Lewis remained ahead of its time for Lifetime audiences as well as the norms of TV production. The film's enduring significance for Black queer fans, to begin with, indicates the arbitrariness of ratings as a measure of value. *Jackie's Back* blazed a trail, moreover, for a television landscape in which Blackness and queerness surpassed the tokenizing, market-driven priorities of "edgy," "risky" product differentiation.

LIFETIME'S TURN TO BLACKNESS

On June 14, 1999, the day *Jackie's Back* debuted, Tarnofsky-Ostroff told *USA Today* that the network was "always looking for ways to diversify [its] movie franchise [. . . and *Jackie's Back*] was a way to [diversify its programming] that was really different and fun."[10] Lifetime was noticing a shift, as *USA Today* eventually reported in 2003, that basic cable channels were becoming "significantly more popular among Black viewers than non-Blacks."[11] Thus, Blackness became key to Lifetime's rebranding strategy. Also on June 14, an ad in *Broadcasting & Cable* featured Lewis in a publicity photo for the film alongside other Black actresses, including Halle Berry (the poster woman for the channel's *Intimate Portrait* [Lifetime, 1994–2005]) and Lorraine Toussaint and Annie Potts from *Any Day Now*.[12] Alongside Leanza Cornett, Kim Coles was also featured, the new replacement for Suzanne Whang in the female interracial duo top lining the second season of the late-night talk show *New Attitudes* (Lifetime, 1985–1991). These programming and casting examples, we argue, heralded Lifetime's commitment to the "risk" Blackness had come to signify within television programming and the media industries.

Part of Lifetime's turn to Blackness and cultivation of quality was its production of *Jackie's Back*. According to script cowriter Brown, the film's budget was $2 million, "which was a lot for television then. Nothing really for a full-length film, though."[13] While Brown suggests that the film's budget was small, it was on par with the $1 million per one-hour episode budget for Lifetime's quality program *Any Day Now*. Centering the network's engagement with "risky" and "edgy" Black content, Lifetime's VP for original movies Laurette Hayden "managed to get [*Jackie's Back*] through the network," Brown recalled, in addition to emphasizing both Lewis's influence and the

It's real.

LIFETIME WOMEN

ENTERTAINMENT
PERFORMANCE
INFORMATION
VALUE
STORIES
RATINGS
STARS
EXPERIENCE
DRAMAS
CONNECTION
COMEDIES
SUBSCRIBER SATISFACTION

Lifetime
Television for Women

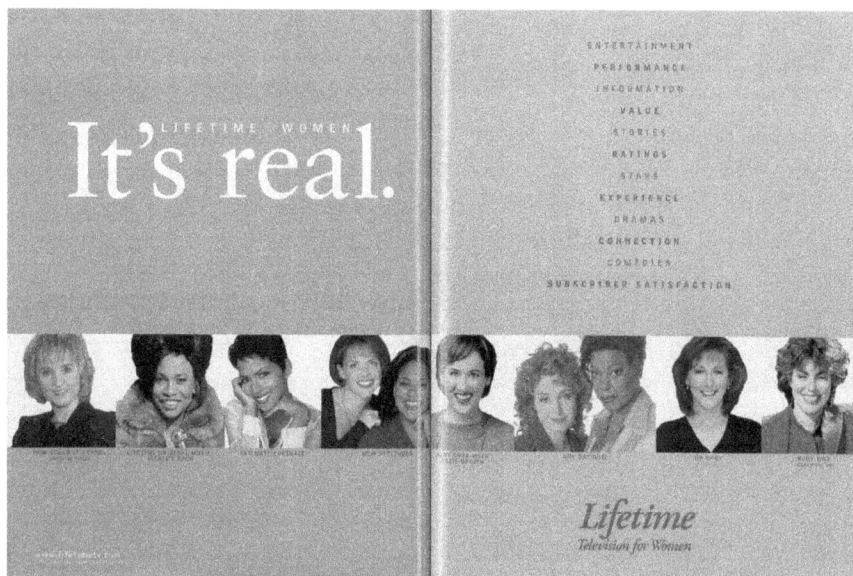

Fig. 12.2 Lifetime's June 14 ad in *Broadcasting & Cable* that telegraphs the network's turn to Black women as a key demographic. Programming and casting choices heralded Lifetime's commitment to the "risk" Blackness had come to signify within television programming and the media industries.

camp persona she had already cultivated: "I mean it was the most loosey-goosey pitch in the world because we just went in. I mean it was sort of a compendium of stuff we'd been talking about for years, and Jackie was sort of a composite of all of Jenifer's cabaret personas because Jenifer was always the diva, but the diva who ended up with egg on her face, but just kept going."[14]

Lewis similarly points to the ways networks, like FOX, UPN, and TBS, turn to Blackness when they are attempting to rebrand.[15] She observes how Hayden "was trying to build up Lifetime" at the time *Jackie's Back* was green-lit and concludes, "You know *Jackie's Back* had no business on Lifetime at all. Like zero, zero, the fuck? But that was what we could get. I wasn't a 'name,' Mark wasn't a 'name.' Barry [Cross, Lewis's then manager] didn't have the [industry] connections. So, we landed at Lifetime."[16] Without explicitly saying so, Lewis gestures toward the risk associated with *Jackie's Back*. Unlike Lifetime's *Any Day Now* (which had Annie Potts, famed for *Designing Women*, a series that had been running in syndication on the network), *Jackie's Back* did not have known talent, or as Lewis puts it, "a name." The only thing the made-for-TV film had was a known format: the female-centered telefilm, which in Lewis, Brown and La Duke's comedic camp treatment deviated even further from Lifetime's familiar territory. The film, particularly at $2 million, was a gamble for a network trying to stake its claim as a player in the original content business.

While *Jackie's Back* was generally well received by critics, the film did not necessarily connect with Lifetime's female viewer base—Black or otherwise. Salon.com's Joyce Millman listed the film as one of her "TV picks," but the last line of her review calls *Jackie's Back* "a diva-watcher's dream," a suggestion of the film's camp style and its appeal to gay men (and perhaps Black gay men specifically) rather than being "Television for Women."[17] In fact, when asked, Brown says the audience and fandom for *Jackie's Back*, particularly in its endurance post-Lifetime, was "gay men, African American [gay] men."[18] As a demographic group, Black gay men were decidedly not Lifetime's target even as the "Gay '90s" had resulted in *Spin City*'s (ABC, 1996–2002) Black gay character Carter Heywood, and millions of viewers were weekly watching the antics of the eponymous characters and costars on *Will & Grace* (NBC, 1998–2006; 2017–2020). Thus, as La Duke suggests, the film "started and ended comedy for Lifetime."[19]

JACKIE'S BACK!: PORTRAIT OF A BLACK CAMP DIVA

In trying to understand *Jackie's Back*'s reception and ratings failure, Lewis located classic elements of camp as well as historically hidden variations. "It was before its time, darling," proclaims Lewis, who punctuates her own affinity with camp-diva fabulousness through the rejoinder "darling" simultaneous to inverting conventional camp wisdom.[20] Susan Sontag famously opined that "so many of the objects prized by camp taste are old-fashioned, out-of-date, démodé."[21] Sontag stresses temporal distance, which produces "detachment" and enables camp fans to revalue an old cultural failure; "Time liberates the work of art from moral relevance" and from "banality. . . . What was banal can, with the passage of time, become fantastic."[22] Considering Lewis's long-standing career as a cabaret star and Hollywood character actor, she was already "fantastic," an intentional camp subject rather than the obliviously camp works and people Sontag prefers, in addition to being "relevant," a Black woman starring in a comedy film on Lifetime. "They weren't ready for me nor were they ready for the drag queen coming out," Lewis continues.[23] Although "the drag queen" she refers to is Jackie Washington's costume designer Kim (Loren Freeman), in light of Lewis's own over-the-top, stylized performance of the irrepressible, incorrigible diva Jackie, it would be easy to assume she was referring to her own inner drag queen "coming out," particularly because Brown suggests that Lewis is, in fact, "a big drag queen."[24]

Far from being démodé, *Jackie's Back* failed to garner high ratings in 1999 because, we argue, it was too new—that is, too Black, too queer, and too campy. For Lifetime audiences used to heroine-in-distress fare like *Mother, May I Sleep with Danger* (1998, dir. Melanie Aitkenhead), it was too Black. For those expecting the network's new Black programming to be quality—that is, serious, realistic, and socially driven, like *Any Day Now*—*Jackie's Back* was too campy and too queer. If "Lifetime was not ready" for Lewis and *Jackie's Back*, the Black queer cult following they have both accrued since 1999 attest to José Esteban Muñoz's formulation for queer camp, in which "failed visionaries, oddballs, and freaks . . . remind queers that indeed they always live out of step with straight time" and whose work presents "a place and time in which potentiality flourished and was extinguished. Yet its example nonetheless promises a return, a reanimation, in a future time and place, a not-yet-here."[25] The criteria of "straight time"—measuring the audience ratings for the film's initial broadcast in 1999—deemed *Jackie's Back!* a failure, but the Black queer reception of the film, enduring and increasing over two decades, effectively locates the "potentiality" of the "not-yet-here" in Lewis's camp antihero and the film's production of camp. Gesturing toward the queer time in which *Jackie's Back* existed, in 2019 Lewis hosted a twentieth-anniversary celebration for the film alongside drag queen (and webseries costar) Shangela in Los Angeles, confirmation of the "return" and "reanimation" of this camp film "failure."

Racquel J. Gates speaks to the historical erasure of "negative" Black popular cultural texts, especially comedies like *Jackie's Back*, and asks, "How, then, are we to 'see' the meaning created in and by negative texts, when society—whether mainstream white culture or black respectability culture—has repeatedly obfuscated or dismissed it?"[26] Gates likens negative texts to camp, in which queer creative "work is disguised as something else, such as stereotypes," a critique of cultural erasure that recalls Muñoz's admonition against the "investment in the 'positive image.'"[27] Correlating both scholars' arguments, *Jackie's Back* personifies a negative camp text, a failure in straight time, that showcases Black and queer and feminist work in its production of camp.

Alongside upsetting the norms of white, liberal-feminist drama that had become Lifetime's calling card and considering Lewis's departure from the camp "common sense" prescribed by Sontag, *Jackie's Back* challenged the white, gay, male hegemony of camp.[28] "Of course it's campy!" exclaims Lewis about *Jackie's Back*, and as she details why, including its casting and the absurdity of its premise, never again repeats the word.[29] The lack of importance Lewis places on the word *camp* recalls Marlon B. Ross's assertion about camp as a historical "resource" for Black queer identification and "how subjects self-consciously identify the ostensible sources of their cultural resources reveals as much about the ideology of resorting to such a selective narrative as about the politics of cultural identification in general."[30] Without reducing her choices to the "selective narrative" of white gay camp, Lewis's dexterous parody of divadom as well as her fearless self-parody speak to Ross's exploration of camp "invective" and its historical, practical resonance with Black cultural practices such as the dozens.[31] "Camp should not be identified solely with white urban homosexuality," Ross avers, "for black homosexuals' inventive use of identity invective reveals a specific interaction between the dozens and camp so indeterminate that defining where one 'site' or 'role' begins and the other ends in their verbal contests would be absolutely impossible."[32] For example, when Lewis recalls how Liza Minnelli becomes involved in the film, an outrageous anecdote unfolds involving one of the reigning divas of canonical white camp, Minnelli, in addition to Lewis's camp zeal to seize the same mantle as well as blur "life" and "theater." "I went to Liza's house. I went to a party of hers. I was drunk as a skunk and everybody was singing. Honey, I was just like, 'Let me get my chords around those notes.' . . . I wouldn't sit down. And I went in there, I went in the room and I came back of course, and told Mark, 'Oh, honey, I picked up Liza's Oscar.' That's how that went in there. I didn't steal her Oscar, but I was playing with it. And I probably told him, 'Man, I'm stealing this shit.'"[33] In the film, the camp invective is escalated when Liza tells this story and, after recounting how Jackie "sang, and she sang, and she sang . . . and sang," reveals that Jackie absconded with her Oscar.

On the one hand, camp remains central to Lewis, from positioning herself alongside Minnelli to her intimate collaborations with gay, white creatives throughout her career. On the other hand, what matters at least as much to her, in the reception of *Jackie's Back* as well as her ascent to stardom as "The Mother of Black Hollywood"—the title of her memoir—is her affinity for Black queer fans. As she commented, "We're gay Black men, I think we've hit it. Look, I'm going to tell you and put it in a nutshell. Gay Black men love me because I love gay Black men. That's the end of the goddamn story. We share the same hopes and dreams. We share the same struggle. That's all, darling. Don't need to elaborate. I think you understand."[34] In collaboration with writers Brown and La Duke, in addition to songwriter Marc Shaiman, director Robert Townsend, and a cavalcade of celebrity friends making cameos, Lewis enlists camp as a stylistic resource for reaching Lifetime audiences in 1999, a strategy that fails commercially but succeeds in locating Black queer audiences who identify with Lewis and the film's camp aesthetic. Referring to *Jackie's Back* as a "Divatastic Cult Classic" in 2019, writer Lester Fabian

Brathwaite celebrated the film as the product of Lewis's camp vision and, despite diminutive ratings, an enduring success: "Despite her minor splash in the summer of 1999, Jackie Washington lives on. Each July 15, fans of the movie commemorate Jackie Washington Day."[35] Brathwaite never directly identifies the Black queer following for the film, but he clarifies this affinity through his own presence as a Black queer cultural critic.

Jackie's Back commits to a kind of camp resignification of Lifetime's *Intimate Portrait*, a "Portrait of the Diva" that magnifies all the excesses of egoistic performance associated with the word, and a performance of the diva that Lewis savors through parody that she unflinchingly aims at herself. The film includes a sequence in which celebrities are asked what the word *diva* means. It begins as a salute to Jackie Washington with Penny Marshall declaring "Jackie is a diva" and Cornelius saying, "I think if you look in the dictionary for the word *diva* you probably see Jackie's picture." It quickly segues into an attack on Jackie's character with Eve Marie Saint arguing that "a diva is a very spoiled singer who lies . . . like Jackie." Lastly, Jackie's sister Ethel (Whoopi Goldberg, who filmed *Jackie's Back* during breaks from filming *Girl, Interrupted* [1999, dir. James Mangold]) says a diva is a "dumb, ignorant, vicious asshole. And if that's what Jackie calls herself, she's right." Thus, Jackie Washington emerges as a camp antihero within *Jackie's Back* because for all her fabulousness, no one really seems to like her much.

Jackie Washington blurs undetectably with Lewis's cabaret personas and her autobiography but also acts as a loving send-up of Black divas. Ross distinguishes the kind of invective that produces flat mockery from camp, which turns people into "the figure of ridiculous fun" as well as "erases the line between the masterful agent of attack and satirized target."[36] For example, one of Jackie's legendary hits "Love Goddess," a camp resignification of Donna Summer's "Love to Love You Baby," begins with Jackie cooing, "Do you want fried rice with that?" When asked where the line originates, Lewis reveals, "That came from when Mark and I were in college together, there was a place called . . . fuck. . . . it was some Chinese place. The woman's name was Ms. Kim. Every time we'd go in there, no matter what you ordered, that bitch would say, 'You want some fried rice with that? You want some fried rice with that?' We'd be like, 'Yeah, bitch. Some fried rice. I ordered fruit, but if you must bring fried rice, bring that shit up.'" A parade of celebrity divas rip at Jackie, including Diahann Carroll—who threatens to sue for libel because Jackie claims Carroll's star persona was stolen from Jackie—and Bette Midler, who calls Jackie "a f****ng nightmare" to work with; Eddie Cibrian adds to this chorus of curses when he claims Jackie attempted to put a dollar in his speedo.

Jackie's Back ultimately takes broad strokes at the egoism of all divas. When Lewis performs the Shirley Bassey–esque song "Look at Me," before an audience of Hollywood luminaries at the Academy Awards, she implicates herself in songwriter Shaiman's pitch-perfect parody of Bassey's "This Is My Life" that gloriously unfolds. Bedecked in a towering wig encrusted with diamonds, pendulous diamond earrings, and a "see-through" gown, Jackie/Lewis belts, "They say to love somebody else / You've got to learn to love yourself / And so I proudly show this face/Like it's an Oscar on the shelf."[37] Jackie's severe facial expression turns to ecstatic upon the word *Oscar* as the song commences into blatant affirmations of self-love: "To hell with all false modesty / If it's perfection you must see / Look at me!" Jackie/Lewis belts the word *me* with the richness and brass of Bassey, having exhumed the narcissism underpinning every diva's persona, and avows, "I only say it 'cause it's you that I adore/My love for you has only made me love me more!"[38] The fact that the film was built around Lewis makes her camping even funnier. Lewis at turns coyly deflects any similarities to Jackie and calls the film a parody of the Bassey documentary *Have Voice Will Travel* (1994) and then admits, "Hold on. How am I not like Jackie?"[39] On the one hand, Lewis's admission that she is like Jackie points to Janet Staiger's assertion that minority authors often create an alter ego to speak for them within a text.[40] On the other hand, this tongue-in-cheek disclosure culminates after Lewis chronicles her collaboration with gay creatives such as Brown, who, Lewis avers, "knew my voice. He had written all my one-woman shows in New York; he knew me."[41] That this collaboration transpired across the constructed boundaries of race and sexuality combines with Lewis's affirmation of both her own self-parody and her creative agency as diva. As she explains, "Here's the thing, we didn't have to try to find the funny. It was just funny because most of the shit was just true. . . . The Blackness was just me being Black."[42]

The Black camp of *Jackie's Back* materializes in its playful ambivalence toward the title character and, by extension, the willingness to make Jackie a camp antihero. Returning to Lewis's reasons for why "Lifetime was not ready" for *Jackie's Back!*, Lewis evidences "the situation with the daughters," a reference to the overarching plotline about Jackie's relationship to her children Antandra (T. V. Blake) and Shaniqua (Tangie Ambrose). Lewis explains that Antandra remained central to Lewis, Brown and La Duke's construction of the plot, not to emphasize Jackie's humanity or her dramatic arc from egoistic to self-sacrificing—the trajectory of most maternal melodramas and many celebrity biopics—but to motivate the punchline, "And make it a double, Antandra."[43] Jackie's treatment of her daughters surely positions the character as a bad mother, a "negative" image considering what is at stake in the history of stereotypical representations of powerful women and maternity, particularly when these representations are overtly racialized.[44] Jackie behaves with Antandra as a star with her beloved acolyte, and she has alienated Shaniqua by refusing to disclose the identity of her daughter's father as well as by vainly resisting the moniker of "grandmother" to Shaniqua's child due to the age it implies. Jackie expresses pride, moreover, in her maternal influence, a gesture that attests to Gates's encapsulation of the "work" represented by Black housewives and mothers on reality television, "the women's resistance to dominant norms of black femininity and the new models of subjectivity that they offer in their place."[45] When Jackie defends her skills as a parental role model to Shaniqua, for example, she gushes, "Her first word was 'mascara,'" then guffaws and adds, "Wonder where she learned that?" Jackie engages camp reasoning to justify her *work* as a diva mama, a "new model of subjectivity" that eschews the "positive image" for fabulousness and fun.

THE SUCCESS OF BLACK CAMP TIME

Although *Jackie's Back!* was a failure according to "straight" and "white" cultural criteria regarding time and quality, it succeeded in Black camp time. The film's Black queer cult following as well as Jenifer Lewis's star turn seal its status as camp: "before its time" and, in Muñoz's words, as a "utopian" harbinger for "animating the desire for a time and place that is not yet here."[46] "You couldn't bring that flavor into a corporate world because they wouldn't understand what the fuck you were talking about," as Lewis sagely put it about "the comedy of *Jackie's Back!*":

> What can I tell you? We spoke from our own truth. You know the language of us? It's our language; it's divas and gays and Black people. It's people that are real. Come on. Child, look, I know the answers that you want. Here, people have asked me this question like, Why do gay men love the Judy Garlands and the Jenifer Lewises, the Bette Midlers? . . . And so, we voiced your souls. Judy Garland voiced your souls. I'm sitting at the edge of that stage and say, "We'll stay all night and sing them all." The generosity of divas not minding that you're gay, knowing that we're singing to the world and that you are part of the world. You couldn't be gay and part of the world. Nobody wants to know you were gay, but Judy knew you were gay. You see?[47]

Jackie's Back brims with "the generosity of divas" in all its camp invective, parody, and self-deprecating humor, to say the least of its roster of female celebrity cameos. Jackie the "divatastic" antihero transforms into a "negative" role model, a "risky," "edgy," and endearingly hilarious figure for Black and queer camp identification. Looking forward to a "not-yet-here" (as far as network television was concerned), Jackie and Jenifer speak "the language of ... divas and gays and Black people. It's people who are real." To access this "real" "language," *Jackie's Back* enlisted the resources of camp to challenge network television's standardized aesthetics of "quality," representations of Blackness, and constructions of audiences.

The epilogue of the film reestablishes these elements. Following Jackie's comeback and reconciliation with her daughters, the narrator informs us that Jackie rerecorded "Look at Me" with new lyrics. A split screen image appears, Jackie in profile on each side, singing to herself, "I found a new philosophy. I'm finally humble, can't you see?! Look at me!"[48] As the two faces of Jackie belt about her newfound humility, each profile alternately smiles and winks at the camera, expressions that illuminate the "generosity" of a diva who gladly includes us in her narcissistic giddiness at being seen. Closing the film, Jackie/Lewis conveys how Black camp sings "to the world and that [Black queers] are part of the world." Ratings could not measure this in 1999, but the pleasure and presence of the film's contemporary fans command, just like Jackie, "Look at me!"

Alfred L. Martin Jr. is Associate Professor of Cinematic Arts at the University of Miami. He is author of *The Generic Closet: Black Gayness and the Black-Cast Sitcom.*

Ken Feil is Associate Professor in the Department of Visual & Media Arts at Emerson College. Ken is the author of *Fearless Vulgarity: Jacqueline Susann's Queer Comedy and Camp Authorship*; *Dying for a Laugh: Disaster Movies and the Camp Imagination*; and *Rowan and Martin's Laugh-In.*

NOTES

1. Eileen R. Meehan and Jackie Byars, "Telefeminism: How Lifetime Got Its Groove, 1984–1997," *Television and New Media* 1, no. 1 (February 2000): 34.

2. Mike Reynolds, "Not Just a Pretty Face: Original Films Brand Image for Networks' Viewers," *Cable World* 11, no. 28 (July 12, 1999): 21.

3. Ibid., 24.

4. Jennifer Fuller, "Branding Blackness on US Cable Television," *Media, Culture and Society* 32, no. 2 (March 2010): 285–305.

5. Jenifer Lewis, interview with Alfred L. Martin Jr., November 20, 2020.

6. Steven Cohan, *Incongruous Entertainment: Camp, Cultural Value, and the MGM Musical* (Durham, NC: Duke University Press, 2005), 1.

7. Kathleen Battles, "This Is UnREAL: Discourses of Quality, Antiheroes, and the Erasure of the Femininized Popular Culture in "Television for Women," *Feminist Media Studies* 20, no. 8 (2020): 1286.

8. David Kronke, "Jackie's Back," *Variety*, June 14, 1999, https://variety.com/1999/film /reviews/jackie-s-back-1117499890/.

9. Marlon B. Ross, "Camping the Dirty Dozens: The Queer Resources of Black Nationalist Invective," *Callaloo* 23, no. 1 (2000): 291; Susan Sontag, "Notes on 'Camp,'" in *Against Interpretation and Other Essays* (New York: Farrar, Straus and Giroux, 1966), 290.

10. Jefferson Graham, "Behind the Bios, Hollywood Rise-and-Fall Sagas' Success Leads to Movies Made for TV," *USA TODAY*, June 14, 1999, https://advance-lexis-com.proxy.lib.uiowa .edu/api/document?collection=news&id=urn:contentItem:3WPP-GJ30-00C6-D3CC-00000 -00&context=1516831.

11. We need the citation for this: *USA Today*, 2003.

12. "Lifetime and Women: It's Real," *Broadcasting & Cable* 129, no. 25 (June 14, 1999): 20–21.

13. Mark Alton Brown and Dee La Duke, interview with Alfred L. Martin Jr., November 11, 2020.

14. Ibid.

15. See Kristal Brent Zook, *Color by Fox: The Fox Network and the Revolution in Black Television* (New York: Oxford University Press, 1999) and Alfred L. Martin Jr., *The Generic Closet: Black Gayness and the Black-Cast Sitcom* (Bloomington: Indiana University Press, 2021) for a more detailed discussion of this history.

16. Lewis interview.

17. Joyce Millman, "Blue Glow," Salon, June 14, 1999, https://www.salon.com/1999/06/14 /glow_49/.

18. Brown and La Duke interview.

19. Ibid.

20. Lewis interview.

21. Sontag, "Notes on 'Camp,'" 285.

22. Ibid.

23. Lewis interview.

24. Brown and La Duke interview.

25. José Esteban Muñoz, *Cruising Utopia, 10th Anniversary Edition: The Then and There of Queer Futurity* (New York: New York University Press, ProQuest Ebook Central, 2019), 149.

26. Racquel J. Gates, *Double Negative: The Black Image and Popular Culture* (Durham, NC: Duke University Press, 2018), 19.

27. Ibid., 149, 20.

28. See also José Esteban Muñoz, "Flaming Latinas: Ela Troyano's Carmelita Tropicana: Your Kunst Is Your Waffen (1993)," in *Ethnic Eye: Latino Media Arts*, ed. Chon A. Noriega and Ana M. López (Minneapolis: University of Minnesota Press, 1996), 129.

29. Lewis interview.

30. Ross, "Camping the Dirty Dozens," 292.

31. Although Ross concentrates on the uses of camp by Black, cisgender men (queer and straight), the core of his premise applies to Lewis as camp performer, the appropriation of camp in *Jackie's Back*, as well as the film's camp reception by Black queer men.

32. Ross, "Camping the Dirty Dozens," 305.

33. Lewis interview.

34. Ibid.

35. Lester Fabian Brathwaite, "Can We Talk About . . .? Divatastic Cult Classic 'Jackie's Back!,'" *New Now Next*, Logo, July 19, 2020, http://www.newnownext.com/can-we-talk -about-jackies-back-20th-anniversary-jenifer-lewis/07/2019.

36. Ross, "Camping the Dirty Dozens," 307.
37. "Look at Me," performed by Jenifer Lewis, written by Marc Shaiman.
38. Ibid.
39. Lewis interview.
40. Janet Staiger, "Authorship and Gus Van Sant," *Film Criticism*, no. 1 (2004): 3.
41. Lewis interview.
42. Ibid.
43. Ibid.; La Duke and Brown interview.
44. Gates, *Double Negative*, 155–56.
45. Ibid., 153.
46. Muñoz, *Cruising Utopia*, 149, 152.
47. Lewis interview.
48. "Look at Me."

BIBLIOGRAPHY

Acham, Christine. *Revolution Televised: Prime Time and the Struggle for Black Power.*
    Minneapolis: University of Minnesota Press, 2004.

Advertisement. *Chicago Defender,* March 24, 1960.

Andreeva, Nellie. "'The Game' Reboot Not Going Forward at the CW." *Deadline,* January 31,
    2020. https://deadline.com/2020/01/the-game-reboot-dead-not-going-forward-the
    -cw-1202847460/.

Apatow, Judd. "Chris Rock: The E-mail Interview." *Vanity Fair,* December 5, 2012.

Attallah, Paul. "The Unworthy Discourse: Situation Comedy in Television." In *Interpreting
    Television: Current Research Perspectives,* edited by Willard D. Rowland Jr. and Bruce
    Watkins, 222–49. London: Sage, 1984.

Aucoin, Don. "An Uncivil War over 'Desmond.'" *Boston Globe,* October 3, 1998.

Auletta, Ken. *Three Blind Mice: How the Networks Lost their Way.* New York: Knopf Doubleday
    Publishing Group, 1992.

Bagdikian, Ben. *The Media Monopoly.* Boston: Beacon Press, 1997.

Bakhtin, Mikhail. *Rabelais and His World.* Bloomington: Indiana University Press, 2009.

Battles, Kathleen. "This Is UnREAL: Discourses of Quality, Antiheroes, and the Erasure of the
    Femininized Popular Culture in 'Television for Women.'" *Feminist Media Studies* 20,
    no. 8 (2020): 1286.

Bauder, David. "UPN's Downturn Makes It a Struggle to Survive." Associated Press,
    November 20, 1998.

Baugh, John. "At Last: Plantation English in America: Nonstandard Varieties and the Quest
    for Educational Equity." *Research in the Teaching of English* 41, no. 4 (2007): 465–72.

Beavers, Herman. "The Cool Pose: Intersectionality, Masculinity, and Quiescence in the
    Comedy and Film of Richard Pryor and Eddie Murphy." In *Race and the Subject of
    Masculinities,* edited by Harry Stecopoulos and Michael Uebel, 253–85. Durham,
    NC: Duke University Press, 1997.

Becker, Ron. *Gay TV and Straight America*. Piscataway, NJ: Rutgers University Press, 2006. https://www.jstor.org/stable/j.ctt5hj2q0.

Beltrán, Mary. "Meaningful Diversity: Exploring Questions of Equitable Representation on Diverse Ensemble Cast Shows." *Flow* (blog), August 27, 2010. https://www.flowjournal.org/2010/08/meaningful-diversity/.

Berlant, Lauren, and Sianne Ngai. "Comedy Has Issues." *Critical Inquiry* 43, no. 2 (2017): 233–49. https://doi.org/10.1086/689666.

Berman, Marc. "The CW Has Some Bright Spots, but Lingering Issues." *Adweek*, November 3, 2008. https://www.adweek.com/convergent-tv/cw-has-some-bright-spots-lingering-issues-110207/.

"Bill Cosby 1964 Stand-up Comedy 2." YouTube. Accessed December 19, 2022. https://www.youtube.com/watch?v=cyyE-q33kGY.

"Bill Cosby with Teens 1965 Comedy Routine." YouTube. Accessed December 28, 2022. https://www.youtube.com/watch?v=Lfe9MCGsYP4&t=47s.

Bonko, Larry. "Fifth Network UPN to Take Off Beginning in January." *Virginian-Pilot*, November 3, 1994.

Borger, Julian. "Black Rage at White House Slavery and Sex Satire." *Guardian*, October 6, 1998.

Boskin, Joseph. *Sambo: The Rise and Demise of an American Jester*. Oxford: Oxford University Press, 1988.

Box Office Mojo. "Bad Boys." Box Office Mojo. Accessed January 10, 2020. https://www.boxofficemojo.com/title/tt0112442/?ref_=bo_se_r_1.

———. "Bad Boys for Life." Box Office Mojo. Accessed January 10, 2020. https://www.boxofficemojo.com/release/rl1182631425/?ref_=bo_yl_table_2.

———. "Big Momma's House." Box Office Mojo. Accessed January 10, 2020. https://www.boxofficemojo.com/title/tt0208003/?ref_=bo_se_r_1.

———. "Blue Streak." Box Office Mojo. Accessed January 10, 2020. https://www.boxofficemojo.com/title/tt0181316/?ref_=bo_se_r_1.

———. "Eddie Murphy: Raw." Box Office Mojo. Accessed January 10, 2020. https://www.boxofficemojo.com/title/tt0092948/?ref_=bo_se_r_1.

———. "Life." Box Office Mojo. Accessed January 10, 2020. https://www.boxofficemojo.com/title/tt0123964/?ref_=bo_se_r_3.

———. "Martin Lawrence: You So Crazy." Box Office Mojo. Accessed January 10, 2020. https://www.boxofficemojo.com/release/rl1836090881/weekend/.

———. "Martin Lawrence Live: Runteldat." Box Office Mojo. Accessed January 10, 2020. https://www.boxofficemojo.com/title/tt0327036/?ref_=bo_se_r_1.

———. "Nothing to Lose." Box Office Mojo. Accessed January 10, 2020. https://www.boxofficemojo.com/title/tt0119807/?ref_=bo_se_r_1.

———. "Richard Pryor: Live on the Sunset Strip," Box Office Mojo. Accessed January 10, 2020. https://www.boxofficemojo.com/title/tt0084597/?ref_=bo_se_r_2.

Boyd, Todd. *Am I Black Enough for You? Popular Culture from the 'Hood and Beyond*. Bloomington: Indiana University Press, 1997.

Bramesco, Charles. "Atlanta: Robbin' Season Review—The Best Show on TV Returns in Style." *Guardian*, February 28, 2018. http://www.theguardian.com/tv-and-radio/2018/feb/28/atlanta-robbin-season-review-the-best-show-on-tv-returns-in-style.

Brathwaite, Lester Fabian. "Can We Talk About . . .? Divatastic Cult Classic 'Jackie's Back!'" *New Now Next*, Logo, July 19, 2020. http://www.newnownext.com/can-we-talk-about-jackies-back-20th-anniversary-jenifer-lewis/07/2019.

Braxton, Greg. "A Controversial 'Diary.'" *Los Angeles Times*, September 19, 1998.

———. "'Desmond Pfeiffer' Is Deep-Sixed." *Los Angeles Times*, November 7, 1998.

———. "Groups Call for Changes in Portrayal of Blacks on TV." *Los Angeles Times*, February 8, 1997.

———. "300 Protest at Studio against TV Comedy Set in Slavery Era." *Los Angeles Times*, October 1, 1998.

———. "UPN Postpones, Reviews Its 'Desmond Pfeiffer' Pilot." *Los Angeles Times*, September 30, 1998.

Breakfast Club Power 105.1 FM. "Will Smith & Martin Lawrence Talk 'Bad Boys' Trilogy, Growth, Regrets + More." Podcast Audio, 2020. https://www.youtube.com/watch?v=wACxobztaXk.

Britt, Bruce. "Leaping Barriers with Laughter: Flip Wilson, a Comic for the Times." ProQuest, November 28, 1998.

Brock, André, Jr. *Distributed Blackness: African American Cybercultures*. New York: NYU Press, 2020.

Bucholtz, Mary. "The Whiteness of Nerds: Superstandard English and Racial Markedness." *Journal of Linguistic Anthropology* 11, no. 1 (2001): 84–100.

"Bud Billiken Talent Show Thrills 25,000 Patrons at Annual Parade." *Chicago Defender*, August 15, 1961.

Calhoun, Lillian S. "Fast-Rising Comedian Bill Cosby Talks about His Different Approach to Comedy." *Chicago Defender*, August 1, 1963.

Caramanica, Jon. "'Game' On: More Real Than Reality TV (Published 2011)." *New York Times*, February 4, 2013. http://www.nytimes.com/2011/01/09/arts/television/09game .html?_r=1&ref=television.

———. "'Key & Peele,' With Keegan-Michael Key and Jordan Peele." *New York Times*, December 26, 2013. https://www.nytimes.com/2013/12/29/arts/television/key-peele-with -keegan-michael-key-and-jordan-peele.html.

Carman, John. "Fox's Fall Leaves Out Black Hits." *San Francisco Chronicle*, May 21, 1997.

Carter, Bill. "Fall Network Schedules Offer Plenty of Choices (At Least for the Young)." *New York Times*, May 27, 1992.

———. "This Fall, the Barely Adult Set Is the Object of Network Desire: Networks Court the Barely Adult Set." *New York Times*, September 10, 1992.

———. "Two Upstart Networks Courting Black Viewers." *New York Times*, October 7, 1996.

Chang, Jeff. *Can't Stop Won't Stop: A History of the Hip-Hop Generation*. New York: Picador, 2005.

Chappelle's Show. Season 2, Episode 1. "Sam Jackson Beer & Racial Draft." Directed by Neal Brennan and Rusty Cundieff. Aired January 21, 2004, on Comedy Central. https://www .cc.com/episodes/3d8tr2/chappelle-s-show-samuel-jackson-beer-racial-draft-season -2-ep-1.

———. Season 3, Episode 2. "Black Howard Dean & Stereotype Pixies." Directed by Rusty Cundieff. Aired July 16, 2006, on Comedy Central. https://www.cc.com/episodes /ynn1mr/chappelle-s-show-black-howard-dean-stereotype-pixies-ep-2.

"Chappelle's Story." Oprah. Last modified February 3, 2006. https://www.oprah.com /oprahshow/chappelles-story.

"Chart History: Martin Lawrence." Billboard. https://www.billboard.com/music/Martin -Lawrence/chart-history/BLP.

"ChrisLacy1990's Review of 'Adore' by Prince." *Album of the Year*. Accessed May 18, 2021. https://www.albumoftheyear.org/user/chrislacy1990/album/284787-adore/.

Chun, Wendy Hui Kyong. *Updating to Remain the Same: Habitual New Media*. Cambridge, MA: The MIT Press, 2016.

Clarke, Michael. "Humor and Incongruity." In *The Philosophy of Laughter and Humor*, edited by John Morreall, 139–55. Albany: State University of New York Press, 1987.

Cobb, William Jelani. *The Devil and Dave Chappelle and Other Essays*. New York: Basic Books, 2007.

Cohan, Steven. *Incongruous Entertainment: Camp, Cultural Value, and the MGM Musical*. Durham, NC: Duke University Press, 2005.

Coleman, Robin R. Means, and Charlton D. McIlwain. "The Hidden Truths in Black Sitcoms." In *The Sitcom Reader: America Viewed and Skewed*, edited by Mary M. Dalton and Laura R. Linder, 125–38. Albany: State University of New York Press, 2005.

Collins, Patricia Hill. *Black Sexual Politics: African Americans, Gender, and the New Racism*. London: Routledge, 2004.

Cook, Kevin. *Flip: The Inside Story of TV's First Black Superstar*. New York: Plume, 2014.

Cooper, Carol. "Someday Your Prince Will Come (1983)." *Beat Patrol* (blog), May 6, 2009. https://beatpatrol.wordpress.com/2009/05/06/carol-cooper-someday-your-prince-will-come-1983/.

Crisafulli, Chuck. "Martin Lawrence: Dr. Dirt or Mr. Clean? Barred by NBC, He's Generally Blue on Stage but Not on TV." *Los Angeles Times*, March 8, 1994.

Dance, Daryl Cumber, ed. *Honey, Hush! An Anthology of African American Women's Humor*. Edition Unstated. New York: W. W. Norton, 1998.

Daniels, Hunter. "Comic-Con: Keegan-Michael Key, Jordan Peele and Director/Producer Peter Atencio Talk 'Key and Peele' Season 4, Animated Spinoffs, FARGO, and More." *Collider*, July 26, 2014. http://collider.com/key-and-peele-season-4-keegan-michael-key-jordan-peele-interview/.

Davies, Christie. *Ethnic Humor around the World*. Bloomington: Indiana University Press, 1996.

Davis, Jenny L., Tony P. Love, and Gemma Killen. "Seriously Funny: The Political Work of Humor on Social Media." *New Media & Society* 20, no. 10 (October 1, 2018): 3898–916. https://doi.org/10.1177/1461444818762602.

de Moraes, Lisa. "L.A. Council Pans 'Desmond Pfeiffer.'" *Washington Post*, October 1, 1998.

———. "'Pfeiffer' Star Lambastes Show's Protesters." *Washington Post*, October 12, 1998.

Del Rosario, Alexandra. "'The Game' Showrunner Devon Greggory Says Dramedy Needed 'an Opportunity to Reboot Itself': Paramount+ Sets Premiere Date—TCA." *Deadline*, August 31, 2021. https://deadline.com/2021/08/the-game-showrunner-devon-greggory-says-dramedy-needed-an-opportunity-to-reboot-itself-paramount-sets-premiere-date-tca-1234824603/.

Demšar, Janez, Tomaž Curk, Aleš Erjavec, Črt Gorup, Tomaž Hočevar, Mitar Milutinovič, Martin Možina, et al. "Orange: Data Mining Toolbox in Python." *Journal of Machine Learning Research* 14 (2013): 2349–53.

Diawara, Manthia, ed. *Black American Cinema*. New York: Routledge, 1993.

Dickson-Carr, Darryl. *African American Satire: The Sacredly Profane Novel*. Columbia: University of Missouri Press, 2001.

Driscoll, Kevin, Alex Leavitt, Kristen L. Guth, François Bar, and Aalok Mehta. "Beyond Big Bird, Binders, and Bayonets: Humor and Visibility Among Connected Viewers of the 2012 US Presidential Debates." *Social Media + Society* 4, no. 1 (January 1, 2018): 2056305118761201. https://doi.org/10.1177/2056305118761201.

Du Bois, W. E. B. *The Souls of Black Folk*. New York: Bantam Books, 1989.

Dudden, Arthur Power. "The Record of Political Humor." *American Quarterly* 37, no. 1 (1985): 50–70. https://doi.org/10.2307/2712762.

Duncan, Stephen A. *The Rebel Café: Sex, Race and Politics in Cold War America's Nightclub Underground*. Baltimore: John Hopkins Books, 2018.

Dungee, Ron. "Unity Works: Black Community Celebrates UPN's Cancellation of 'Desmond Pfeiffer.'" *Los Angeles Sentinel*, December 3, 1998.

Easterling, Paul. "Biracial Butterflies: 21st Century Racial Identity in Popular Culture." In *Color Struck: Teaching Race and Ethnicity*, edited by Lori Latrice Martin, Hayward Derrick Horton, Cedric Herring, Verna M. Keith, and Melvin Thomas, 123–42. Rotterdam: Sense Publishers, 2017.

Eastman, Max. *Enjoyment of Laughter*. London: Routledge, 2009.

———. *Enjoyment of Living*. New York: Harper, 2022.

———. *The Sense of Humor*. New York: Charles Scribner & Sons, 1921.

Farley, Christopher John. "Dave Speaks." *Time*, May 14, 2005. http://content.time.com/time/magazine/article/0,9171,1061512,00.html.

"Filthy Words by George Carlin." January 23, 2011. https://web.archive.org/web/20110123114427/, http://www.law.umkc.edu/faculty/projects/ftrials/conlaw/filthywords.html.

Fiske, John. *Media Matters: Race and Gender in US Politics*. Minneapolis: University of Minnesota Press, 1996.

Fleetwood, Nicole R. *On Racial Icons: Blackness and the Public Imagination*. New Brunswick, NJ: Rutgers University Press, 2015.

The Flip Wilson Show. 1970. Season 1, Episode 7. Directed by Tim Kiley. Aired October 29, 1970 on NBC.

Florini, Sarah. "Enclaving and Cultural Resonance in Black 'Game of Thrones' Fandom." *Transformative Works and Cultures* 29 (March 15, 2019). https://doi.org/10.3983/twc.2019.1498.

———. "Tweets, Tweeps, and Signifyin' Communication and Cultural Performance on 'Black Twitter.'" *Television & New Media* 15, no. 3 (March 1, 2014): 223–37. https://doi.org/10.1177/1527476413480247.

Foster, Gwendolyn A. *Performing Whiteness: Postmodern Re/constructions in the Cinema*. Albany: State University of New York Press, 2003.

Freitas, Dudu. "Prince on American Bandstand 1980." YouTube, 2017. https://www.youtube.com/watch?v=krEXzOEsP9I.

Freud, Sigmund. *The Joke and Its Relation to the Unconscious*. New York: Penguin Books, 2002.

———. "Three Essays on the Theory of Sexuality (1905)." In *The Standard Edition of the Complete Psychological Works of Sigmund Freud, volume VII (1901–1905): A Case of Hysteria, Three Essays on Sexuality and Other Works*, edited by James Strachey and Anna Freud, 125–245. London: Hogarth Press, 1953.

Fuller, Jennifer. "Branding Blackness on US Cable Television." *Media, Culture & Society* 32, no. 2 (2010): 285–305. https://doi.org/10.1177/0163443709355611.

Gambino, Childish. "Bonfire." Recorded 2011. Track 3 on *Camp*. Glassnote, digital.

———. "Fire Fly." Recorded 2011. Track 2 on *Camp*. Glassnote, digital.

———. "Not Going Back." Recorded circa 2010–2011. Track 5 on *EP*. Glassnote, digital.

Gandy, Oscar H. *Communication and Race: A Structural Perspective*. London: Arnold, 1998.

Gardaphé, Fred. "We Weren't Always White: Race Ethnicity in Italian American Literature." *Lit: Literature Interpretation Theory* 13, no. 3 (2010): 185–99. https://doi.org/10.1080/10436920213855.

Gates, Henry Louis, Jr. *The Signifying Monkey: A Theory of African American Literary Criticism*. Reprint ed. New York: Oxford University Press, 1989.

———. *The Signifying Monkey: A Theory of African American Literary Criticism*. 25th anniversary ed. New York: Oxford University Press, 2014.

Gates, Racquel J. "Bringing the Black: Eddie Murphy and African American Humor on Saturday Night Live." In *Saturday Night Live & American TV*, edited by Nick Marx, Matt Sienkiwicz, and Ron Becker, 151–72. Bloomington: University of Indiana Press, 2013.

———. *Double Negative: The Black Image and Popular Culture*. Durham, NC: Duke University Press, 2018.

Gill, Mark Stuart. "He's Half Macho Man, Half Teddy Bear." *New York Times*, August 1, 1993.

Gillota, David. "Black Nerds: New Directions in African American Humor." *Studies in American Humor*, no. 28 (2013): 17–30. JSTOR.

———. *Ethnic Humor in Multiethnic America*. New Brunswick, NJ: Rutgers University Press, 2013.

Glover, Donald, writer. *Atlanta*. Season 2, Episode 1. "Alligator Man." Directed by Hiro Murai, featuring Donald Glover, Brian Tyree Henry, and LaKeith Stanfield. Aired March 1, 2018.

Goodale, Gloria. "Cult Fans Bring 'The Family Guy' Back to TV." *Christian Science Monitor*, April 22, 2005. http://www.csmonitor.com/2005/0422/p12s01-altv.html.

Goodman, Tim. "'Atlanta Robbin' Season': TV Review." *Hollywood Reporter* (blog), February 28, 2018. https://www.hollywoodreporter.com/news/general-news/atlanta-robbin -season-review-1088898/.

"Gossip Girl Reviews at Metacritic." *Metacritic*, September 1, 2008. http://www.metacritic .com/tv/shows/gossipgirlseason2?q=gossip%20girl.

Graham, Jefferson. "Behind the Bios, Hollywood Rise-and-Fall Sagas' Success Leads to Movies Made for TV." *USA Today*, June 14, 1999. https://advance-lexis-com.proxy.lib.uiowa .edu/api/document?collection=news&id=urn:contentItem:3WPP-GJ30-00C6-D3CC -00000-00&context=1516831.

———. "Protest Greets UPN's New Season." *USA Today*, October 5, 1998.

Gray, Herman. *Cultural Moves: African Americans and the Politics of Representation*. Berkeley: University of California Press, 2005.

———. *Watching Race: Television and the Struggle for Blackness*. 2nd ed. Minneapolis: University of Minnesota Press, 2004.

Gray, Jonathan. *Watching with 'The Simpsons': Television, Parody, and Intertextuality*. London: Routledge, 2012.

Gray, Jonathan, Jeffrey P. Jones, and Ethan Thompson, eds. *Satire TV: Politics and Comedy in the Post-Network Era*. New York: NYU Press, 2009.

Gregory, Dick. *Nigger*. New York: Plume, 2019.

Guerrero, Ed. "The Black Image in Protective Custody." In *Black American Cinema*, edited by Manthia Diawara, 237–46. New York: Routledge, 1993.

Guerrero, Lisa. "Can I Live? Contemporary Black Satire and the State of Postmodern Double Consciousness." *Studies in American Humor* 2, no. 2 (2016): 266–79. JSTOR.

Haas, Nancy. "A TV Generation Is Seeing Beyond Color." *New York Times*, February 22, 1998. 1.

Haggins, Bambi. *Laughing Mad: The Black Comic Persona in Post-Soul America*. New Brunswick, NJ: Rutgers University Press, 2007.

Hall, Stuart. "Encoding/Decoding in the Television Discourse." In *Channeling Blackness: Studies on Television and Race in America*, edited by Darnell M. Hunt, 46–59. New York: Oxford University Press, 2005.

Harris-Lacewell, Melissa Victoria. *Barbershops, Bibles, and BET*. Princeton, NJ: Princeton University Press, 2010. https://www.degruyter.com/document/doi/10.1515/9781400836604 /html.

Hartzell, Stephanie L. "Whiteness Feels Good Here: Interrogating White Nationalist Rhetoric on Stormfront." *Communication and Critical/Cultural Studies* 17, no. 2 (2020): 129–48. https://doi.org/10.1080/14791420.2020.1745858.

Hawksey, Martin. "Twitter Archiving Google Sheet." TAGS. Accessed February 11, 2021. https://tags.hawksey.info/.

Henderson, Felicia. "The Culture behind Closed Doors: Issues of Gender and Race in the Writers' Room." *Cinema Journal* 50, no. 2 (2011): 145–52.

Hicks, Jonathan. "Russell Simmons Taps Street Culture to Build an Empire in Entertainment." *New York Times*, June 14, 1992.

Higgins, John M. "Viacom Stands behind Valentine." *Broadcasting & Cable*, November 9, 1998.

Hilmes, Michele. "Invisible Men: *Amos 'n' Andy* and the Roots of Broadcast Discourse." *Critical Studies in Mass Communication* 10, no. 40 (1993): 301–21.

Hinton, Elizabeth. *From the War on Poverty to the War on Crime: The Making of Mass Incarceration in America*. Cambridge, MA: Harvard University Press, 2016.

Hobbes, Thomas. *Human Nature*. Vol. 4, of *The English Works of Thomas Hobbes of Malmesbury*, edited by William Molesworth. London: J. Bohn, 1841.

Hood, Cooper. "Beverly Hills Cop: Why Eddie Murphy Replaced Sylvester Stallone." Screen Rant, October 24, 2020. https://screenrant.com/beverly-hills-cop-eddie-murphy-replaced-sylvester-stallone.

hooks, bell. "The Oppositional Gaze: Black Female Spectators." In *Black Looks: Race and Representation*, 115–31. Boston: South End Press, 1992.

Horowitz, Joy. "Snookums! Steve Urkel Is a Hit." *New York Times*, April 17, 1991.

Hswen, Yulin, Xiang Xu, Anna Hing, Jared B. Hawkins, John S. Brownstein, and Gilbert C. Gee. "Association of '#covid19' Versus '#chinesevirus' With Anti-Asian Sentiments on Twitter: March 9–23, 2020." *American Journal of Public Health* 111, no. 5 (March 18, 2021): 956–64. https://doi.org/10.2105/AJPH.2021.306154.

Ill Mami. "#2: Prince 'Adore.'" *Soul Bounce*, August 28, 2008. https://www.soulbounce.com/2008/08/2_prince_adore/.

Iverem, Esther. "Lawrence to Appeal MPAA Rating of 'You So Crazy.'" *Los Angeles Times*, February 16, 1994.

James, Caryn. "A Corrosive Comedy of Hip-Hop Manners: Aiming Gags about Prison Rape and Feminine Hygiene at the Mainstream." *New York Times*, April 27, 1994.

Johnson, Allan. "Integration? TV's Black 'Ghetto' Opens Its Doors to White Characters." *Chicago Tribune*, September 30, 1998.

———. "With 'Brothers,' UPN Aims to Rebuild Black Audience." *Chicago Tribune*, January 19, 1999.

Johnson, E. Patrick. *Appropriating Blackness: Performance and the Politics of Authenticity*. Durham, NC: Duke University Press, 2003.

Johnson, Steve. "Is Television Reverting to Black & White?" *Chicago Tribune*, August 27, 1996.

Jones, Bomani. "Rock's Last Great Double Album." *Ottawa Citizen*, May 23, 2002.

Joseph, Mike. "Prince's 'Adore' Is the Love Song to End All Love Songs." *Diffuser*, February 23, 2018. https://diffuser.fm/prince-adore/.

Kapur, Sahil. "Stephen Miller Reveals Trump's Immigration Agenda If He's Re-Elected." NBC News, October 30, 2020. https://www.nbcnews.com/politics/immigration/trump-adviser-stephen-miller-reveals-aggressive-second-term-immigration-agenda-n1245407.

Karnow, Stanley. "Bill Cosby: Variety Is the Life of Spies." *Saturday Evening Post* 238, no. 19 (1965): 86–88.

Kessell, Martina, and Patrick Merzinger. Introduction to *The Politics of Humour: Laughter, Inclusion in the Twentieth Century*. Toronto: University of Toronto Press, 2012.

Key & Peele. Season 1, Episode 3. "Das Negros." Directed by Peter Atencio. Aired February 14, 2012, on Comedy Central. https://www.cc.com/episodes/eytrvv/key-peele-das-negros-season-1-ep-3.

———. Season 3, Episode 1. "Les Mis." Directed by Peter Atencio. Aired September 18, 2013, on Comedy Central. https://www.cc.com/video/4p0coy/key-peele-hoodie.

———. Season 3, Episode 11. "The Power of Wings." Directed by Peter Atencio. Aired December 4, 2013, on Comedy Central. https://www.cc.com/episodes/ho3vr3/key -peele-the-power-of-wings-season-3-ep-11.

———. Season 4, Episode 1. "Alien Imposters." Directed by Peter Atencio. Aired September 24, 2014, on Comedy Central. https://www.cc.com/episodes/apyii9/key-peele-alien -imposters-season-4-ep-1.

———. Season 4, Episode 2. "Little Homie." Directed by Peter Atencio. Aired October 1, 2014, on Comedy Central. https://www.cc.com/episodes/lgsnos/key-peele-little-homie -season-4-ep-2.

———. Season 5, Episode 11. "The End." Directed by Peter Atencio. Aired September 9, 2015, on Comedy Central. https://www.cc.com/episodes/ho3vr3/key-peele-the-power-of -wings-season-3-ep-11.

Kimball, Trevor. "*The Game*: Season Four Starts on BET in January 2011." Canceled & Re-newed TV Shows, *TV Series Finale*, October 12, 2010. https://tvseriesfinale.com/tv -show/the-game-season-four-bet-18759/.

King, Don Ray. "Martin Lawrence's Monologue." SNL Transcripts Tonight, updated October 8, 2018. https://snltranscripts.jt.org/93/93nmono.phtml.

Kitwana, Bakari. *The Hip Hop Generation: Young Blacks and the Crisis in African American Culture*. New York: Basic Civitas Books, 2002.

Kloer, Phil. "Struggling UPN Gives Black Actors a Home." *Atlanta Journal-Constitution*, July 20, 1999.

Koltnow, Barry. "Crazy Like a Fox: Martin Lawrence Puts a Positive Spin on Criticism." *Chicago Tribune*, March 27, 1994.

Kronke, David. "Jackie's Back." *Variety*, June 14, 1999. https://variety.com/1999/film/reviews /jackie-s-back-1117499890/.

Kubey, Robert. *Creating Television: Conversations with the People behind 50 Years of American TV*. New York: Routledge, 2009.

Lawrence, Martin. *Funk It!*. East West, 1995.

———. "Got to Be Real." *VIBE*, April 1994.

———. *Martin Lawrence: You So Crazy*. Directed by Thomas Schlamme. New York: HBO Independent Productions, 1994.

———. *Martin Lawrence Live: Doin' Time: Uncut*. Directed by David Raynr. New York: Show-time Networks, 2016.

———. *Martin Lawrence Live: Talkin' Shit*. East West Records, 1993.

———. "Martin Lawrence Makes the Jump from TV to Film." *Entertainment Weekly*, February 4, 1994. https://ew.com/article/1994/02/04/martin-lawrence-makes-jump-tv-film.

Lee, Linda. "Attack of the 90-Foot Teen-Agers." *New York Times*, November 9, 1997.

Levin, Sam. "Mike Bloomberg Hangs with 'Gossip Girl' Cast." *Village Voice*, August 27, 2018. https://www.villagevoice.com/2012/01/26/mike-bloomberg-hangs-with-gossip-girl-cast/.

Lhamon, W., Jr. *Raising Cain: Blackface Performance from Jim Crow to Hip Hop*. Cambridge, MA: Harvard University Press, 1998.

"Lifetime and Women: It's Real." *Broadcasting & Cable* 129, no. 25 (June 14, 1999): 20–21.

Littleton, Daryll. *Black Comedians on Black Comedy*. New York: Applause Theatre and Books, 2006.

Lotz, Amanda D. "Segregated Sitcoms: Institutional Causes of Disparity among Black and White Comedy Images and Audiences." In *The Sitcom Reader: America Viewed and*

Skewed, edited by Mary M. Dalton and Laura R. Linder, 139–50. Albany: SUNY Press, 2005. https://www.sunypress.edu/p-4180-the-sitcom-reader.aspx.

Louis, Pierre-Antoine. "Jaleel White Wants to Sell You 'Purple Urkle.'" *New York Times*, May 8, 2021. https://www.nytimes.com/2021/05/08/us/jaleel-white-purple-urkle.html.

Lu, Jessica H., and Catherine Knight Steele. "'Joy Is Resistance': Cross-Platform Resilience and (Re)Invention of Black Oral Culture Online." *Information, Communication & Society* 22, no. 6 (May 12, 2019): 823–37. https://doi.org/10.1080/1369118X.2019.1575449.

Luconi, Stefano. "The Impact of Italy's Twentieth-Century Wars on Italian Americans' Ethnic Identity." *Nationalism and Ethnic Politics* 13, no. 3 (August 16, 2007): 465–91. https://doi.org/10.1080/13537110701451637.

Mabley, Moms. "Don't Sit on My Bed, 1948." YouTube. Accessed December 19, 2022. https://www.youtube.com/watch?v=4hot_teqE_E.

Manning, Brandon J. *Played Out: The Race Man in Twenty-First-Century Satire*. New Brunswick, NJ: Rutgers University Press, 2022.

Maragakis, Lisa Lockerd. "Coronavirus Disease 2019 vs. the Flu." April 29, 2021. https://www.hopkinsmedicine.org/health/conditions-and-diseases/coronavirus/coronavirus-disease-2019-vs-the-flu.

Martin, Alfred L., Jr. "Doing Double Duty: Toward a Theory of 'Compound Otherness' on Television." *Flow*, August 18, 2011. https://www.flowjournal.org/2011/08/doing-double-duty/.

———. "FOX Formula 3.0? TBS, Cougar Town, and the Disappearing Televisual Black Body." *Antenna*, June 18, 2012. http://blog.commarts.wisc.edu/2012/06/18/fox-formula-3-0-tbs-cougar-town-and-the-disappearing-televisual-black-body/.

———. *The Generic Closet: Black Gayness and the Black-Cast Sitcom*. Bloomington: Indiana University Press, 2021.

———. "Notes from Underground: WGN's Black-Cast Quality TV Experiment." *Los Angeles Review of Books*, May 31, 2018. https://lareviewofbooks.org/article/notes-from-underground-wgns-black-cast-quality-tv-experiment/.

———. "The Tweet Has Two Faces: Two-Faced Humor, Black Masculinity, and RompHim." *Journal of Cinema and Media Studies* 58, no. 3 (2019): 160–65. https://doi.org/10.1353/cj.2019.0031.

Marx, Nick. "Expanding the Brand: Race, Gender, and the Post-Politics of Representation on Comedy Central." *Television & New Media* 17, no. 3 (March 2016): 272–87. https://doi.org/10.1177/1527476415577212.

Maus, Derek C. Introduction to *Post-Soul Satire: Black Identity after Civil Rights*. Jackson: University Press of Mississippi, 2014.

McAllister, Marvin. "Bob Cole's Willie Wayside: Whiteface Hobo, Middle-Class Farmer, White Trash Hero." *Journal of American Drama and Theater* 14, no. 1 (2002): 64–77.

———. *Whiting Up: Whiteface Minstrels and Stage Europeans in African American Performance*. Chapel Hill: University of North Carolina Press, 2011.

McDonald, Soraya Nadia. "'Atlanta,' the Weirdest, Blackest Show on TV, Finally Gets a Return Date." *Andscape* (blog), January 6, 2018. https://andscape.com/features/atlanta-the-weirdest-blackest-show-on-tv-finally-gets-a-return-date/.

McKinney, Megan. "When Chicago Was a World-Famous Party Town." *Classic Chicago Magazine*, July 1 2018. https://classicchicagomagazine.com/mister-kellys-london-house-and-all-that-jazz/.

Meehan, Eileen R., and Jackie Byars. "Telefeminism: How Lifetime Got Its Groove, 1984–1997." *Television and New Media* 1, no. 1 (February 2000): 34.

Mekeisha Madden, Toby. "The Rise of the Black Nerd in Popular Culture." CNN, March 31, 2012. https://edition.cnn.com/2012/03/31/showbiz/rise-of-black-nerds/index.html.

Mifflin, Laurie. "Black Protest Delays Sitcom Episode." *New York Times*, October 3, 1998.

Miller, Liz Shannon. "'Atlanta': Donald Glover Wants You to Feel What It's Like to Be Black." *IndieWire* (blog), August 9, 2016. https://www.indiewire.com/2016/08/donald-glover -atlanta-fx-hiro-murai-trump-1201714877/.

Millman, Joyce. "Blue Glow." Salon, June 14, 1999. https://www.salon.com/1999/06/14 /glow_49/.

Mills, Brett. *The Sitcom*. Edinburgh: Edinburgh University Press, 2009.

———. *Television Sitcom*. London: Palgrave Macmillan, 2005.

Mittell, Jason. "A Cultural Approach to Television Genre Theory." *Cinema Journal* 40, no. 3 (2001): 3–24.

Monk-Payton, Brandy. "#LaughingWhileBlack: Gender and the Comedy of Social Media Blackness." *Feminist Media Histories* 3, no. 2 (April 1, 2017): 15–35. https://doi.org /10.1525/fmh.2017.3.2.15.

Morgan, Danielle Fuentes. *Laughing to Keep from Dying: African American Satire in the Twenty-First Century*. Urbana: University of Illinois Press, 2020.

Morreall, John. *Comic Relief: A Comprehensive Philosophy of Humor*. Malden, MA: John Wiley & Sons, 2009.

Morris, Wesley. "The Year We Obsessed over Identity." *New York Times*, October 6, 2015. http://nyti.ms/1j2L3uC.

Muñoz, José Esteban. *Cruising Utopia, 10th Anniversary Edition: The Then and There of Queer Futurity*. New York: New York University Press, ProQuest Ebook Central, 2019.

———. "Flaming Latinas: Ela Troyano's Carmelita Tropicana: Your Kunst Is Your Waffen (1993)." In *Ethnic Eye: Latino Media Arts*, edited by Chon A. Noriega and Ana M. López, 129–42. Minneapolis: University of Minnesota Press, 1996.

Murry, Jawn. "The Game Sitcom's Return on BET." *AOL Black Voices*. Accessed April 22, 2009. http://www.bvbuzz.com/2010/03/15/the-game-sitcoms-return-on-bet-nearly-finalized.

Neal, Mark Anthony. *Soul Babies Black Popular Culture and the Post-Soul Aesthetic*. New York: Routledge, 2002.

Neale, Steve, and Frank Krutnik. *Popular Film and Television Comedy*. New York: Routledge, 1990.

Newman, Michael Z., and Elana Levine. *Legitimating Television: Media Convergence and Cultural Status*. New York: Routledge, 2012.

Nilsen, Don L. F. "The Social Functions of Political Humor." *Journal of Popular Culture* 24, no. 3 (Winter 1990): 35.

"Nipsey Reaches Main Event." *Chicago Defender*, November 15, 1962.

"Nipsey Views the Regal." *Chicago Defender*, August 1, 1962.

O'Connor, John J. "Blacks on TV: Scrambled Signals." *New York Times*, October 27, 1991.

———. "The Curse of Incessant Cursing." *New York Times*, July 31, 1994.

———. "Onstage at the Outer Limits of the Outrageous: Russell Simmons's Def Comedy Jam." *New York Times*, July 8, 1993.

Paletz, David L. "Political Humor and Authority: From Support to Subversion." *International Political Science Review* 11, no. 4 (October 1, 1990): 483–93. https://doi.org /10.1177/019251219001100406.

Paramount+. "The Game Season Two Kicks of Dec 15 on Paramount+." Posted October 21, 2022. https://www.paramountplus.com/shows/the-game-2021/news/1010495/the -game-season-2-kicks-off-dec-15-on-paramount-plus/.

Petrović, Tanja. "Political Parody and the Politics of Ambivalence." *Annual Review of Anthropology* 47, no. 1 (2018): 201–16. https://doi.org/10.1146/annurev-anthro-102215-100148.

Poniewozik, James. "Review: 'Atlanta' and the Surreal Larceny of Life." *New York Times*, February 28, 2018. https://www.nytimes.com/2018/02/28/arts/television/atlanta-robbin -season-review.html.

Porter, James. "Before the Civil Rights Act, Herman Robert's Club Defined Black Nightlife on the South Side." *Chicago Reader*, December 1, 2014. https://chicagoreader.com/music /before-the-civil-rights-act-herman-robertss-club-defined-black-nightlife-on-the -south-side/.

Pressler, Jessica, and Chris Rovzar. "The Genius of Gossip Girl." *New York Magazine*, April 18, 2008. http://nymag.com/arts/tv/features/46225/index1.html.

Prince. "Prince & The Revolution – Kiss (Official Music Video)." YouTube, 2017. https://www .youtube.com/watch?v=H9tEvfIsDyo.

Reed-Danahay, Deborah E. *Auto/Ethnography: Rewriting the Self and the Social*. Oxford: Berg, 1997.

"Regal Spends $150,000 For Live Summer Shows." *Chicago Defender*, July 1, 1959.

Reynolds, Mike. "Not Just a Pretty Face: Original Films Brand Image for Networks' Viewers." *Cable World* 11, no. 28 (July 12, 1999): 21.

Richardson, Kartina. "'Key & Peele's Edge-Less, Post-Racial Lie." Salon, February 21, 2012. https://www.salon.com/2012/02/21/key_peeles_toothless_post_racial_lie/.

Rickford, John R. "The Creole Origins of African American Vernacular English: Evidence from Copula Absence." In *African American English*, edited by Salikoko S. Mufwene, John R. Rickford, Guy Bailey, and John Baugh. London: Routledge, 1998.

Robinson, Louie. "The Evolution of Geraldine—Flip Wilson's TV Creation Is a Classic Comic Character." *Ebony* 26, no. 2 (December 1970): 176–78, 180, 182.

Robinson, Stefani, writer. *Atlanta*. Season 2, Episode 5. "Barbershop." Directed by Donald Glover, featuring Brian Tyree Henry and Robert S. Powell III. Aired March 29, 2018.

Rogan, Joe. *The Joe Rogan Experience*. Episode 1712. "Bert Kreischer (Part 2)." Podcast Audio, September 2021.

Rosenberg, Howard. "Where Are Critics of 'Def Comedy'?" *Los Angeles Times*, April 15, 1994.

Ross, Marlon B. "Camping the Dirty Dozens: The Queer Resources of Black Nationalist Invective." *Callaloo* 23, no. 1 (2000): 291.

Russell, Nipsey. *Confucius Told Me* (1959). YouTube. Accessed December 28, 2022. https:// www.youtube.com/watch?v=tS_bR-ePWIc&t=347s.

Salinger, Tobias. "'Darling Nikki': How Prince's Lyrics Angered Tipper Gore and Led to the Parental Advisory Label." *New York Daily News*, April 21, 2016. https://www .nydailynews.com/entertainment/music/prince-lyrics-led-parental-advisory-label -article-1.2610382.

Samuels, Allison. "Inside the Weird, Industry-Shaking World of Donald Glover." *Wired*, January 19, 2017. https://www.wired.com/2017/01/childish-gambino-donald-glover/.

Saturday Night Live. Season 19, Episode 14. Directed by Lorne Michaels. Aired February 19, 1994, on NBC. https://www.nbc.com/saturday-night-live/video/martin-lawrence -monologue/n10550.

Saunders, Doris E. "Confetti." *Chicago Defender*, August 23, 1967.

"The Season at a Glance." *TV Guide*, September 12, 1998.

Semmes, Clovis E. *The Regal Theater and Black Culture*. New York: Palgrave Macmillan, 2006.

Shabazz, David L. "Barbershops as Cultural Forums for African American Males." *Journal of Black Studies* 47, no. 4 (May 1, 2016): 295–312. https://doi.org/10.1177/0021934716629337.

Snell, Kelsey. "Trump Halts Coronavirus Relief Talks Until after the Election." NPR, October 6, 2020. https://www.npr.org/sections/latest-updates-trump-covid-19-results/2020/10/06/920828075/trump-pausing-coronavirus-stimulus-talks-until-after-the-election.

Sontag, Susan. "Notes on 'Camp.'" In *Against Interpretation and Other Essays*, 275–292. New York: Farrar, Straus and Giroux, 1966.

Spaulding, Norman. *History of Black-Oriented Radio in Chicago, 1929–1963*. Champaign: University of Illinois Press, 1981.

Spencer, E. A., and K. Mahtani. "Hawthorne Effect." Catalogue of Bias 2017, Sackett Catalogue of Bias Collaboration. Accessed August 22, 2021. https://catalogofbias.org/biases/hawthorne-effect/.

Squires, Catherine R. "Rethinking the Black Public Sphere: An Alternative Vocabulary for Multiple Public Spheres." *Communication Theory* 12, no. 4 (2002): 446–68. https://doi.org/10.1111/j.1468-2885.2002.tb00278.x.

Staiger, Janet. "Authorship and Gus Van Sant." *Film Criticism*, no. 1 (2004): 3.

Stanley, T. L. "'Buffy' to Slay Small Screen; New Action Thriller for the WB Television Network." *Mediaweek*, February 17, 1997.

Stecopoulos, Harry, and Michael Uebel, eds. *Race and the Subject of Masculinities*. Durham, NC: Duke University Press, 1997.

Steele, Catherine Knight. "The Digital Barbershop: Blogs and Online Oral Culture within the African American Community." *Social Media + Society* 2, no. 4 (October 1, 2016): 2056305116683205. https://doi.org/10.1177/2056305116683205.

Stelter, Brian. "'The Game' Is a Winner, Helped by BET Loyalists." *New York Times*, January 17, 2011. https://www.nytimes.com/2011/01/17/business/media/17bet.html.

Sterngold, James. "A Racial Divide Widens on Network TV." *New York Times*, December 29, 1998.

Sutherland, Meghan. *The Flip Wilson Show*. TV Milestones Series. Detroit, MI: Wayne State University Press, 2008.

Swartz, Tracy. "Hot Mess Cubs Inspired Two Iconic 'Key and Peele' Characters." *Chicago Tribune*, August 5, 2016. https://www.chicagotribune.com/entertainment/ct-key-peele-meegan-andre-20160805-story.html.

"Talkin' Shit." Billboard. https://www.billboard.com/music/martin-lawrence/chart-history/TSL/song/177370.

Tampa Bay Times. "SNL Went Too Far, Viewers, Censor Agree." *Tampa Bay Times*, March 22, 1994. https://www.tampabay.com/archive/1994/02/22/snl-went-too-far-viewers-censor-agree/?outputType=audit.

Time Magazine. "Comedian Flip Wilson: TV's First Black Superstar." *Time Magazine*, January 31, 1972.

"Time Warner Plans Its Own TV Network, Battling Paramount." *Austin American Statesman*, November 3, 1993.

Tinsley, Justin. "'Atlanta' Recap: Season 2, Episode 1: The Family Scars That Bind." *Andscape* (blog), March 2, 2018. https://andscape.com/features/atlanta-recap-season-2-episode-1-the-family-scars-that-bind/.

"Tivoli Theater." Cinema Treasures. Accessed December 14, 2020. http://cinematreasures.org/theaters/943.

Tobenkin, David. "Plotting WB-ification." *Broadcasting and Cable*, July 25, 1994.

Towers, Andrea. "'The Game' Returns to TV after 6 Years with New and Old Cast Members." *EW*, May 13, 2021. https://ew.com/tv/the-game-returns-to-television-revival/.

Tucker, Ken. "The Secret Diary of Desmond Pfeiffer." *Entertainment Weekly*, October 9, 1998.

Tucker, Terrence. *Furiously Funny: Comic Rage from Ralph Ellison to Chris Rock*. Gainesville: University Press of Florida, 2018.

Turan, Kenneth. "Martin Lawrence's Family Values." *Los Angeles Times*, April 27, 1994.

"UPN Pulls 'Desmond Pfeiffer' from Monday Lineup." *Jet*, November 9, 1998.

Valley, Dylan. "Key and Peele Unchained." *Africa Is A Country*, January 17, 2013. https://africasacountry.com/2013/01/key-and-peele-unchained/.

Vásquez, Sam. "Television Satire in the Black Americas: Transnational Border Crossings in *Chappelle's Show* and *The Ity and Fancy Cat Show*." In *Post-Soul Satire: Black Identity after Civil Rights*, edited by Derek C. Maus, and James J. Donahue, 254–68. Columbia: University Press of Mississippi, 2014.

Warner, Kristen J. "A Black Cast Doesn't Make a Black Show: *City of Angels* and the Plausible Deniability of Color-blindness." In *Watching While Black: Centering the Television of Black Audiences*, edited by Beretta Smith-Shomade, 49–62. New Brunswick, NJ: Rutgers University Press, 2012.

———. "In the Time of Plastic Representation." *Film Quarterly* 71, no. 2 (2017): 32–37.

Washington, Bryan. "Atlanta Robbin' Season Recap: A Good Day." *Vulture*, March 30, 2018. https://www.vulture.com/2018/03/atlanta-recap-season-2-episode-5-barbershop.html.

Watkins, Mel. "Flip Wilson, Outrageous Comic and TV Host, Dies at 64." *New York Times*, November 27, 1998. https://www.nytimes.com/1998/11/27/arts/flip-wilson-outrageous-comic-and-tv-host-dies-at-64.html.

———. *On the Real Side: A History of African American Comedy from Slavery to Chris Rock*. Chicago: Chicago Review Press, 1999.

———. *On the Real Side: Laughing, Lying, and Signifying—The Underground Tradition of African American Humor that Transformed American Culture from Slavery to Richard Pryor*. New York: Simon & Schuster, 1994.

Wayne, Michael L. "Ambivalent Anti-Heroes and Racist Rednecks on Basic Cable: Post-Race Ideology and White Masculinities on FX." *Journal of Popular Television* 2, no. 2 (October 1, 2014): 205–25. https://doi.org/10.1386/jptv.2.2.205_1.

———. "Critically Acclaimed and Cancelled: FX's *The Bridge*, Channel as Brand and the Adaptation of Scripted TV Formats." *VIEW Journal of European Television History and Culture* 5, no. 9 (August 1, 2016): 116–25. https://doi.org/10.18146/2213-0969.2016.jethc107.

Weaver, Simon. "Humor and Race." In *The Wiley Blackwell Encyclopedia of Race, Ethnicity, and Nationalism*, edited by A. D. Smith, X. Hou, J. Stone, R. Dennis, and P. Rizova. Hoboken, NJ: Wiley, 2015. https://doi.org/10.1002/9781118663202.wberen455.

West, Abby. "Dick Gregory's Provocatively Titled Memoir Is Still Causing a Stir Decades Later." *Audible* (blog), January 29, 2020. https://www.audible.com/blog/dick-gregory-provocatively-titled-memoir-is-still-causing-a-stir-decades?pf_rd_p=47170265-da9c-4883-8b6f-59516e7875b5&pf_rd_r=3RY9CTPGDFZ5DPYZVHGW.

"Where to Go." *Chicago Defender*, January 5, 1963.

Whitaker, Mark. *Cosby: His Life and Times*. New York: Simon & Schuster, 2014.

White, Jack. "Dumb and Dumber." *Time*, October 12, 1998.

White, Mimi. "Ideological Analysis and Television." In *Channels of Discourse: Television and Contemporary Culture*, 2nd ed., edited by Robert C. Allen, 161–202. Chapel Hill: University of North Carolina Press, 1992.

"Why We Should Build the R&B Music Hall of Fame Museum," YouTube. Accessed December 14, 2020. https://www.youtube.com/watch?v=voHveKbg6ZU.

Wilkerson, Isabel. "Black Life on TV: Realism or Stereotypes?" *New York Times*, August 15, 1993.

Winford, Donald. "On the Origins of African American Vernacular English—A Creolist Perspective: Part I: The Sociohistorical Background." *Diachronica* 14, no. 2 (January 1, 1997): 305–44. https://doi.org/10.1075/dia.14.2.05win.

Wocjik, Pamela Robertson. *Guilty Pleasures: Feminist Camp from Mae West to Madonna*. Durham, NC: Duke University Press, 1996.

Wynter, Leon E. "TV Programmers Drop 'Black-Block' Lineups." *Wall Street Journal*, September 2, 1998.

Yahr, Emily. "'The Game' Is over and Everybody Won: How BET's Comedy Helped Make TV History." *Washington Post*, July 28, 2015. https://www.washingtonpost.com/lifestyle/style/changing-the-game-how-the-bet-comedy-helped-make-tv-history/2015/07/28/6245ed08-3546-11e5-94ce-834ad8f5c50e_story.html.

Yam, Kimmy. "Anti-Asian Hate Crimes Increased by Nearly 150% in 2020, Mostly in N.Y. and L.A., New Report Says." NBC News, March 9, 2021. https://www.nbcnews.com/news/asian-america/anti-asian-hate-crimes-increased-nearly-150-2020-mostly-n-n1260264.

Zook, Kristal Brent. *Color by Fox: The Fox Network and the Revolution in Black Television*. New York: Oxford University Press, 1999.

Zurawik, David. "Races Diverging in Viewing Habits." *Baltimore Sun*, May 2, 1996.

INDEX

FOR INDIANA UNIVERSITY PRESS

Tony Brewer, *Artist and Book Designer*

Brian Carroll, *Rights Manager*

Allison Chaplin, *Acquisitions Editor*

Emma Getz, *Editorial Assistant*

Sophia Hebert, *Assistant Acquisitions Editor*

Brenna Hosman, *Production Coordinator*

Katie Huggins, *Production Manager*

David Miller, *Lead Project Manager/Editor*

Dan Pyle, *Online Publishing Manager*

Leyla Salamova, *Artist and Book Designer*

Stephen Williams, *Marketing and Publicity Manager*

www.ingramcontent.com/pod-product-compliance
Lightning Source LLC
Chambersburg PA
CBHW030329270326
41926CB00010B/1560